D0301362

PUBLIC POLICY FOR THE 21ST CENTURY

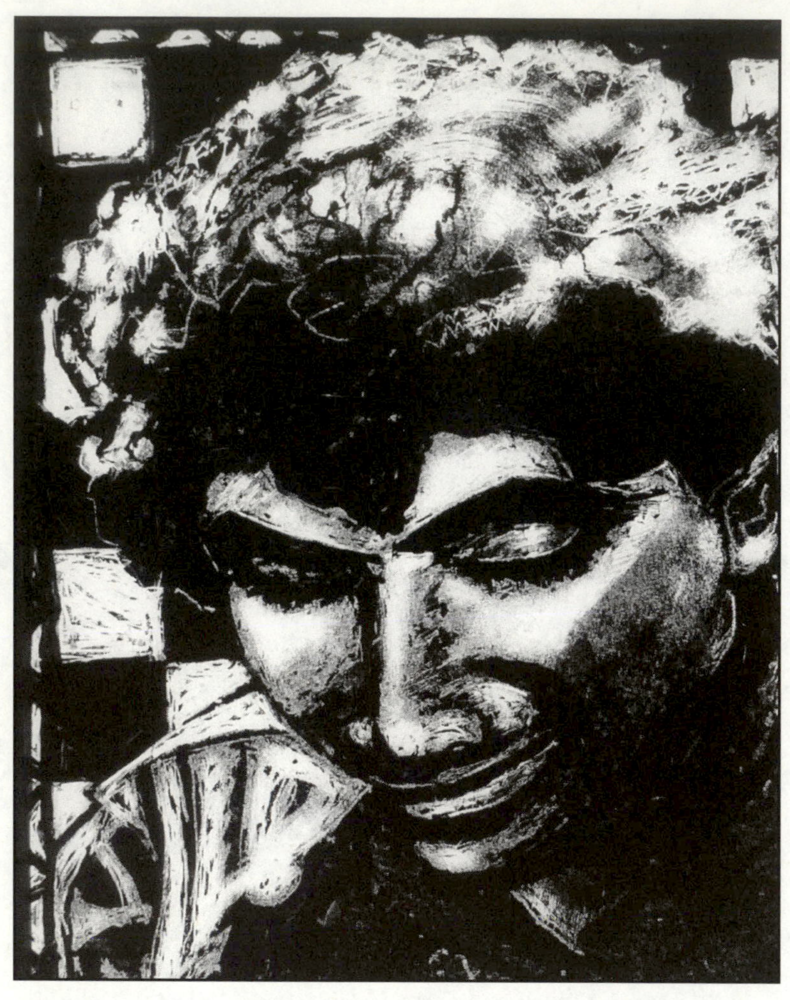

Portrait of Henry Neuburger, taken from a stained glass window by Rosalind Grimshaw

PUBLIC POLICY FOR THE 21ST CENTURY

Social and economic essays in memory of Henry Neuburger

Edited by Neil Fraser and John Hills

First published in Great Britain in December 2000 by

The Policy Press
34 Tyndall's Park Road
Bristol BS8 1PY
UK

Tel +44 (0)117 954 6800
Fax +44 (0)117 973 7308
e-mail tpp@bristol.ac.uk
www.policypress.org.uk

British Library Cataloguing in Publication Data

A catalogue record for this book is available from the British Library

ISBN 1 86134 268 3 hardback

Neil Fraser is Senior Lecturer in Social Policy at the University of Edinburgh and **John Hills** is Professor of Social Policy and Director of the ESRC Research Centre for Analysis of Social Exclusion at the London School of Economics.

Cover design by Qube Design Associates, Bristol.

The Policy Press works to counter discrimination on grounds of gender, race, disability, age and sexuality.

Printed and bound in Great Britain by Hobbs the Printers Ltd, Southampton.

Contents

Acknowledgements

Earlier drafts of the papers contained in this volume were discussed at a seminar held at the Economic and Social Research Council (ESRC) Centre for Analysis of Social Exclusion, London School of Economics, in April 2000. As well as most of the contributors to the volume, participants included Anna Brueton, Tania Burchardt, Dan Corry, Karen Gardiner, Sue Himmelweit, Ursula Huws, Emma Maclennan, Louisa Neuburger, Tom Sefton, and Holly Sutherland. The editors and authors are very grateful to them for the many helpful comments and suggestions they made which have led to substantial improvements in the final collection included here. They are also very grateful to Jane Dickson and particularly Rebecca Morris for their support in assembling the collection and preparing the typescript.

London and Edinburgh
July 2000

Notes on contributors

Christopher Allsopp is a Fellow and Tutor in Economics at New College, Oxford. He has been a member of the Bank of England's Monetary Policy Committee since June 2000. He has been editor of the *Oxford Review of Economic Policy* since 1985.

Iain Begg is Professor of International Economics at South Bank University, London, and is joint editor of the *Journal of Common Market Studies*. He is currently leading research projects on how economies deal with economic problems under European Monetary Union (EMU), and social protection. Recent publications include work on the EU budget (a book entitled *Paying for Europe*), reform of the Structural Funds (including editing a special issue of *European Planning Studies*), the political economy of EMU, and economic adjustment under EMU.

Andrew Burchardt teaches at Oxford University's Department of Continuing Education. He has contributed to various journals including the *Economic Journal* and the *International Journal of Computers in Adult Education and Training*. His book on industrial economic policy and the role of economist civil servants, *The Broyd Papers*, was published by Spokesman in 1997. He knew Henry Neuburger for 35 years.

Hugh Davies was Senior Lecturer in Economics, Birkbeck College, University of London. He died in October 2000, as this book was going to press. His interests included family economics, and gender and income distribution. He was the major author of the simulation model of lifetime income used in this book and for the Cabinet Office report on *Women's incomes over the lifetime* (The Stationery Office, 2000).

Meghnad Desai is Professor of Economics and Director of the Centre for the Study of Global Governance at the London School of Economics (LSE). He has written extensively on macroeconomics, monetary theory and policy, development and international political economy. He is a long standing advocate of basic income and is a backbench Labour peer.

Neil Fraser is Senior Lecturer in Social Policy at the University of Edinburgh. He is the author with Henry Neuburger of *Economic policy analysis: A rights-based approach* (Avebury, 1993). He has written on employment policies, the economics of childcare, and the economics of breast-cancer screening.

Anne Harrison is Counsellor on Sustainable Development in the statistics directorate of the Organisation for Economic Co-operation and Development (OECD) in Paris. She was involved in the preparation of the *1993 System of National Accounts* and is currently editing the revised version of the *System of Environmental and Economic Accounting Manual*. She has a number of publications in the area of national accounts and environmental accounting.

John Hills is Professor of Social Policy and Director of the ESRC Research Centre for Analysis of Social Exclusion at the London School of Economics. His interests include: income distribution, the distributional impact of taxation and social security, the welfare state, and housing finance. Recent publications include *Paying for health, education and housing: How the centre pulls the purse strings* (co-author, Oxford University Press, 2000), and *Private welfare and public policy* (co-author, Joseph Rowntree Foundation, 1999).

Heather Joshi is Professor of Economic Demography at the Institute of Education, London University where she is also Deputy Director of the Centre for Longitudinal Studies. Her duties include providing academic access to the Office for National Statistics (ONS) Longitudinal Study and establishing the ESRC Millennium Cohort Study. Many of her publications are analyses of longitudinal data on issues of gender, the family and health inequalities. Previous employment includes the Government Economic Service, London School of Hygiene, Birkbeck College and City University.

Peter Mackie is a Professor in the Institute for Transport Studies, University of Leeds. He was a colleague of Henry Neuburger in the Ministry of Transport in the period 1968-70. He has worked and published extensively in the fields of transport appraisal and regulation, and is a member of the Standing Advisory Committee on Trunk Road Assessment.

David Metcalf is Professor of Industrial Relations at the LSE. He is Director of the Leverhulme Trust programme on the Future of Trade

Unions in Modern Britain. He has written extensively on the economics of unions and pay. He is a Commissioner on the Low Pay Commission, which recommends the level of the minimum wage. He owns a leg of a successful National Hunt racehorse and is a Jockey Club Steward.

Gavin Mooney is Director of the Social and Public Health Economics Research Group (SPHERe) and Professor of Health Economics at the Universities of Sydney and Curtin (Perth). His main research interests are in health economics, particularly Aboriginal health, equity more generally and in eliciting community values in healthcare.

Chris Nash is Professor of Transport Economics and currently Director of the Institute for Transport Studies, University of Leeds. His interest in appraisal techniques goes back to his appointment as lecturer in Economics at Southampton University in 1971, where his collaboration with David Pearce led ultimately to a textbook *The social appraisal of projects* (Macmillan, 1981). More recently he has worked extensively on rail transport, including appraisal and infrastructure pricing issues.

Jenny Neuburger is the eldest daughter of Henry Neuburger. She is currently working as a housing advisor with the Notting Hill Housing Trust and taking a postgraduate degree in International Housing at the London School of Economics.

Mark Wickham-Jones is Senior Lecturer in Politics, University of Bristol. He is the author of *Economic strategy and the Labour Party* (Macmillan, 1996) and co-editor of *New Labour's foreign policy* (Manchester University Press, 2000). He is currently inching his way towards a book on Labour and Europe.

Simon Wren-Lewis began his career as an economist in HM Treasury. In 1981 he moved to the National Institute of Economic and Social Research where as a Senior Research Fellow he constructed the first versions of the world model NIGEM, and as Head of Macroeconomic Research he supervised development of this and the Institute's domestic model. In 1990 he became a Professor at Strathclyde University and built a new UK econometric model, COMPACT. Since 1995 he has been a Professor at Exeter University. He has published papers on macroeconomics in a wide range of academic journals.

ONE

Introduction: For the purposes of the future

Neil Fraser and John Hills

For many people, economics – if not the 'dismal science' it was once said to be – is a subject both sterile and remote from the real world. Although frequently complex in the techniques used, it is often seen as being over-simplified in its assumptions about human behaviour and narrow in its concerns. Where it does touch on matters of great public concern, its practitioners sometimes seem to do more to mystify than to explain, and to close down debate as being a matter only for properly qualified technicians, rather than providing the analysis which could open up discussion.

This collection of essays has been written to try to show that these preconceptions need not be true, and as a tribute to the memory of a man for whom they certainly were not. Henry Neuburger was a much loved economist whose sadly foreshortened career as a government economist covered half a dozen government departments and who was, for much of the 1980s, an advisor to the Labour Party when it was in opposition. He had hugely varied interests (see Chapter Fifteen, and the bibliography of his published output) and made contributions to economic policy analysis in many areas, including all those represented here and several others besides. The contributors all knew Henry and his work and were sympathetic to his concerns. They are active in a collection of fields which together span the central concerns of economic policy, so that the collection also serves as an introduction both to recent developments in policy analysis and to economic policy making at the start of the new century.

The collection is divided into four parts. The first looks at some of the tools of the economist's trade, drawing attention to ways in which they have developed in recent years (not always for the better in some contributors' views). It shows how economic analysis can be widened beyond narrow concerns with market goods and the money economy. The second looks at policy issues in three areas affecting the economy as a whole: macroeconomics, taxation and public spending (particularly social security), and the impact of European integration. The third examines current issues in four sectors of the economy: the labour market, transport, housing, and healthcare. The final part looks at Henry Neuburger's own contribution, both as part of Labour Party policy making in the 1980s, and in his more general career.

The tools for analysing policy

Developments in economic policy analysis explored in Part One include macroeconomic modelling, the framework of national accounting, the economics of project appraisal, understanding what is happening within the household, and the fundamental objectives of policy, going beyond cash or standard economic notions of 'utility'.

For a long time the construction and output of large macroeconomic models was the most prominent form of economic analysis. In Chapter Two Simon Wren-Lewis traces the history of macroeconomic modelling from the 1970s and asks why such models have become less dominant, and why the attention given to them has declined. He considers but rejects various culprits, including the change in beliefs about macroeconomic policy under the Conservative governments of the 1980s and 1990s, and failures in the models' performance in forecasting. One conclusion is that alternative approaches have proved more attractive both to some users and to academic economists. He argues that this is unfortunate. Large macroeconomic models can provide a crucial bridge between economic theory and empirical reality, allowing policy options to be tested against the best structurally consistent evidence. Central issues of contemporary economic policy – such as the consequences of entry into European Monetary Union (EMU) – need illumination by the analysis that can be provided by macroeconomic modelling.

The system of national accounts is the raw material for much economic policy analysis[1]. As Anne Harrison argues in Chapter Three, most people have heard of GDP (Gross Domestic Product), but few understand the framework from which it is derived, or the potential for creative analysis which recent developments allow. She discusses what can be created in the new international system of national accounting both through the rearrangement of existing data within the accounts ('internal satellite accounts') and through links to additional data ('external satellites').

Examples of the former include: varying ways of examining the distribution of who ultimately pays tax or benefits from subsidies; allowing for services 'in kind' like health and education; and more sophisticated treatment of the relationship between flows of income and the stock of capital (including the difficult issues around human capital and training). Under external satellite accounts she discusses developments of great interest to policy analysis in the new century, for instance: distinguishing between different kinds of households, so that national accounts shed light on income distribution; 'green' accounts which take into account environmental effects and compute the true cost of the exploitation of natural resources; and accounts which allow for production within the home not intended for sale on the market (an issue returned to in two of the subsequent chapters).

At the other end of the discipline, microeconomics, cost–benefit analysis is one of the best known economic tools, providing a way of comparing different projects – for instance, government transport investments. But, as Neil Fraser examines in Chapter Four, there are flaws in this approach, and some of its findings can be too sweeping. Drawing on joint work with Henry Neuburger (1993) he reviews different forms of project appraisal for the public sector. He takes issue with the 'willingness to pay' criterion of cost–benefit analysis and argues instead for cost effectiveness analysis, where several outcomes are left in non-monetary form, rather than reduced to a single money total. More ambitiously this can be developed into what they call democratic decision analysis. Through this kind of approach the relationship between analyst and policy maker can become interactive and transparent, as against important decisions on trade-offs between objectives being hidden in the analyst's implicit decisions. He uses the example of alternative anti-poverty policies to illustrate the complexity that arises when multiple objectives have to be confronted.

The next two chapters develop the theme of taking analysis beyond simple valuations of goods traded in the market. In Chapter Five Heather Joshi and Hugh Davies give an example of analysis which goes beyond cash incomes, which looks at lifetimes rather than just snapshots, and which looks within what is often the 'black box' of the household. By using simulated biographies (constructed to be consistent with contemporary survey data) for high, middle, and low earning couples, they explore the costs and impact of parenthood. They measure these not just in terms of the direct costs of providing for children, but also the indirect costs of foregone earnings and changes in the use of unpaid time. They examine the impact of being a parent on the allocation of time and other costs between the father and mother, showing that one cannot generalise about the ways different couples balance between family and working life – a finding of great importance for current policy.

Meghnad Desai takes this concern with activities within the household and with time much further. He argues that economic analysis, and with it policy towards reform of the welfare state, has been too concerned with what he describes as 'outside' goods – the products and services which are traded in the market. Yet true measures of wellbeing will actually depend much more on 'inside' goods – activities taking place within the household and between people without a monetary transaction. Rather than traded private goods, or even the public goods we supply collectively, our central concern should be with 'social goods' – the activities of living involving human interaction. Wellbeing, he argues, comes from the production and consumption of these social goods. From this perspective, measures like GDP or counts of the numbers with low incomes are poor measures of wellbeing and its distribution. In particular, they neglect the time people have available for producing social goods. This leads to mistaken policies, for instance welfare reforms which increase the cash incomes of groups helped or pressed into paid work, but at the cost of their 'net living time', such as that of lone parents with their children.

The economy as a whole

In Chapter Seven, Christopher Allsopp reviews what has changed and what remains the same in policies for inflation and employment (macroeconomic policies) over the last four decades of the twentieth century – the subjects of the models discussed in Chapter Two. He describes the major swings in the macroeconomic environment in Britain over this period, organising his account around the changing approaches to the control of inflation. At the end of this period, however, both the problems and the policies bear a remarkable similarity to those at its start. An abiding issue explored here is whether policy makers have enough instruments for the different targets of macropolicy.

A second part of the overall analysis of the economy is the impact of government through its policies towards tax and public spending. Recent developments in these are analysed by John Hills in Chapter Eight, following the philosophy that the two can only be understood together. He examines: changes in the level and composition of taxation in Britain by comparison with that in other industrialised countries; the changing balance between taxation, spending, public borrowing and public assets since the 1970s; the composition of taxation and its distributional effects; and social attitudes to taxes and public spending. Against this background he uses the results of microsimulation modelling to examine the distributional effects of changes in tax and benefit policy since the 1997 election, comparing their impact with what would have resulted from alternative strategies.

Increasingly, domestic economic – and other – policies have to take account of membership of the European Union. In Chapter Nine Iain Begg describes how national economic policy making is changing with the evolution of policy making in the European Union. This is not just a matter of the 'internal market' after the reforms of 1992, or of EMU and its implications for fiscal as well as monetary policies. As he describes, new attempts also are being made to coordinate policy in a number of areas, the most developed of which is employment policy. To ignore the constraints and opportunities for policy of European frameworks would, he argues, be asking for trouble.

Sectoral issues

The operation of the labour market is central to both production and distribution. In Chapter Ten David Metcalf (a member of the Low Pay Commission) examines a new institution, the National Minimum Wage introduced from April 1999, and the impact of an older one, the unions. He shows that both have made important differences to the distribution of pay. He charts the impact of the minimum wage on the 1.7 million workers who were previously earning lower wages, and examines whether it has had adverse side effects. He then looks at the impact of unionisation on pay structures, in particular on differentials in wages by gender, health status and ethnicity. As his analysis illustrates, institutions can make a difference to economic outcomes, rather than there being unstoppable market pressures.

Chris Nash and Peter Mackie's account of economic appraisal in transport in Chapter Eleven can be seen as an application of the project appraisal techniques introduced in Neil Fraser's essay, Chapter Four of this book. Analysis of road schemes is the most systematic use of project appraisal in the British public sector. The chapter describes how the systems for appraisal have become more sophisticated since the 1960s. Analysis by transport economists now incorporates some of the issues which were previously neglected, for instance: allowing for congestion and traffic growth induced by new roads; environmental impacts; economic development effects; and the distribution of costs and benefits. An important recent development has been greater openness in publishing the factors used in appraisal, allowing external examination of the implicit weightings used in decisions, and taking the system a little nearer the democratic decision analysis advocated by Neuburger and Fraser.

Housing and planning policy are vital for parts of the environmental agenda. In Chapter Twelve Jenny Neuburger examines the debate around the 'urban renaissance' called for by the government's Urban Task Force, particularly around the land density of new developments, and the use of existing housing. In common with other contributors, she argues for more attention to distribution, as well as to the consequences of policy for the supply of homes affordable by those with low incomes, rather than concentration on the simple '3.8 million new homes' total of new housing units implied by changing household numbers. Policy has to focus on the existing stock, with incentives to make best use of it, including reform of property taxation to put more of a price on its use by the already well housed, and wider policies to revive areas where existing housing is in low demand.

Following the discussion in previous chapters of social security, transport and housing, Chapter Thirteen examines economic analysis and policy making in healthcare. Gavin Mooney begins with the academic development of cost effectiveness analysis (and its variant, cost utility analysis) in health. He asks why in practice this has not been much applied to investment decisions on treatment methods. His main argument is that such appraisal does not fit the framework of health services, which require a community focus, a citizen's voice.

Henry Neuburger's contribution

As each contributor explains, the previous chapters take as their starting point some of Henry Neuburger's contributions to the specific area. The final part of the book discusses his contribution more widely. In Chapter Fourteen Mark Wickham-Jones provides a political scientist's perspective on the Labour Party's economic policy making during the 1980s. At this time, when Labour was in opposition and Mrs Thatcher and the Conservatives in government, Henry Neuburger was at the centre of that policy making. The party made radical changes in policy over the period, by the end anticipating New Labour. Drawing on internal documents as well as the published statements by the Labour Party, Mark Wickham-Jones gives a fascinating account of how the policies of political parties evolve – and the role of the advisor within that process. Finally, Andrew Burchardt provides a summary and personal appreciation of Henry Neuburger's career, accompanied by a bibliography of his publications prepared by Tania Burchardt.

As contributors and editors we hope that this book will serve as an introduction to central parts of the economic debate at the start of the new century. Economic analysis need not take the form of routine application of textbook techniques. As Henry's career shows, the role of the analyst can also be to challenge orthodoxy – if the evidence supports such a challenge. As the contributions stress, the questions to be addressed and the tools available are changing all the time, as is the evidence. John Maynard Keynes wrote that the role of the economist is, "to study the present, in the light of the past, for the purposes of the future". We hope that the collection may also act as an inspiration for those who would like, as Henry did, to contribute to those purposes.

Note

[1] It is also a way into economics – cf the textbook by Sir John Hicks (1942).

References

Hicks, J. Sir (1942) *The social framework*, Oxford: Oxford University Press.

Neuburger, H. and Fraser, N. (1993) *Economic policy analysis: A rights-based approach*, Aldershot: Avebury.

Part One:
The tools for analysing policy

TWO

The decline of macroeconomic modelling

Simon Wren-Lewis[1]

Introduction

In the UK Treasury in the late 1970s I was lucky, as a new recruit straight out of university, to work on the Treasury model at the same time as Henry Neuburger. Henry was not only central to the Treasury's modelling work over this period, but he retained his interest in macromodelling during his subsequent period working for the Labour Party, establishing an informal working group from the main modelling organisations[2].

Although Henry's interest in macromodelling never declined, this cannot be said of the academic, policy and political community. Whereas once the properties of macromodels like the Treasury model appeared to directly influence policy, now they attract very little interest. In the early 1980s the Treasury model was discussed in Parliament on a number of occasions. At the end of the 1990s the Bank of England published details of its core macromodel, and hardly anyone noticed.

This chapter charts this decline, and asks why it has occurred[3]. There are a number of potential candidates, including the role of the Conservative government in the 1980s, and forecasting failures in the early 1990s. I shall argue that the underlying cause is neither of these, but instead it is due to a change in the way academic economists go about their trade.

I will also argue that the decline of macromodelling presents serious dangers for macroeconomic policy making in the 21st century. We know from the past that policy makers are too often tempted by economic theories which have little or no empirical backing. As the UK discovered with monetarism and entry into the Exchange Rate Mechanism (ERM), implementing these theories can have disastrous consequences. By providing a vital link between economic ideas and empirical reality, econometric macromodels provide one line of defence against similar disasters happening again. If the decline in macromodelling is not reversed, there is a serious danger that the quality of macroeconomic policy advice will decline with it.

The golden age of macromodelling

In the 1970s in the UK, when Henry was directly involved in macromodelling at the Treasury, the model was king. The Treasury model was the vehicle through which nearly all macroeconomic issues were discussed within the Treasury. It not only produced the forecast, but also the macroeconomic policy analysis on which budget decisions were based. A large amount of the time of macroeconomists working in the Treasury was spent estimating equations for the Treasury model.

The dominant position of the model within the Treasury was reflected in the importance attached to macromodels outside, including academia. Many of the key macroeconomic debates in the UK in the 1970s were conducted as contests between models. The 'New Cambridge' critique of short-term demand management was mediated through the Cambridge Policy Group's macromodel. The adoption of international monetarism within the London Business School model helped in the formulation of the 1979 government's Medium Term Financial Strategy (MTFS) (see Kenway, 1994, for example).

What exactly are these models that played such an important role in policy making? They are a system of equations explaining many key macroeconomic variables (for instance consumer prices, unemployment, exchange rates). The structure of the equations (which variables determine what) comes from economic theory, but the parameters of the equations (the strength of the influences) come from examining the historical evidence of how these variables have moved in the past (econometrics). However good the equations are, a large part of past behaviour remains unexplained (the equations are 'stochastic'), but the model quantifies this uncertainty[4].

Econometric macromodels were originally seen by many academics as the concrete manifestation of a progressive research programme that would see a steady increase in the extent to which we understood, and could predict and manipulate the national economy. The 1970s also saw the introduction of optimal control techniques from engineering into economics, and the idea that the management of the economy could ultimately be automated like an industrial process.

The role of econometrics in building these models was central and taken for granted. Before new theory could be introduced into a model, it had to be tested against the historical evidence, and if it failed that test, it would not be part of the model. A large amount of important work took place attempting to integrate theoretical ideas with statistical methods of analysis, such as the research by the LSE group of econometricians.

Contrast this with the position today. With independence, the focus of interest in short-term demand management has now shifted to the Bank of England. The Bank employs many economists, but a small minority work on their traditional macroeconometric model. The Treasury model is increasingly seen by economists working there as a means of producing a forecast, rather than as a way of organising ideas.

Among the UK academic community, the Economic and Social Research Council's macromodelling consortium, a collaboration between the ESRC, the Treasury and the Bank, provided the core funding for macromodelling in the 1980s and 1990s. The efforts of the various modelling institutions were compared and analysed by the ESRC Macromodelling Bureau at Warwick University. In 1999 the consortium came to an end, and with it the Warwick Bureau. The demise of the consortium reflected the culmination of growing disquiet among a number of academics over the amount of funding going to macromodelling.

Is this decline to be welcomed or lamented? An answer may lie in establishing the reasons for the diminished role of traditional macromodels. There are a large number of possible suspects in the case of who killed macromodelling, but I will suggest that a number are less important than they might at first appear.

Suspect 1: Mrs T

It is tempting to attribute a large part of the decline of macromodels in the UK to the election of Mrs Thatcher. The new Conservative government's macroeconomic policies were radical and opposed to the dominant Keynesian consensus – recall the famous *Times* letter from 364 economists in 1981 which attacked deflationary policies during a recession. To a first approximation, the Treasury macromodel reflected the previous consensus. This model was clearly 'not one of us'.

The antipathy between the new Conservative government's monetarism and the Treasury model did not just give civil servants a headache. As a result of the efforts of Jeremy Bray MP in the late 1970s, the Treasury model now had to be published and could be used by others.

Contradictions between the model and government policy could be, and sometimes were, exploited by the government's opponents, including Henry (see for example the chapter by Mark Wickham-Jones in this volume). In these circumstances it was natural for Conservative ministers to attack the whole macromodelling enterprise.

However, the antipathy between the Conservative government and macroeconometric modelling did not last, because both sides changed. The Treasury model was gradually adapted in the 1980s so that money could play a more prominent role, and the transmission mechanism (from money to prices) became clearer. Indeed this was already the case in the international monetarist version of the London Business School model (one of whose architects, Terry Burns, became Chief Economic Advisor at the Treasury in 1981), and in Patrick Minford's new macromodel (see Kenway, 1994).

Government policy changed in the sense that the belief that inflation could be controlled by setting money growth targets both quickly and at little cost was blown apart by the 1980/81 recession. From a macromodelling point of view, the really radical part of the MTFS was not the central role assigned to money, but the implication that demand management was no longer a problem. If the MTFS had worked, then the consequences for macromodelling would have been serious. Macroeconometric models were built around the idea that policy had a role to play in short-term demand management, so a model was required both to understand how policy worked and also to predict what would happen to the economy without any policy change. If demand management was dead, then macroeconometric models became much less interesting. Events in 1980–81 showed that money was not a reliable thermostat for the economy, and so demand management might still be needed.

Unfortunately for the UK, the attempt to do away with demand management had one last fling after monetarism, when we entered the ERM in 1990. After this second failure, demand management was no longer a dirty word, and it describes exactly what the Bank of England, the US Federal Reserve and the European Central Bank are all now trying to do. If the Conservative government's attack on demand management had been responsible for the decline in macroeconometric modelling, then we should now be seeing a revival. Instead, as the recent events outlined above suggest, the decline has continued.

Before moving on to other possible suspects, I would like to note one fact during this period that I will use later in macromodelling's defence.

The recessions of 1980-81 and 1990-92 were both associated with attempts to move to an 'intermediate target' approach to macropolicy, where the target was money and the exchange rate respectively. In both cases UK macroeconomic models could have been used, and in some cases were used, to foresee the output consequences of these policies. It is by now well known that an internal Treasury forecast after the first Conservative budget predicted a fall in GDP close to that which occurred in 1980–81, although it got the details of the recession wrong. A study by Church (1993) at the Warwick Bureau showed that the main UK macromodels all suggested that the entry rate of 2.95 DM/£ was significantly overvalued, and at least one model was used to suggest this publicly before the event (see Wren-Lewis et al, 1991). In both cases the theory used by the models to make these predictions was neither sophisticated nor controversial. The key was to confront the policy with historical evidence in a structural way[5].

Suspect 2: Forecast failure

So if Mrs T was not the cause of macromodelling's demise, what was? I suspect the answer that most outsiders would come up with would relate to forecasting performance. Put simply, macromodels failed to deliver good macroeconomic forecasts.

Perhaps the clearest example of forecast failure was the 1990-92 recession. Earlier disasters, although not necessarily predicted, could be blamed on something else or excused. As we have already noted, the 1980-81 recession, although at least as traumatic, was clearly seen as the result of a policy experiment (monetarism) and, as I noted above, Treasury internal forecasts did predict its consequences. The rise in UK inflation in the mid 1970s could be directly laid at the door of forecast failure[6], but in this case forecasters could convincingly argue that they could not have foreseen what happened to oil prices.

There seemed to be no easy excuses in the late 1980s and early 1990s. As a number of studies have shown (for example Pain and Britton, 1992) forecasters missed the strength of the late 1980s boom, and the extent of the subsequent recession. Indeed a major cause of the initial boom, the willingness of consumers to take up unusually high levels of debt, remains unexplained to this day, with a number of alternative theories still competing with each other. Was this the last straw that showed the fallibility of macromodelling forecasts?

In an important sense this and earlier forecast failures should not have come as a surprise. Macroeconomic models actually predict that macroeconomic forecasts are highly unreliable, and that the occasional major failure will occur. Any individual equation in a model will not track past events exactly even in hindsight: there is always a large part of aggregate behaviour that remains unpredictable. With a bit of work, this historical uncertainty for individual equations can be translated into expected uncertainty for the predictions of the model as a whole[7]. We can ask, even if the equations in the model were completely correct (that is they were based on relevant theory with the true parameters), what would be the uncertainty in the forecasts implied by the uncertainty in the past? If we do this, we come up with numbers that are of the same general magnitude as the actual forecast errors made. In other words, the poor forecasting record should not be a surprise – it was entirely predictable given the models being used[8].

Forecasters over this period can with some justification be accused of being rather economical with these facts. Fifteen years ago, as I know from personal experience, it was very difficult to get forecasters to present their forecasts in a way that gave an accurate indication of the uncertainties involved. It is not surprising therefore, that the public and politicians should have become disenchanted with forecasts, when they were not clearly presented with information on the known uncertainties involved.

So macroeconomic forecasts based on models were always going to be seriously unreliable, and sometimes seriously wrong. However, there is also considerable evidence that they are better than informed guesswork: the model helps a bit. As the advantages of even a bit of extra knowledge in this area are great, a macroeconomic forecasting industry where the industry leaders still use conventional macromodels survives. Today some of the major forecasters have become more responsible in the way they present their predictions, in much the same way as weather forecasters now occasionally tell us the expected probability of rain or sunshine. A well known example is the Bank of England's 'fan chart' for expected inflation. Forecasters have realised that to be honest and explicit about uncertainty is in their own self interest.

Of course the inevitable uncertainty involved in forecasting makes it a prime target. It is easy to suggest that the world is changing too rapidly to be pinned down in any set of equations. Structural change is a serious problem, but it is not a fatal problem. While it is important to be alive to the possibility of structural change, it is possible to explain a good deal of past macroeconomic behaviour in a fairly simple way. Some have suggested that forecast failure indicates some deep malaise in economics itself, and that radical changes in economic theory are required (for instance Ormerod, 1994). In reality economics is applied in a useful way every day in countless firms and other organisations. As a discipline it appears controversial partly because it often lies at the heart of political debate (Neuburger, 1996, commenting on Ormerod). While some criticisms of economic theory and theorising may be legitimate (see , for example, my discussion on page 21 of how reluctant much modern macroeconomic theory has been to incorporate Keynesian price rigidities), economics is a progressive science, typically building on existing ideas.

I believe we can discount the idea that forecast failure indicated some fundamental flaw in the macromodelling enterprise. Instead it simply reflects the perhaps inevitable uncertainties involved in predicting human behaviour. Once we accept this, then it is difficult to see forecast failure as the prime cause of macromodelling's decline. Henry often found comparisons with weather forecasting instructive. After the 1987 hurricane devastated large parts of South East England, the inability of the Met Office to predict that event led to *more* resources, not less, being devoted to modelling the weather.

Econometric macromodels are used probably as much today as they were ten or twenty years ago to produce forecasts. The decline in the use and attention paid to conventional macromodels is mainly concentrated in the area of policy analysis rather than forecasting[9]. Yet, for reasons explained above, unreliability in forecasting does not logically imply unreliability in policy analysis. Forecasting errors may simply reflect the uncertainty 'built into' the model, and the model itself could be completely correct. As a result, the model may still provide our best guide to the effects of policy intervention. Although forecast failure undoubtedly harmed the public reputation of macromodels, I would guess that if macroeconomists had stood by them as the best way to conduct policy analysis, their use in this area would not have declined.

Suspect 3: Rational expectations

In academic economics the United States leads in many areas, including macroeconomics. Widespread scepticism of macromodelling in the United States had become well entrenched in the late 1980s. Mankiw (1990) describes how large-scale macromodels had become something of a joke in academic circles. The proximate cause appeared to be very specific – the concept of rational expectations.

Expectations are crucial to many macroeconomic relationships, yet until the 1970s macroeconomists had modelled these expectations in very simple ways. In the most popular model, for example, agents simply adjusted their predictions by a fraction of their previous error, ignoring all other information. Here agents seemed to behave in a naive fashion, ignoring in particular information that economic theory suggested was important.

In contrast, the Rational Expectations Hypothesis (REH) suggests individuals will use the best means at their disposal to make economic guesses. It extends to expectations formation the optimisation assumption that lies behind most economic theories, for example that firms maximise profits, or consumers maximise utility. The REH implies individuals maximise the predictive power of available information.

The REH caused something of a revolution in academic macroeconomics in the 1970s. It turned out that the dominant Keynesian paradigm at the time depended critically on expectations not being rational. Furthermore, Lucas and others showed that a failure to explicitly model expectations rationally would make any model incapable of analysing the effects of any change in policy regime (the Lucas critique, 1976). So rational expectations became the main weapon for those who wished to challenge Keynesian orthodoxy. By the late 1980s, the REH was used almost universally, and theories or models that used earlier expectations theories, including conventional macromodels, were largely discredited. To many, therefore, the large-scale US macromodels appeared to resemble dinosaurs: large cumbersome beasts based on outmoded ideas that could no longer survive.

In fact, in the US the 'dinosaurs' live on. They did not adapt by incorporating the REH, but neither did they die out as a result. By the 1980s the major US macromodels had become focused on selling forecasting services, and partly as a result had become very large through greater disaggregation. (Greater disaggregation increases the amount of potentially relevant information you can incorporate in your forecast, and it also gives you more appeal to sector-specific clients.) Incorporating the REH into macromodels involved a number of difficult technical problems, problems which increased with the size of the model concerned. In this sense it may be the case that the large US forecasting models were indeed incapable of adapting to the new academic climate.

On the other hand from a forecasting point of view the incentive and need to adapt to the REH was not compelling. While rational expectations had critical implications for policy analysis, it was far less clear that it would enable economists to produce better forecasts, except perhaps after a distinct change in policy regime. There is no evidence that models that incorporate rational expectations do better at forecasting than those that do not, and there has been no overwhelming demand from clients of forecasting models to adopt the REH.

Could rational expectations help explain why the decline in the use of conventional macromodels is confined to policy analysis rather than forecasting? While I think the REH has a role to play in any explanation, it alone cannot be the whole story for two simple reasons. First, Keynesian economics did recover from the rational expectations revolution. It became clear fairly quickly that it was possible to reformulate Keynesian models of the business cycle in a manner that was quite consistent with the REH (New Keynesian economics). In the US, John Taylor constructed a New Keynesian global econometric model, and other examples followed on both sides of the Atlantic. Second, it was also possible to construct non-Keynesian econometric macromodels that incorporated rational expectations, of which Patrick Minford's model based at Liverpool University is the pioneering example.

In the UK, unlike the US, the main traditional macromodels did adapt to include the REH. The models of the National Institute, the London Business School and the Treasury all incorporated the REH to a greater or lesser extent in the 1980s. The difference between the UK and US experience can be related directly to differences in funding. Whereas the US models depended mainly on private sector funding through the sale of forecasts, in the UK funding through the ESRC consortium was critical. The major influence in the consortium was from academic macroeconomists, and it therefore became important for the UK models to incorporate the REH to some degree. Of course the Treasury model was not subject to these funding pressures, but Treasury economists did recognise the importance of keeping pace with what the other UK models were doing.

The simple fact that there are now many examples of econometric macromodels that embody the REH suggests that this idea alone cannot account for the decline in macromodelling. It is true that the REH made macromodelling technically more difficult, but set against this have been advances in computer technology that made model use much easier[10]. To find out what really killed academic interest in macromodelling, we need to look at some more general academic devolopments over the last 20 years.

Suspect 4: An academic divide?

Macroeconometric models involve a perpetual compromise between theory and evidence. They are places where econometric techniques and economic theories are applied, but they are unlikely to be the source of innovation in either. An outsider might imagine that models provide the arena where alternative theories get tested. However, the uncertainties involved in forecasting cited earlier mean that it would take us many years, possibly decades, before we knew whether one model had predicted better than another for reasons other than chance. For the applied macroeconomist, it is generally easier to look at one part of a model, rather than the model as a whole, to test particular ideas.

Partly as a result, building macromodels is extremely unlikely to generate articles in the top journals (see Smith, 1994). While over the last ten years the most influential economics journals have contained countless papers on macroeconomics, virtually none use or describe structural econometric macromodels. For this reason there has to be some other reason why academics should be interested in macromodels. In the past one important reason was policy. To put it crudely, in the 1970s to influence UK macropolicy you had to influence the Treasury model, or persuade officials why the results of that model were wrong.

In the 1970s and 1980s two new ways emerged of providing practical policy prescriptions. Single equation reduced forms (for instance an equation relating prices to money whose properties were entirely data-determined) had always been a competitor of macromodels, but they used so little information that they were unlikely to be a serious rival. In 1980 Sims introduced VAR (Vector Autoregression) analysis, which is essentially a reduced form generalised to a small collection of variables. In introducing VARs, Sims (1980) directly attacked the plausibility of the restrictions placed on the data in structural macromodels. VARs allowed us to examine the historical evidence on macroeconomic interactions without being tied down to any particular theory.

VARs provided a natural focus of interest for the econometrician concerned with macropolicy. They were also much easier to construct than conventional models. They became the basis for a whole econometric research programme. For the econometrician, or the econometrically minded macroeconomist, they provided an alternative to traditional macromodels that was more attractive in many ways[11].

VARs were unlikely to appeal to the macro theorist, however, because by construction they contained very little theoretical content. The alternative to econometric macromodels and VARs for this group was the calibrated system.

Small parameterised macroeconomic systems were constructed which were related very closely to an analytical model, but whose parameters did not come directly from econometric estimation. Models of this type were central to the Real Business Cycle programme, which attempted to explain business cycles using classical rather than Keynesian ideas. 'Explanation' in this case meant that the model as a whole produced fluctuations in key variables that fitted the stylised facts about the business cycle. (Sims, 1996, provides a critique of this rather selective approach to evidence.)

These calibrated systems, which are now generally termed Stochastic Dynamic General Equilibrium (SDGE) models, had various advantages over conventional macromodels for the macro theorist. First, the theoretical structure of the model was both clear and unadulterated by any attempt at econometric estimation. Second, because econometrics was not used, the model builder needed to know nothing about econometric techniques[12].

The emphasis that these models put on a set of consistent theoretical foundations fitted in well with a trend in macroeconomic theory to provide microfoundations for macroeconomics. It no longer became acceptable to justify macroeconomic equations on the basis of plausibility alone: instead they had to be grounded in individual optimising behaviour. The REH can be seen as just one, albeit very important, example of this trend.

The danger with this research programme is that internal theoretical consistency with core microeconomic theory may become more important than consistency with the facts. These models are in danger of becoming more like parables than true stories[13]. An example of this might be the length of time it has taken for these calibrated models to adopt Keynesian price rigidity. We now have many theories about why firms do not change prices quickly, even under the REH, and how this can lead to aggregate economic fluctuations (New Keynesian theories of the business cycle). However, these theories tend not to fit easily and elegantly into the paradigm of optimising representative agents. As a result, introducing price rigidity into a theoretical macromodel is always going to appear a little unsatisfactory from a microfoundations perspective, and at worst 'ad hoc'. Only recently have many SDGE modellers discovered that price rigidity makes it much easier for these models to fit the facts[14]. Similar problems mean that these models are likely to remain relatively closed to the introduction of political or sociological influences. (Neuburger, 1983, argues strongly why such variables should be introduced into macromodels.)

The attractions of theory based, calibrated models were enhanced by the lack of theoretical credentials of many existing econometric macromodels. As I have noted earlier, some of the major models had become quite large and cumbersome. This had two negative consequences. First, it was often difficult to work out what the overall theoretical structure of the model was. Sometimes the complexity of the model had allowed mistakes to be introduced which impacted on overall model properties without model proprietors being aware of what was going on. Of course complexity can be theoretically interesting, but only if we know what is going on (Wren-Lewis et al, 1996). Second, the large size of the models made it more difficult to incorporate theoretical innovation. As the pace of theoretical advance quickened with the REH and other developments, conventional macromodels could easily get left behind.

So both the macro theorist and the macroeconometrician now have an alternative to conventional macromodels that more closely suit their interests and needs. Of course much applied macroeconomic research still involves econometric estimation of individual structural relationships, but there is little incentive for the researcher to go on to place that relationship within a complete econometric macromodel. So there is no need for any academic macroeconomist to become involved with conventional econometric macromodels, and the internal incentives (for publication) certainly point in different directions. As a result, only a few macroeconomists on either side of the Atlantic are involved with conventional macromodels.

These alternative ways of modelling the macroeconomy can be represented as shown in Figure 2.1.

Figure 2.1: The macromodelling spectrum

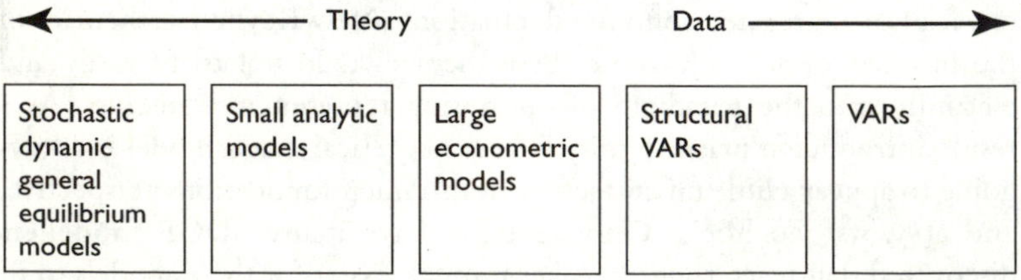

← Theory Data →

Stochastic dynamic general equilibrium models	Small analytic models	Large econometric models	Structural VARs	VARs

Thirty years ago, before econometric models went out of favour with academics, theoretical macroeconomists tended to use small analytic models. Like SDGE models these tend to be calibrated rather than estimated, but their relationships need not all come from a consistent theoretical framework, and could instead be based on relationships that have proved to be empirically robust. Although they are still widely used today, in SDGE model terms they would be described as 'ad hoc', and partly for this reason SDGE models tend to dominate small analytic models in the current academic literature. Structural VARs represent a new attempt to incorporate some degree of theoretical structure (normally involving long run relationships) within a VAR framework. Econometricians appear to be less averse to using theory than some theorists seem to be to using econometrics!

Today academic research is concentrated at either end of this spectrum. This does not of course imply that theorists ignore the real world, or that econometricians dismiss theory, but it does encourage what could be described as unbalanced development. To see how this has and may continue to impact on policy, we need to examine current practice in policy-making institutions.

Implications for policy?

The year 1999 saw the publication of *Economic models at the Bank of England* (Bank of England, 1999) which provides a comprehensive account of how the body currently charged with short-term UK macroeconomic management uses models. The most immediate and important insight is that the book describes not one model but many. The book is divided into chapters, which roughly correspond to the items in the spectrum in Figure 2.1, and the introduction describes a similar spectrum. Only one chapter describes a traditional econometric model, but that model is described as the 'core model', and it provides the basis for forecasting.

The Bank is probably unusual among central banks and similar institutions in formalising this diversity of modelling practice, but something approaching this probably takes place elsewhere. What is clear is that the conventional econometric model continues to play a central role in most institutions involved in macroeconomic policy in the major industrialised countries, including international bodies like the International Monetary Fund (IMF) or the Organisation for Economic Co-operation and Development (OECD). Within policy-making institutions, and in contrast to academia, the importance of the traditional macromodel may have declined but it is far from dead.

The position that the conventional econometric model has within the policy-making process at the Bank of England is in my view entirely appropriate. It was never healthy to rely exclusively on a single model, or a single modelling technique, to provide policy advice. I have argued elsewhere that it may be appropriate to use different models for forecasting and for policy advice (Wren-Lewis, 2000). Using a single model militated against new ideas, and did little to ensure that policy was robust to uncertainty.

The difficulty for macroeconomic policy making in this century is whether the current position is sustainable. The outcome I fear is that the influence of econometric macromodels within policy institutions will continue to decline, so that the macromodelling spectrum in policy institutions will look increasingly like the current academic scene. This is unlikely to be the result of a deliberate strategy, as policy makers find econometric macromodels particularly useful, for reasons I outline below. It will occur because policy-making institutions cannot or will not devote the resources required to maintain the quality and relevance of these models.

As I noted above, academic support for either end of the modelling spectrum is substantial and both the Bank and (since 1997) the Treasury are very active in using that support. Academic ideas and economic events move too rapidly for any economic policy-making body to be able to contemplate isolation, and it would be very difficult to imagine any situation in which isolation was desirable. Academic support in the area of econometric macromodelling, however, has largely disappeared. I suggested above that academics face incentives to generate innovations in theory or econometrics, and this is unlikely to come from building traditional macromodels.

Econometric models that are maintained by policy-making institutions require outside support for two reasons. First, although it is the case that conventional macromodelling is basically derivative, it nevertheless involves issues and problems that are specialised (like solution techniques for non-linear models under rational expectations) and which are essentially academic in nature and solution. Second, macromodels cannot afford to stand still: they need constant development to keep pace with theoretical or econometric innovations.

Academics have argued that if research on econometric macromodels is of primary interest to policy-making institutions or forecasters, then those bodies should fund that research directly. This is both unrealistic and undesirable. Commercial forecasters are rarely in the position to fund fundamental research: research institutions, such as the National Institute, that also forecast are not able to fund model development from the returns from forecasting. The Treasury or Bank could in principle greatly expand their in-house macromodelling teams, but this is unlikely to happen in practice, partly because it would appear to be moving back to the time when econometric macromodels were dominant.[15] Even if it did, however, it would not be desirable, because it would create an unhealthy monopoly in providing a key vehicle for policy advice. While it may be difficult to say just how many UK econometric models are required to provide informed debate and robust policy advice, the answer is certainly not only one, particularly if that one is subject to the inevitable sensitivity to disclosure and criticism that comes with any policy-making institution.

Unfortunately, the argument that the academic sector should not provide the research support for econometric macromodelling has in practice won the day[16]. Without this support, the quality of the models maintained within policy-making institutions will gradually decline. Econometric macromodels are unlikely to disappear completely, partly because they are a useful way of collecting and using large amounts of information in forecasting. However, if macroeconomic theory continues to advance at anything like its recent pace, then these models will also need considerable development just to keep up, and without outside help this is unlikely to occur. As these models fall further behind current macroeconomic theory, then either policy makers will become increasingly reluctant to use them for policy analysis, or the quality of advice these models provide will become outdated.

If this does come to pass, would it really matter? After all, we would still be getting advice on macroeconomic theory from theorists, and the evidence from the past from econometricians. By cutting out the middle from the macromodelling spectrum, are we just losing one particular form of policy analysis among many? Would governments or central banks really be more likely to adopt bad policies as a result?

Unfortunately the evidence from the past suggests we would. Policy makers are often tempted by economic theories which have dubious empirical backing, but which offer an easy or quick fix to important problems. Krugman (1994) relates how the Laffer curve – the idea that tax cuts could be self financing – was used by Reagan to justify the large US fiscal expansion in the early 1980s, even though nearly all economists rejected the idea. He argues that economic policy is not chosen by finding the best economists and acting on their advice, but instead through the activities of what he describes as "policy entrepreneurs", whose economic understanding may be relatively limited. The UK monetarist experiment in the early 1980s might be another example, although in this case the minority of economists backing the policy was both larger and more significant. As both these examples illustrate, the presence of econometric macromodels on their own will not prevent these flights of fancy turning into policy if the policy maker is determined enough, but they certainly discourage this tendency. As I noted above, the Treasury model did predict the consequences of the MTFS for UK unemployment, and it made life uncomfortable for the Conservative government in a way that was probably more effective than a letter from 364 economists. While the academic economists on their own may be no match for the successful policy entrepreneur, their collective wisdom encapsulated in a model can provide some defence.

It is worth exploring the monetarist example in more detail, because it helps explain why structural econometric models are so useful in policy analysis, and what would be lost if they were no longer used. The idea that gradually reducing the money supply would bring about a gradual and painless reduction in inflation had clear theoretical credentials, even though the majority of economists at the time thought that the theory was inadequate. Theoretical debate alone was never going to disprove monetarism. The data based evidence, relating money to prices, appeared mixed. In 1980 the Treasury was asked to examine this evidence, and I was the Treasury economist who was asked to do the work. To its credit the Treasury published what I found, but without any interpretation or conclusion. After publication Tim Congdon claimed in *The Times* that I had found clear evidence to support the MTFS, while Peter Shore (who was advised by Henry) wrote in a letter immediately afterwards that I had done exactly the opposite. From the policy maker's point of view, the evidence could simply be labelled controversial. (To find out who I believe was right and who was wrong, see Wren-Lewis, 1984, which was published after I had left the Treasury.)

The advantage of an econometric model is that it tells a structural story that is much more difficult to mystify. Reducing the money supply ahead of inflation required higher interest rates, leading to an appreciation in the exchange rate and an uncompetitive manufacturing sector. To suggest otherwise required prices and wages to fall in line with the money supply, while all the historical evidence showed that a much more gradual adjustment would occur. In this case the empirical evidence was more compelling, because it related to the actual behaviour of firms and workers, rather than the 'black box' transmission from money to prices. It was of course still possible to discount this evidence on the grounds that the very existence of the MTFS would change people's behaviour, but the argument that the world has (just) changed is an argument of last resort.

Econometric models are so useful to policy makers because they bring theory and evidence together in a structural way. We can examine in detail the process by which policy instruments influence objectives, and use both the theory and evidence we have about these individual processes. There is simply no other way, for example, of combining what knowledge we have about each aspect of macroeconomic behaviour to present a picture of how interest rates influence inflation[17].

At the beginning of the 21st century, the key macroeconomic issue facing the UK is entry into the EMU. The entry rate is a key issue, with Sterling in early 2000 even more overvalued than our ERM central parity. Here the advice coming directly from either theory or the data is mixed. While some data based studies confirm Sterling is overvalued and the Euro undervalued (for instance Alberola et al, 1999) others are less clear (Wadhwani, 1999), and both newspapers and politicians have on occasion suggested that UK manufacturing is 'learning to live' with the high pound. The most basic theory we have (Purchasing Power Parity) suggests that our ERM entry rate is now about right.

In this situation a structural analysis based on a macroeconometric model would be extremely helpful. Not only would it provide additional evidence, but it could also be used to move the debate forward. Is there evidence from recent export behaviour, for example, to suggest that the UK is learning to live with a high pound? The models in the Treasury and the Bank could provide an answer, but if this analysis has been done it has not been made public. In one of its last papers before it closed (Church, 1999), the Warwick Bureau published research based on the Treasury model that suggested an EMU entry rate well below current or ERM parities[18].

Macroeconometric models, particularly if they are in the public domain, can contribute to debates of this kind. Perhaps more importantly, they at least have the potential (by linking data and theory directly in a structural manner) of helping to isolate the cause of conflicting advice and move a debate forward. Without them I fear macroeconomic policy analysis will become more fragmented, and the chances of major mistakes being made will increase.

To avoid this happening requires a change in attitude from both policy institutions and academic economists. Policy advisors, who by and large do recognise the importance and utility of econometric macromodels to policy making, need also to recognise that research on these models needs active encouragement. Academic macroeconomists, on the other hand, need to appreciate that, by cutting themselves off from research on econometric macromodels, they are losing a critical and effective means of getting macroeconomic ideas into policy making. If these models continue to be used but are not kept up to date with new ideas, techniques and evidence, then they become an electronic embodiment of Keynes' academic scribbler[19]. If, as a result of academic neglect, their influence declines, then policy becomes more susceptible to being hijacked by economic ideas that may be politically attractive but turn out to be both wrong and damaging.

Conclusion

Macroeconometric models appear to be much less important today than they were in the 1970s. To analyse whether this will help or hinder policy making in the future, we can consider why this decline in influence has occurred. In this chapter I have argued that it reflects the emergence of alternative ways of modelling the macroeconomy, and this greater diversity in the forms of evidence available on its own is to be welcomed.

Unfortunately developments within academic macroeconomics suggest that the decline in econometric macromodels will go too far, such that they no longer play a useful role in macroeconomic policy debates. Macromodels provide a crucial link between theory and evidence which is in danger of being lost, and the quality of macroeconomic policy decisions will suffer as a result.

Notes

[1] I am grateful to the other contributors to this volume, and to Ron Smith, for helpful comments on an earlier draft.

[2] 'Modellers for socialism'.

[3] Christopher Allsopp in Chapter Seven charts what was happening to macroeconomic policy itself over this period.

[4] These models tend to be large in size, but this is a consequence of their use rather than a defining characteristic, and there are many examples of small econometric macromodels (e.g. Desai and Weber, 1988). The activity of building and using such models is typically referred to as macromodelling, although as I will discuss later there are now other important ways of modelling the macroeconomy.

[5] The 'theory' in both cases was the relationship between the exchange rate and aggregate demand.

[6] In particular the failure to see that the indexation clauses agreed as part of the incomes policy would be triggered

[7] Using the technique of stochastic simulations. Optimism in the early days of macromodelling might have hoped that the amount of uncertainty would have decreased steadily as models improved, but recent improvements seem to have been modest at best.

[8] Actual errors will be greater than predicted errors because theories or parameters may be wrong, but on the other hand judgmental intervention by forecasters using models tends to go in the opposite direction.

[9] In a forecast, everything is predicted unconditionally. In policy analysis, the effects of a policy change are analysed conditional on other things being equal. The Bank of England might use a macromodel to forecast what will happen to the economy with current interest rates (a forecast), but it could also use a macromodel to examine what effect a change in interest rates would have (policy analysis).

[10] It remains the case, however, that macroeconometric models take time to build from scratch (my own model, COMPACT, took about six person years), and they are relatively expensive in resource terms compared to some of the alternatives I outline below. Such costs are of course trivial compared to the costs of major macroeconomic policy errors.

[11] Of course econometricians are interested in testing theory against the data. However once we allow the possibility of a large degree of system interaction, as Sims (1980) suggested we should, then the VAR becomes the natural starting point for analysis.

[12] As both time series econometrics and macroeconomic theory were developing fast and were internally controversial, an attempt to master both was costly.

[13] One economist described one of my own published efforts in this area as 'not quite Kosher', and I think this gives exactly the right flavour of the value systems being adopted. Henry argued that this theoretical introspection stemmed in part from the lack of a clear policy framework (Neuburger, 1996). An alternative view might be that such introspection is encouraged because it keeps macroeconomics close to a rather simple theoretical framework which supports a laissez-faire outlook.

[14] The other main reason why calibrated models were slow to incorporate price rigidity was ideological: Real Business Cycle theorists who pioneered the use of this modelling approach formed part of the New Classical, anti-Keynesian school.

[15] In my experience another problem is that most macromodelling resources in policy making institutions tend to be absorbed in the day to day needs of forecasting – it is all too easy to put off investment in model development when there are immediate policy needs (see Wren-Lewis, 2000).

[16] When the ESRC replaced its programme of support for macromodelling with a much more general, inter-disciplinary research programme on macroeconomics, its documentation focused on the need to embrace the new developments in modelling techniques that I outlined above. What the ESRC did not address, however, was the fact these new methods were already heavily researched within the academic community, while work on macromodelling was not.

[17] If advice only came from either end of the macromodelling spectrum, then it is unclear how differences between theory and evidence would be resolved. If theory suggested interest rates should influence prices quickly, but the data suggested a long lag, then which parts of the theory need modifying? The obvious way to answer this is to compare each element of the theory with the evidence, which is exactly what a structural econometric model does!

[18] It should be obvious that I consider the decision by the ESRC not to continue supporting the Warwick Bureau or an equivalent successor to be a major error.

[19] "Practical men, who believe themselves to be quite exempt from any intellectual influences, are usually the slaves of some defunct economist. Madmen in authority,

who hear voices in the air, are distilling their frenzy from some academic scribbler of a few years back" (Keynes, 1936).

References

Alberola, E., Cervero, S.G., Lopez, H. and Ubide, A. (1999) 'Global equilibrium exchange rates', *IMF working paper*, 99/175.

Bank of England (1999) *Economic models at the Bank of England*, London: Bank of England.

Church, K.B. (1993) 'Properties of the fundamental equilibrium exchange rate in models of the UK economy', *National Institute Economic Review*, no 141, pp 62-70.

Church, K.B. (1999) 'Properties of the fundamental equilibrium exchange rate in the Treasury model', *National Institute Economic Review*, no 169, pp 96-104.

Desai, M. and Weber, G. (1988) 'A Keynesian macro-econometric model of the UK: 1955-1984', *Journal of Applied Econometrics*, vol 3, pp 1-33.

Kenway, P. (1994) *From Keynesianism to monetarism: The evolution of UK macroeconometric models*, London: Routledge.

Keynes, J.M. (1936) *The general theory of employment, interest and money*, London: Macmillan.

Krugman, P. (1994) *Peddling prosperity*, New York, NY: Norton.

Lucas, R.E. (1976) 'Econometric policy evaluation: a critique', *Carnegie-Rochester series on Public Policy*, no 1, pp 19-46.

Mankiw, N. (1990) 'A quick refresher course in macroeconomics', *Journal of Economic Literature*, vol 28, pp 1645-60.

Neuburger, H. (1983) 'The use and limitations of economic forecasting models', *Socialist Economic Review*, vol 3, pp 259-75.

Neuburger, H. (1996) 'Life after economics', *New Economy*, vol 3, no 1, pp 39-42.

Ormerod, P. (1994) *The death of economics*, London: Faber.

Pain, N. and Britton, A. (1992) 'The recent experience of economic forecasting in Britain', *National Institute Discussion Paper*, no 20, London: NIESR.

Sims, C. (1980) 'Macroeconomics and reality', *Econometrica*, vol 48, no 1, pp 1-48.

Sims, C. (1996) 'Macroeconomics and methodology', *Journal of Economic Perspectives*, vol 10, pp 105-20.

Smith, R. (1994) 'The macromodelling industry: structure, conduct and performance', in S. Hall (ed) *Applied economic forecasting techniques*, Hemel Hempstead: Harvester/Wheatsheaf.

Wadhwani, S. (1999) 'Sterling's puzzling behaviour', *Bank of England Quarterly Bulletin* (November), pp 416-27.

Wren-Lewis, S. (1984) 'Omitted variables in equations relating prices to money', *Applied Economics,* vol 16, pp 483-96.

Wren-Lewis, S. (2000) 'Conflicts between macroeconomic forecasting and policy analysis', in F.A.G. den Butter and M.S.Morgan (eds) *Empirical models and policy making: Interaction and institutions*, London: Routledge (forthcoming).

Wren-Lewis, S., Darby, J., Ireland, J. and Ricchi, O. (1996) 'The macroeconomic effects of fiscal policy: linking an econometric model with theory', *Economic Journal*, vol 100, pp 756-72.

Wren-Lewis, S., Westaway, P., Soteri, S. and Barrell, R. (1991) 'Evaluating the UK's choice of entry rate into the ERM', *Manchester School*, Money Study Group Conference, vol LIX Supplement, pp 1-22.

THREE

National accounts for policy analysis

Anne Harrison

A new system of accounts

Even those with little knowledge and less interest in economics have heard of gross domestic product, at least in its abbreviated form of GDP. Few of those who quote GDP knowledgeably are aware of the whole system from which it is drawn and the richness this system provides, for instance to demonstrate the interaction of production with the demand for capital and labour, or the process by which income from employment is transformed into a different capacity to purchase the outputs of the production allowing for the redistributive effect of taxes and benefits.

This wider framework, the system of national accounts (SNA) was revised in 1993 and now, in 2000, is just being implemented world wide. The new system (referred to as SNA93) gives a much greater scope for flexibility and imaginative use than the previous one published in 1968. Henry Neuburger was one of the first to seize enthusiastically on the possibilities of this flexibility as a means of demonstrating the usefulness of the whole system to economists and of persuading the statisticians producing the accounts to exploit this new liberation from a statistical straitjacket in order to develop alternative presentations of the material in the accounts in a manner more responsive to analytical needs.

Non-standard accounts are described in the SNA93 as 'satellite' accounts to emphasise they are complementary to the standard accounts and not replacements for them. They incorporate flexibility in one of two ways. Either the existing material is rearranged to show the same phenomena in a different light, or new material is added as a supplement to extend the basic framework. Henry named these two alternatives internal and external satellites. His vision, and mine, was to develop an interlinked set of internal and external satellites which could address policy issues in a manner more intelligible to a wide range of analysts not indoctrinated with all the national accounting mystique. This chapter gives an overview of the sorts of possibilities which have been or could be developed by describing first three internal satellites and then three external ones. Macroeconomics is where modellers start. The goal here is to form simple bridges to particular policy issues including tax policy, income distribution and poverty, the provision of public services such as health and transport, and ultimately to welfare; all issues taken up in other chapters in this volume.

Paying for government

Government intervenes in the operation of the market to increase the prices of goods and services by levying taxes on these products. The revenue raised is then used to pay, in part, for the services that government provides. To some extent, therefore, there is double counting in a measure of GDP which includes both the taxes on products and the services provided by government. The UK has been almost alone in continuing to refer to the measure of GDP 'at factor cost' which eliminates this double counting by excluding all taxes on products. In most international work, and in many national contexts including for the UK, it is GDP at market prices which is generally used.

Not only is there double counting in GDP at market prices, but the extent of double counting varies as the tax structure changes. If, for example, the government raises VAT and lowers income tax rates in a way that is revenue neutral, GDP still increases on a market price basis. On the other hand, if VAT is increased but rates on offices and factories drop exactly to compensate, GDP is unaltered. Not only are these consequences for GDP counter-intuitive to some observers, they are inconsistent with the idea that VAT is a tax on consumption rather than a tax related to production.

In an internal satellite account, though, we may change some of the conventions on how taxes are recorded in SNA93 to derive a presentation where taxes are separated into taxes paid by producers, taxes paid by consumers, taxes paid on income and taxes paid on capital. Taxes on producers would include rates on buildings, any taxes levied on the labour force and any taxes on products which a producer pays as part of his operating costs, for example non-deductible VAT and the excise tax levied on fuel oil. Taxes on consumers include most VAT and excise duties on drink, tobacco and on their use of petrol, for example.

A table such as Table 3.1 can be drawn up showing the composition of

Table 3.1: Tax incidence

	Corporations	Households
Total income	225	1,424
Taxes on income	34	178
Taxes on consumption		115
% of income	15.1	20.6

the tax burden for enterprises and households allowing helpful comparisons to be made for different parts of the economy or showing how the burden alters over time. This is particularly useful when a government is thinking of changing the structure of taxes – as in Australia at the present time where plans to introduce a general sales tax (operating like VAT) are well advanced.

Not only does the SNA93 contain no taxes on consumption in its main tables, it also has no consumer subsidies. This too can give rise to somewhat anomalous changes in GDP as a result of changing government policies. 'Small' subsidies are regarded as being paid to producers. They reduce prices below what they would otherwise be and thus GDP at market prices is less than it would be in the absence of the subsidy. By extension, an increase in a small subsidy reduces GDP at market prices. 'Large' subsidies are treated differently. When most of the costs of an enterprise are covered by subsidies from government, the enterprise itself is regarded as being part of the government sector and the goods and services it produces are treated as part of government output and are valued at cost. In this case, increasing a large subsidy *increases* GDP. Now, if it is known that government is going to increase (or decrease) the subsidy on a particular range of products, the impact on GDP cannot be predicted unless it is known whether the subsidies in question count as 'small' or 'large'. Clearly the borderline between small and large is debatable, but however it is drawn, having an enterprise pass from being in receipt of one to receiving the other has quite anomalous results for the estimation of GDP.

If we follow the path indicated above for taxes on products and identify subsidies which primarily benefit consumers, a much tidier and intuitive picture emerges. If government gives a subsidy to a producer to allow elderly people to travel free, this should be seen as a subsidy to consumers and any increase in taking advantage of these subsidies would result in an increase of GDP regardless of how important this section of the market is to the transport enterprise.

Table 3.2: Alternative portrayal of subsidies

Government consumption	**412**
Collective consumption	*192*
– own production	156
– bought from enterprises (producer subsidies)	36
Individual consumption	*220*
– own production	212
– bought from enterprises (consumer subsidies)	8

Just as we have subsidies benefiting consumers, we may also have subsidies benefiting producers (Table 3.2). Government may offer inducements to an enterprise to operate in a particular area or to employ particular classes of people. Should we think of these simply as means of reducing the prices (or maintaining the profits) of the enterprise? An alternative is to view the enterprise as carrying out government regional or employment policy and being recompensed for doing it. An increase in these sorts of subsidies would also increase GDP but this time by increasing the costs of implementing government policy. Thus we reach the position that any increase in subsidies increases GDP in much the same way that any other increase in government spending on goods and services does.

Making services visible

The SNA93 introduces an important and interesting distinction concerning consumption. Consumption expenditure shows who pays for the items concerned; actual consumption shows who benefits from them. Thus government health and education expenditures are paid for by government but benefit households. Government actual consumption is reduced to cover only pure public goods such as administration and defence; household actual consumption expands to include all health and education, both government funded and privately paid. Such a presentation makes for interesting comparisons across time and country and brings us closer to a measure of household wellbeing (to which we will return towards the end of the chapter).

Within an internal satellite, we may extend this notion of separating who pays for and who benefits from certain types of expenditure. For years a debate has raged about the appropriate recording of television funded by advertising. Should it not be regarded as a kind of final consumption by the enterprises paying for the advertising? No, came the answer, this cannot be because enterprises do not have final consumption. Now we can find a way round this. We can have final consumption expenditure of enterprises on television, or sports sponsorship and so on, and actual consumption by households. This we achieve in the same way that we have a bifocal view of health expenditure, we allow social transfers in kind to be paid by enterprises to households which reduce actual consumption by enterprises to zero but increase actual consumption by households by the same amount.

So far, the SNA93 uses social transfers in kind only to augment household consumption. But we may generalise this also. We considered above treating subsidies paid to enterprises as a means of paying enterprises to undertake government policy in return for reimbursement. Increasingly, however, government implements policy by imposing regulations on enterprises. Restrictions on permissible levels of air and water emission to protect the environment is one example. The conventional SNA presentation simply shows the enterprise internalising the costs as part of intermediate consumption. If instead we identify the activity as the provision of environmental services funded by the enterprise, we may treat these as public goods provided by enterprises without explicit charge. Since public goods are 'consumed' by government on behalf of the community at large, we introduce the idea of social transfers in kind receivable by government as well as those payable by them. In this way we may then show public goods provided by enterprises as final consumption expenditure of enterprises but actual consumption of government.

Another area which has caused endless but unresolved discussion is how to account for increases in human capital in the national accounts. If a firm pays for training, should this not be reflected as a sort of capital expenditure by the firm? One problem is that it is not quite the same sort of capital formation as the purchase of a fleet of vehicles. The vehicles are owned by the enterprise and may be sold by them; usually they are gradually used up over a period of time. Training is not used up, but forms the foundation for further increments in human capital. Training is embodied in the employees; it cannot be sold by the employer and may be lost to him (though not the community) if the employee leaves the enterprise which provided the training.

Within our satellite account we may deal with this by a further level of generalisation. We allow the distinction between who pays and who benefits to be extended to capital formation as well as to expenditure. Government current expenditure is divided into that part benefiting

Table 3.3: Examples of transfers in kind

Type of expenditure	Unit that pays	Unit that benefits
Final consumption		
TV funded by advertising	Corporations	Households
Environmental services mandated by legislation	Corporations	Government (representing the community at large)
Fixed capital formation		
Investment in public corporations	Government	Corporations
Education	Government and corporations	Households

individuals and that part benefiting the whole community. We may extend this to capital expenditure, saying that education expenditure is not only capital in nature but is undertaken by government on behalf of individuals. On the other hand, provision of road- and street-lighting, for example, benefits the community as a whole and so can be regarded as 'collective' capital expenditure. There is a third class of government capital expenditure though; purchase of computers for government staff, like computers bought by enterprises for their staff, constitutes capital formation to be used in the production process and is therefore to be regarded as 'enterprise' capital expenditure. A similar distinction can be made for enterprises. Most of their expenditure is for use in their own production processes. Some may be of a collective nature, for example major environmental clean-ups or restoration of public spaces. Training by enterprises can be seen as fixed capital formation expenditure by them and as individual capital formation by households (see Table 3.3).

In input–output tables, it is usual to allow enterprises to produce different types of goods. One is designated the principal product and the others secondary products. With the exception of distribution and construction, though, it is usual to treat all the services produced by a goods manufacturer as 'ancillary', that is not sold to anyone else and simply to merge all the costs associated with these ancillary services as overheads into the operational costs of the enterprise. The pattern of ancillary services has changed over time with more government legislation, greater emphasis on training and increased outsourcing of certain activities. Essentially what we are suggesting in this satellite is to pay attention to the ancillary services and to identify them explicitly. This allows us to obtain pictures of all training undertaken – both that outsourced and that provided internally; all environmental protection expenditure – both that funded by government and that undertaken by firms in response to government legislation or even by voluntary agreement. At the same time, the costs to the firm not wrapped into an ancillary service relate more closely to the technological process of making the principal and secondary products of the firm. Attempts over many years to explain the evolution of the movements of technological coefficients have failed to come up with plausible paths. One reason may be the changing role of ancillary services. Separating these activities gives insight into the full extent of 'support' services but may also lead the way to understand better the costs of the firm's main business.

Accounting for income

It is accepted as a truism that economic activity can be measured as the sum of value added, the sum of all final expenditures or the sum of all income generated as a result of production. Under 'paying for government' we saw that including the production of government services in both output and expenditure involves some degree of double counting and suggested an alternative means of recording taxes to avoid this. Under 'making services visible' we explored how we may have two patterns of expenditure, one showing who pays for it and one who benefits from it. In our third and last internal satellite, we turn our attention to the third measure of GDP, that of income.

The SNA93 includes all forms of income, those arising directly from production, those paid in respect of lending out assets to another unit (property income), and those given without a *quid pro quo* (transfers, including taxes on income). These flows appear in a strict sequence of accounts, one element at a time leading to a measure of disposable income which is then accounted for by final consumption or capital formation in accordance with all the best economic textbooks. This process, however, is not well suited to understanding how wealth accumulates because capital gains and losses are rigorously excluded from a measure of income forced to be dependent on a concept of production which excludes such gains. This satellite, therefore, assembles all the elements of income together in a different set of accounts and adds in holding gains so the impact on changing wealth can be seen.

Nowhere in the SNA is profit mentioned, nor does the cost of using fixed or financial capital enter into the production account. Our first account is a production account modified to include all costs associated with the use of capital. These costs include interest paid on financial loans, a measure of the cost of services provided by fixed capital and other costs not recorded in the conventional SNA accounts, such as costs of depleting natural capital – either renewable (such as natural forests) or non-renewable (such as mineral deposits). The inclusion of the cost of capital services provides a link to productivity studies. Use of natural resources leads into 'green' accounting as will be seen below (p 44). The residual item on the account, income from production, is close to a measure of 'pure' profit or loss.

The next account is a use of assets account, showing who owns assets and therefore earns income from them. Those payments occurring in connection with production are covered in the preceding account, others such as interest payment on consumer debt are recorded as an outgoing in this present account.

The third account looks at how capital evolves. Is it used up in production? Does it produce a return which enhances its value? Is natural capital enhanced by timber growth or new discoveries of mineral deposits? Most importantly, how does the value of capital assets change in response to absolute and relative price changes? All these changes can be anticipated and can be construed as forming part of income as Hicks defined it. In addition exceptional events such as catastrophic losses, even though not anticipated, must be accounted for if the balance sheet value of assets is to reflect all changes which occur.

We can now assemble the various types of income, compensation of employees, enterprise income from production (the pure profit element), income from the use of assets and change in the value of assets including real holding gains and losses. The next step is to look at the effect on this initial distribution of total income of receipts of income via the redistributive processes of tax and benefits systems.

Total income after redistribution is used either for current consumption or is further redistributed by exchanging assets and acquiring new ones. This process is shown in the last of our supplementary accounts. A summary table such as Table 3.4 brings all these elements together. It enables us to see where the income of each sector of the economy comes from and how far each sector finances its own capital formation and how far it is dependent on borrowing from another sector.

'As if people mattered'

In 1973 E.F. Schumacher published a book called *Small is beautiful* which caught the public imagination. Many of the attitudes it endorsed which

Table 3.4: Sources of income and capital accumulation

	Corporations	Government	Households	Total
Compensation of employees			766	766
Income from production	–241	–19	447	187
Income from the use of assets	466	52	211	729
Taxes on producers		120		120
Total income	**225**	**153**	**1,424**	**1,802**
Transfers received				0
Taxes		328		328
Social contributions	54	268		322
Social benefits			332	332
Other transfers	2	127	3	132
Income after redistributive receipts	**281**	**876**	**1,759**	**2,916**
Transfers paid				0
Taxes	34		294	328
Social contributions			322	322
Social benefits	42	290		332
Other transfers	14	113	5	132
Income after redistributive payments	**191**	**473**	**1,138**	**1,802**
Final consumption		412	1,015	1,427
Saving	191	61	123	375
Capital transfers	10	–28	18	0
Capital formation	265	83	27	375
Net borrowing (+)/ net lending (–)	64	50	–114	0

seemed revolutionary have become commonplace, not least the idea caught in its subtitle: *A study of economics as if people mattered.*

The normal accounts of the SNA93 describe economic processes but people hardly feature in them. True there is a sector comprising households, all of which consume and some of whom produce, but they are featureless and anonymous. Yet even before *Small is beautiful* was published, Richard Stone, pioneer of the national accounts, had developed a Social Accounting Matrix (SAM) which added a disaggregation of households by important characteristics to the main national accounts. Over thirty years, a number of SAMs have been constructed but mainly in developing countries and most often as one-off exercises. There are several reasons why the notion of a SAM has lain dormant for so long. One is that they are typically very data demanding. Not only do they require data on households as well as data on industries but the linking factor, employees, have to be reconcilable between the two data sets. Often, even when good alternative data sets existed, the strain of matching the linking variables distorted one or both basic sets unacceptably. A second reason was that the notion of a SAM is deliberately openminded about what determining characteristics for households should be selected. Typically each new SAM used a new household breakdown so those trying to learn from past experience were not always sure how to adapt the choices to new circumstances. Lastly, a SAM is constructed as a large interrelated matrix which gives a valuable picture of interrelationships but only for a single time period, yet many analyses depend on the time series element for greatest relevance.

Recent work has shown that harmonising household data with the macroeconomic aggregates from national accounts on a regular basis may be more easily within reach than has been the case in the past. If to this work we add a simple, but standard, disaggregation of households, we may be able to make a bridge to other data sets relating to people and households with recognisable characteristics. A starting point is to consider households where the main income earner is in employment, or is of working age but not in employment, or is retired. These three categories coincide to a large (but not exhaustive) extent with income from employment, social security benefits (other than pensions) and pensions (whether from the state or an occupational pension scheme).

A breakdown, such as that shown in Table 3.5, though simple, is key to two of the most important debates on social policy. Are there sufficient jobs for everyone of working age who wants one? How will the economy be able to provide for an increasing number of households of retired persons? If we can set up this disaggregation of households we may further disaggregate it. We could, for example, separate state pensioners from others and the latter between those in receipt of an occupational pension scheme and those having other sources of incomes. But the disaggregation need not stop there. Non-working households could be divided between fulltime students, single parents with young children not actively seeking work and others.

Clearly the correlation between the three sorts of household and three sorts of income is not exact. Not only must we allow for 'non-typical' income receipts, we must also allow for other items such as interest receipts and inheritances. We may also add in other considerations such as entitlement to government services for health and education. If we can

Table 3.5: Income distribution within the SNA?

Status of reference person	Employed	Not employed	
		Of working age	**Not of working age**
Numbers			
Households	*	*	*
Adults of working age	*	*	
Adults not of working age			*
Children	*	*	
Money values			
Compensation of employees	*		
Income from self-employment/ mixed income	*		
Pensions – state			*
Pensions – other			*
Unemployment benefits		*	
Child benefits	*	*	
Property income receivable	*		*
Property income payable	*		*

Key: Households to be classified by reference person (main income earner); expected significant entries are shown by *; an empty cell here does not necessarily imply a zero entry in practice; row totals corresponding to national totals to be included also.

also distinguish the actual take-up of these services, we can see whether the state services do provide more security to poorer families (as usually presumed) because their take-up is higher than their equitable entitlement or whether it is the somewhat wealthier and often more articulate households who make fullest use of their entitlement.

Further elaboration of these accounts is also possible. One matter for examination is how far distribution of expenditures provides insights into the standard of living of different groups of households in ways complementary to the view given by distribution of income alone. While income may be seen to be a characteristic of an individual, a fact increasingly recognised in income tax legislation and data coming from tax sources, levels of expenditure are inextricably linked to household characteristics since this is the way in which patterns of sharing some forms of expenditure (housing, utilities, food) are captured. From here it is a small step to examine expenditure patterns in relation to both household composition and income levels and to consider the option of calculating cost of living indices for different household groups.

Greening the accounts

The 1970s saw a concern not only with putting people into the accounts but also to think more carefully and explicitly about the interaction between the economy and nature. The national accounts have always taken natural resources for granted. Subsoil deposits, natural forests, fish stocks in the ocean were there for the taking, 'free'. Similarly the land, air and water could assimilate the residuals generated by economic production 'without cost'. Increasingly this view of nature has come to be seen as overly simplistic and pressure has grown to produce a 'green GDP' where the natural resources exploited by production processes are costed and accounted for in the same way as products generated by the economy.

The interaction between the economy and the environment is two way. Much of the pressure to calculate a figure for green GDP comes from a desire to know what impact unsustainable use of the environment will have on the economic potential in the future. Evocatively, this is sometimes expressed in terms of ensuring this generation should not imperil the economic potential of future generations by recklessly running down the stock of natural capital without building up other capital to preserve the total wealth of the nation to be bequeathed to the future.

The contribution of the environment to the economy is exceedingly difficult to quantify in economic terms. Some commentators reject in rather absolute terms the need even to attempt this. It is sufficient, they say, to point out the dangers of global warming and measure carbon dioxide emissions quantitatively without trying to put a money value on them. There is much force in this argument but moral pressure alone is not sufficient to invoke universal environment-friendly behaviour. Quantification in terms of money is needed to answer the questions 'how much will environment-friendly behaviour cost us?' or 'what will happen to the growth rate of the economy if we use less X or pay more for Y?' in order to inform the political debate involving trade-offs between desirable but competing objectives. (But see Neil Fraser's discussion of some of the problems raised by translating all costs and benefits into monetary terms in Chapter Four).

An international accounting handbook describing how a set of measures of GDP adjusted to varying degrees for environmental concerns could be calculated was also issued in 1993. This manual is currently being revised and will represent a particularly important external satellite of the SNA.

The first step will be to discuss the depletion of natural resources, those elements drawn into the economy and subsequently transformed into other products, crude oil to petroleum, forest trees to wooden furniture, fish to fish fingers. Two different types of depletion are normally considered, those where natural replenishment leads to renewal (forests and fish, for example) and those such as mineral deposits where renewal does not occur on a human timescale. The conventions for when and how to make deductions from GDP in these cases are close to agreement by the statisticians who have been discussing this over recent years.

The second step concerns degradation of natural resources by their use as an environmental sink. We may think of the air as an 'asset' but it is difficult to imagine putting a comprehensive value on it or to agree who owns which part of it. One question which can be asked is how much would it cost to stop the air being polluted? Sometimes the answer is that no amount of money is sufficient; some damage done cannot be reversed at any cost. Sometimes a reasonable cost may solve 95% of the problem but removing the last 5% is punitively expensive. Would the 95% solution be acceptable? Almost always, the question is not well phrased. Instead of asking what the cost to households for water would be if it were all metered, should we not be asking how much water would households demand if the water were metered? At the margin we may ask how much would something cost, but not when introducing prices for a previously free commodity which would cause a radical shift in supply and demand; then even the hypothetical answer may not be very illuminating.

An alternative approach is not to ask how much clean air is worth but to ask how much damage polluted air causes. The damage to buildings, for example, should in principle already be included in the national accounts. The damage to human health is not. If we regard human capital as a necessary factor of production, though, we could include an estimate of the effects on health as a cost of air pollution and say that in line with a Hicksian view of income where capital is kept intact this is a cost to be deducted from national income. This moves the discussion forward but does not solve all the problems. No unequivocally correct way of estimating the damage is yet agreed and there are second order problems. Is it only the health of people still in the labour force that matter? Nevertheless this is the route which seems most promising at present.

Increasingly the assumption that there is no cost associated with the use of environmental resources is invalid. Governments who started by invoking legislation (later voluntary agreements) to control natural resource use are increasingly changing to using economic instruments for bringing about the desired effect. One example is the introduction of emissions permits or fishing quotas which can be sold on the market to limit damage to the environment. Another is the use of environmental taxes and reduction in subsidies to bring market forces into play in controlling use of the environment. A third strand of the new environmental accounting manual thus will be to explore how to identify such environmentally relevant parts of the existing national accounts.

One hallmark of this satellite account will be that there are indeed some issues where non-monetary data is at least as illuminating as the monetary work and the complementarity of the two accounting units should be emphasised and exploited. So far, only non-monetary values can be used to measure the non-economic values of biodiversity. Even for aspects such as the amenity value of landscapes, monetary values alone capture only a part of the non-economic value placed on them by economic beings.

Economics and the feel-good factor

This last thought leads us into the area of measuring welfare and the quality of life. National accountants complain loud and long when people take GDP to be the measure of welfare. Some may concede that it is *a* measure of welfare but hasten to add that it is an imperfect measure. One reason is that it makes no attempt to measure consumer surplus. Another is simply that the range of activities covered by the accounts is quite restricted.

A particular case in point is the role of services provided within the household and consumed by the household. There are activities such as house cleaning, child rearing and care of elderly people where market alternatives may exist but the current market prices reflect the fact that for the most part these are performed without direct cost at home. Then there are other aspects of family life such as companionship where market equivalents are hardly applicable. For several years there has been vocal demand that excluding household services was to neglect a very important part of welfare and it is undoubtedly the case that the measurement of growth of an economy, swollen by increased participation of women in the labour force without any diminution of household services, does overstate the growth of production.

One way to address this issue is to include information in the accounts of the role of people in terms of their input in time into different production processes. This can be done through a series of labour accounts where demographic factors and (paid) employment opportunities are explicitly recognised. Another is via time use surveys where the twenty-four hours available to everyone are assigned to one of several categories, paid employment, unpaid work, leisure, 'maintenance' (eating, washing and sleeping). Each of these can then, in principle, be given a value which allows the extension of the accounts to include any or all of the last three categories.

Demography affects not only early years when people are below the age for participation in the labour force and years which may be devoted to child rearing but increasingly the number of years spent post employment. Much of the talk of the 'new economy' focuses on the possibilities unleashed by technology but much of the future of economies in OECD countries may be centered around very old skills – entertaining those not in work and caring for elderly people no longer able to care for themselves. Here again the question of health recurs, bringing with it health accounts and measures not only of life expectancy but also of the quality adjusted life expectancy.

Our view of education also has changed. It is no longer something that takes place only in designated learning institutions but includes learning from others, whether in the home or workplace, whether formal or informal. Increasingly attention is given not just to numbers of students' hours but to attainment of basic literacy skills. Nor is education only about making people more useful labourers in paid employment but again is about improving the quality of life outside and beyond the workplace.

For all these issues we need to consider expanding the accounts, sometimes in monetary terms, but increasingly by bringing together measures relating to numbers of people, to hours spent in particular activities and to qualitative rather than quantitative measures.

Conclusions

The aim of this chapter has been to give the flavour of the possibilities of, and the excitement of, extending the present set of national accounts to make them more alive and more relevant to non-specialists. Three examples represented ways in which the present accounts could be represented in novel forms to permit easier analysis to users. Three examples show how the accounts may be adapted to come closer to measures of welfare. This is a daunting task. Many national accountants are rather conservative and, exhausted by the effort of implementing the 1993 SNA, the last thing they wish to hear is enthusiasm for more changes or, perhaps worse, suggestions for optional extras. Nevertheless, if national accounts are to retain their pride of place as the system which unites a wide range of facets of economic interactions within a single, coherent, consistent framework, the challenge is to address policy and analytical issues and not just measurement problems; a challenge to be addressed squarely and with enthusiasm.

Further reading

Papers elaborating the topics of the first four sections are available from the author. The new manual on environmental accounting is due for completion early in 2001; again details on this are available from the author. The last area is the most ambitious and most diffuse. Other chapters in this volume address some of the issues. They represent some of the most vibrant areas for exploration in terms of expanding the national accounts, areas with which Henry Neuburger would undoubtedly have wished to have been associated and where his equally certain enthusiasm would have encouraged the rest of us enormously.

References

Schumacher, E.F. (1973) *Small is beautiful: A study of economics as if people mattered*, London: Blond and Briggs.

FOUR

Economic policy analysis

Neil Fraser

Introduction

Typical economic policy analysis involves trying to understand factors affecting policy objectives like the rate of employment, inflation, national product, the health of the nation, or numbers in poverty. The method is called modelling and involves theory and statistical verification. It also enables policy makers to explore the implications of the form objectives take, for example defining poverty in different ways. The Cabinet Office has recently been trying to improve such economic policy analysis within British government departments (Cabinet Office, 2000). What I am discussing in this chapter is further analysis which builds on the results of modelling to rank policy options for government. It is often called project appraisal – analysis of choices involving using resources. I will particularly discuss, as my example, ranking projects to reduce the number of children in poverty.

Discussions of project appraisal usually start with public sector approaches as variants of private sector project analysis based on a goal of profit maximisation ('discounted cash flow'). But public sector projects have to deal with a wider range of public interest objectives such as health or poverty reduction. The most ambitious approach is that of cost–benefit analysis.

Cost–benefit analysis (CBA)

Cost-benefit analysis embodies a utilitarian approach to policy – the adding up of positive and negative consequences on a common scale of monetary valuations. What is measured, in the form of CBA known as the 'potential Pareto' criterion, is the money beneficiaries are willing to pay for their benefits and the compensation required by the losers to put up with their losses. By valuing both benefits and costs in the same terms, they can be compared. Then the test is whether the willingness of the beneficiaries to pay exceeds the compensation required by the losers. If compensation were paid there would be gainers and no losers; if it were not paid then at least gainers potentially could have compensated losers. This is said to be meeting an objective of 'economic efficiency'.

In 1993 Henry Neuburger and I published *Economic policy analysis: A rights-based approach* (Neuburger and Fraser, 1993). In this book we criticised cost–benefit analysis and argued instead for 'cost effectiveness analysis' (CEA) and a generalising of CEA which we called democratic decision analysis (DDA). Cost–benefit analysis was criticised in particular for the use of 'willingness to pay' to value outcomes, that is using the values of the market for benefits not allocated through the market. We objected to the way policies are seen only in terms of correcting market failures. Economic efficiency cannot incorporate all the objectives of public policy, particularly where distribution is an issue. 'Willingness to pay' is partly a matter of 'ability to pay' – indeed, in much policy individual wants and the existing income distribution are deliberately not the basis for public choice. And as compensation is never paid in full to losers of policies there are always some losers and so equity is always an issue (for a fuller critique of CBA see Chapter Eleven by Chris Nash and Peter Mackie).

Further, we argued that it is legitimate to reject valuation by individual preferences where 'needs' and 'rights' and more political valuations are thought appropriate. Public policies provide an opportunity to give certain things a higher valuation than we might choose to give them in our private market behaviour – an opportunity which should be welcomed not denied (Kelman, 1981). A notable example is the valuation of life itself for CBA of policies affecting the risk of death.

Cost–benefit analysis is not in fact widely used in Whitehall (see the review by Florio, 1990, although the case studies in the Cabinet Office report in 2000 suggest some CBA work in new areas, for instance on the government's air quality strategy). The one example where there is routine use of CBA is in decisions on major roads (see Chapter Eleven). This involves a surrogate market as use of roads is typically unpriced. The methodology has grown in sophistication. Originally the monetary value of benefits was derived from only estimates of time savings and the decrease in risk of accidents. Willingness to pay for time savings was based on the employer cost of work time and 40% of that figure in the case of non-work time. Willingness to pay for accident reduction was based on healthcare costs, lost earnings and a figure of half a million pounds for deaths. Now benefits and costs include noise and pollution effects, induced traffic and economic development effects. Road projects are then ranked by benefits minus costs. Distributional issues are not pursued except, as Nash and Mackie note, that average values of time are applied rather than varying with actual incomes in valuing time saving.

It should be said that there is a version of CBA which uses decision makers' valuations in place of individuals' valuations when decision makers – democratically accountable decision makers – judge against the assumptions in the use of individual valuations (Sugden and Williams, 1978). This is closer to the argument in Neuburger and Fraser (1993). The implication of this approach, that there should be a lot of dialogue between analysts and policy makers about the assumptions in any analysis, seems to me well founded (Williams, 1993). In practice, CBA in Britain does tend to have a decision-making rather than a pure potential Pareto focus – see, for example, the Treasury Manual (HM Treasury, 1991).

Cost effectiveness analysis

Henry Neuburger and I argued that CEA is an appraisal technique which avoids the main problems of CBA by leaving benefits (outcomes) in a non-monetary form. Instead of subjective valuations, outcomes are measured in objective terms such as the characteristics of people (for example their health). This involves working out a ratio between outcomes so measured and cash expended from a budget. Ratios can then be compared for different projects with similar outcomes. The method seeks the efficient production of final outcomes, using as criteria maximising outcomes for a given budget or minimising costs per unit of outcome. The most common way in which this is applied at present is to compare two policies within the same field. One example is the comparison of outcomes of alternative policies of the same cost, for example two healthcare policies are compared in terms of 'years of life saved' for say £100,000 spent on each policy.

There are in fact various appraisal methods which leave output in non-money form. The matrix or multicriteria approach quantifies different outputs without aggregating. When comparing projects, however, analysis needs to go towards CEA, with outputs put on a common footing. If there is one dominant output, CEA may be used with that output, for instance as with the comparison of job schemes in terms of cost per person off the unemployment register. But that is liable to have a distorting effect because there are in practice usually more outputs than one. This leads to combining outputs into one by 'weighting and scoring' (the terms used in HM Treasury, 1991). Cost–benefit analysis, of course, also combines outputs into one using money weights. It is important to note that there is no technical, value-free way to perform such aggregation. Finally, and most ambitiously, different outcomes throughout public policy may be aggregated in a social welfare function, as suggested in our book (Neuburger and Fraser, 1993).

The best example of weighting and scoring with CEA (also known as cost-utility analysis) is the measure of health gain in healthcare appraisal – quality adjusted life years (QALYs). The Department of Health has been quite keen on the development of a league table of treatments by cost per QALY, an approach which Henry worked on for them in the early 1990s (see Chapter Thirteen by Gavin Mooney). However, there has been only very limited use in practice of such techniques by Health Boards. Doctors' scepticism has undoubtedly held back their use. This is one area where there is quite a lot of consensus among economists in favour of CEA rather than CBA, probably because equity is such a consideration in healthcare, and QALYs, with their assumption that a QALY is the same for everyone, embody a kind of equity. In fact though the assumption that five QALYs for one person are equivalent to one QALY each for five persons is a carry-over from the utilitarianism of CBA and can be questioned. But still, health goes much further than transport in this country in challenging the existing income distribution in appraisal methods (as Williams, 1993 has noted; but see also Christopher Nash and Peter Mackie, Chapter Eleven on this issue).

The weighting and scoring in QALYs is because of the need to combine years of life and quality of life, and within quality to combine indicators like pain and restricted function. How this is done is a matter of social or political judgement for which there is no technical answer. However, one criticism is that QALYs do not capture all the output of healthcare – that it is hard for them to be applied to anxiety or in health promotion or for equity aspects like equal access. Another criticism is that they are 'ageist' because the young, with more life years available to be saved, will be favoured. However, this is not so true when used for investment decisions on treatments where QALYs are averaged across patients of different ages, as is usual in league tables of treatment.

Although healthcare is the area where most CEA with final social outcomes has been pursued, there are others. There are several studies of the balance of care between domiciliary and residential care; for instance one study which measures outcomes like social integration, independence and morale, is Davies and Challis (1986). Educational studies are dominated by the human capital or rate of return approach, attempting to measure outcomes in production terms rather than educational attainment or health and so on, but there have been some 'production function' studies with educational outcomes in the USA and UK and studies of policies for literacy in developing countries. Employment policies are typically evaluated in terms of 'cost per person off the unemployment register'. This can be a rather narrow view of outcomes – although still inherently difficult to estimate, with 'deadweight', 'substitution' and 'displacement' to deal with (OECD, 1993). Some comments on cost effectiveness for anti-poverty policies, including employment policies, are given in the next section. A pioneering study of a factory closure (the steelworks in Corby) attempted to estimate employment effects on mortality, health and crime (Rowthorn and Ward, 1979).

The matrix, or multicriteria approach to appraisal involves leaving output measures uncombined. The decisionmaker is provided with a profile of a policy with different output measures as the aid to decisions but no single output for cost effectiveness comparisons. If the matrix approach were to be used in healthcare evaluation, predicted years of life and quality of life would be left separate, so that there would not be cost per health gain comparisons. This seems quite a limitation. However, this approach is found widely in urban planning, environmental policies and hospital building choices (option appraisal). Nash (1997) gives a sympathetic assessment of the strengths and weaknesses of this approach in an article reviewing CBA and Neuburger and Fraser (1993) (see also Chapter Eleven by Nash and Mackie).

Anti-poverty policies

The alleviation of poverty is an example of a policy area which is cross-departmental and where the present British government has an explicit policy. In March 1999 Tony Blair, the Prime Minister, gave a commitment to end child poverty within twenty years (Walker, 1999, includes the speech). The annual monitoring of targets for poverty and social exclusion began with a report in September (DSS, 1999).

As we are primarily dealing with transfer or distributional policies in the CEA of anti-poverty policies, 'cost' is not real resource costs but cash expended from a budget[1]. The policy problem is maximising the poverty reduction with a given budget (as in Atkinson, 1998, p 123).

It is first necessary to note that alleviating poverty is not the only aim of policies which have an impact on poverty. For example, social security measures are also concerned with preventing unexpected falls in living standards and with enabling people to redistribute their income over the life cycle. Policies are also concerned with minimising disincentives to take paid work. Second, the exact form of the poverty target is crucial to the design of policies. Even among income measures, there are headcount measures (giving the number below a line) and poverty gap measures (measuring how far they fall short of it) and differences created by the way one gives weights for family size. Lately a headcount measure based on a ratio of average household income has been popular – but there is still the choice of ratio (half, 60%) and whether the average is the median or mean.

A wide range of policies can impact on poverty numbers. The Blair speech (Walker, 1999) included policies for low pay such as the minimum wage and in-work benefits, policies for employment like the New Deals, education and childcare, plus social security and tax policies like child benefit and the new children's tax credit. Employment policies are important, but so is support for families with no member in work.

In practice policy analysis tends to focus on social security policies. It might appear that 'poverty gap' calculations, which estimate the total shortfall in income below a poverty line, tell us the cost of bringing people up to the line through benefit payments, but no actual policy is going to have 100% 'efficiency' in poverty alleviation in those terms. Beckerman and Clark (1982) pioneered the calculation of the efficiency of social security payments – how much of social security goes to poverty reduction – but they stressed that poverty reduction is not the only aim of social security. In fact they concluded that the increasing efficiency of social security through time could be seen as a failure of policy rather than a success – reflecting the increasing proportion of benefit expenditure via means-tested Income Support rather than National Insurance benefits, which were designed to insure the population against loss of work income. This study was based on using Income Support (Supplementary Benefit as it was then) as the poverty line. Atkinson (1998, pp 119-26) reviews the Beckerman and Clark work and goes on to develop a theoretical treatment of the cost effectiveness of different designs of transfer policy in terms of poverty alleviation.

John Hills, in Chapter Eight of this book, describes simulations with a powerful tool for assessing the impact of tax and benefit changes, POLIMOD (Cambridge University Microsimulation Unit model), which uses a large sample of families from the Family Expenditure Survey. He compares the impact on different income decile groups (tenths of individuals arranged in order of income) of two policies, that of the actual Labour budgets since 1997 and of an alternative policy of simply uprating taxes and benefits in line with incomes. He also refers to another source using POLIMOD which measured the impact on numbers in poverty (especially children) of the Labour budgets, and the impact on the poverty gap of different components of them (Piachaud and Sutherland, 2000). This uses as the poverty line one-half of mean equivalised disposable income. In terms of the ratio, reduction in poverty gap to cost, the changes in Child Benefit and Income Support were more cost effective than the introduction of Working Families' Tax Credit (at least without considering the jobs effect or the politics of the size of the available 'budget' for different uses).

The New Policy Institute has a model of factors influencing poverty numbers using the same 'below half average income' poverty measure (Howarth et al, 1999). They give a 'ready reckoner' cost effectiveness estimate of the effect on numbers in poverty (adults and children) of different policies with a similar cost. For example, they claim a 20% rise in child benefit would cost £1.5 billion and reduce poverty by 120,000-180,000 people, whereas a 10% rise in Income Support would cost the same and reduce poverty by between 350,000 and 550,000 people. One of the important conclusions their modelling reaches is that benefit improvements are needed to reduce numbers in poverty by the 'numbers below half average income' definition, because otherwise the linking of benefit uprating to prices rather than wages is always tending to increase numbers in households below half average income. This is also discussed in John Hills's chapter. In Piachaud (1999), there are estimates of how much of the cost of the new government's initial policies for poverty were just compensating for this factor.

This is a policy area where there are dangers in the target approach – because policies have other aims, targets can be distorting and much depends on their exact specification. It is surely wrong that money going to people above the poverty line ('spillover') should be treated as a cost of *no* benefit. Weighting and scoring so that spillovers receive some credit is one possibility (Atkinson, 1998, p 126). Giving different weights to alleviating different poverty gaps is another. A policy of highly targeted income-related benefits is always likely to look best if government is just focusing on poverty alleviation. This conclusion will be altered when other aims are recognised. Consideration of work incentives leads to less emphasis on targeting, because of the poverty trap which arises when benefits are sharply cut as income rises. Consideration of administrative effectiveness is also significant in systems using means tests (Atkinson, 1998, p 130). But I would argue that the existence of multiple objectives is not a reason for abandoning attempts at CEA, though it does point to care in its use and to the combining of objectives.

Estimating the impact of social security measures is the most tractable part of analysing anti-poverty policies, especially in the short term when changes in people's behaviour are likely to be small. Budget estimates of policies, and POLIMOD estimates, are of this kind. But anti-poverty policies are not all of this kind (and social security policies can have longer-term impacts). Policies aiming at changing employment are particularly difficult to evaluate. They involve two stages. First, an estimate of the change in labour supply, for example of willingness of single parents to look for work. Second, an estimate of the change in employment following the change in labour supply, for example through adjustments in wages or skills sought. The Institute for Fiscal Studies has pioneered the modelling of employment effects of tax and benefit changes in this country (Blundell and Reed, 1999) and the Treasury also reports work (HM Treasury, 2000). The subsidy for childcare costs under the Working Families' Tax Credit is a further example of a 'welfare-to-work' policy with an anti-poverty aim but uncertain employment impact. There had been modelling work on such policies (Duncan, Giles and Webb, 1995) but the Treasury must still have considered the policy somewhat experimental. Childcare is also potentially an anti-poverty policy, like education, through its effects in the long term on the upbringing of disadvantaged children – effects which are particularly hard to assess in terms of income poverty but which research has begun to identify for other aspects of poverty and social exclusion (Waldfogel, 1999).

The government has published many targets in relation to poverty (DSS, 1999). Their primary income target appears to be based on numbers below half of average income – though it is clearly not an absolute target before which all other goals are sacrificed. The government could be criticised for setting too many targets, although this may reflect initial uncertainties in this policy area. There are targets for social exclusion and targets for poverty which probably go together but may not. Further, as this is an interdepartmental issue, it is desirable to translate poverty targets into targets for individual departments, for instance showing what targets for DSS outputs and what targets for DfEE (Department for

Education and Employment) outputs fit the overall targets and are compatible with each other – a very complex analysis question.

Democratic decision analysis

Henry Neuburger and I argued that cost effectiveness analysis does not have to be limited to decisions with one or two outputs within one sector of policy. We argued for an approach which we called 'democratic decision analysis' (DDA), involving certain key final outcomes in public policy, which could be aggregated in a 'social welfare function' without valuations in money terms. We suggested these should be in terms of characteristics of people, especially opportunities or freedoms, what Sen calls 'capabilities' (Sen, 1984; 1999). We argued that there was a logical order to key final outcomes starting with life and health, followed by civil, political and social 'rights' like literacy, nutrition, shelter, and work/participation. A similar approach is that of Doyal and Gough (1991) who derive their key final outcomes from the basic needs of survival/health and autonomy. Giving content and valuations to such a list of key final outcomes must be a matter of political debate and different political parties will give different valuations to the final outcomes. We argued that a goal of social planning should be an index of key outcomes in terms of which the outputs of projects and the resources they use are measured.

As far as poverty reduction as an objective is concerned, Sen argues that poverty should be seen as deprivation of basic capabilities rather than lowness of income (Sen, 1999, chapter 4). As a result education and health policies are not seen as anti-poverty policies only because of their effect on incomes, but also because education and healthcare directly reduce poverty. Henry Neuburger argued very similarly (Neuburger and Fraser, 1993, chapter 7).

Democratic decision analysis allows CEA to operate intersectorally. With an index of social welfare involving outcomes like health and education one can maximise the outcome of health and education from the combined budget of the two or maximise total social welfare from the full public expenditure budget. This requires a measure of the opportunity cost of general budget spending (the value of say £1 million of resources of 'general public expenditure' which is sacrificed by a particular proposed use) expressed as the same index of final outcomes by which policy is being appraised. The 'shadow price' for these resources involves valuations and technical possibilities. We suggested it could be approached through, first, macroeconomic forecasting models (see Simon-Wren Lewis, Chapter Two) for the impact on jobs, inflation and so on of general public expenditure – according to financing by taxation or borrowing. Second, one needs to use research linking jobs and inflation with the key outcomes, health, education, social exclusion and so on (cf Brenner, 1981, for example) to estimate the impact of general budget spending on key outcomes. Then, third, valuations are required for the outcomes, making them into an index of social welfare. The appraisal of new policies then has an opportunity cost measured in terms of the index of final outcomes to compare with the estimated impact of the policy on those outcomes (Neuburger and Fraser, 1993, chapter 8). Rather than the ratio of outcome to money cost as in CEA, this approach shows which policies make a positive contribution to net social welfare outcome (direct contribution minus opportunity cost from lost general public expenditure or from extra taxation/borrowing).

The method is designed to give a ranking to a range of policies according to their contribution to the index of key outcomes. For mutually exclusive policies one would then choose the one ranked highest, and for policies not mutually exclusive they would be chosen in rank order until the budget was exhausted. Attention has to be paid to complementarities between policies. Budget allocation should also pay attention to the cut-off cost effectiveness level of different budgets to attempt to bring their marginal contribution to the index of key outcomes into line.

There is no doubt that this approach to policy analysis is very demanding ('utopian' as one reviewer called it). It is demanding, first, in its modelling requirements. Not only do we need to be able to predict how particular policies affect health, life and so forth, but also how general public expenditure affects these outcomes via its impact on macroeconomic variables. Second, it is demanding in political valuations. There have to be political valuations of the key final outcomes – in relation to each other and in relation to general consumption expenditure. This applies to the component indices like pain and restriction of activity as well as final outcome indices like the state-of-health, life and shelter. The only way to approach such political valuations is through analysis of the implications of different choices being presented to policy makers and the public. The theory for how this might be done is given in a publication of the United Nations Industrial Development Organisation (UNIDO, 1972, chapter 12). They try to refine the valuations politicians put on different projects by displaying the implications of those valuations for the ranking of projects. A system of dialogue goes on between analyst and politicians with different sets of values producing different hypothetical rankings of projects. In the end they believe this process will yield a set of politically determined weights for the important social objectives. This can be questioned because politicians can be very reluctant to go public on hypothetical choices (and it is not very democratic if there is no public debate).

Conclusion

The current Labour government shows a commendable commitment to economic policy analysis – to the monitoring of performance against objectives, to modelling policy relationships. Henry Neuburger showed this commitment throughout his career. This chapter has reviewed policy appraisal methods, beginning from the critical position Henry took about the assumptions of CBA. I concluded with the ambitious alternative he developed, DDA, to give a basis for comparing projects throughout the public sector without the willingness-to-pay valuation or acceptance of current income distribution inherent in CBA. I would argue that it is worth working towards but it is not feasible for a while. I have tried to discuss in relation to anti-poverty policies what sort of analysis can be done now.

Note

[1] There is, of course, a question as to how the 'costs' are defined, for instance when the same policies can be implemented through social security spending or through tax credits or allowances (see John Hills, Chapter Eight).

References

Atkinson, A.B. (1998) *Poverty in Europe*, Oxford: Blackwell.

Beckerman, W. and Clark, S. (1982) *Poverty and social security in Britain since 1961*, Oxford: Oxford University Press.

Blundell, R. and Reed, H. (1999) *The employment effects of the working families tax credit*, Institute for Fiscal Studies Briefing Note, 6/99, London: IFS.

Brenner, M.H. (1981) 'Importance of the economy to the nation's health', in L. Eisenberg and A. Kleinman (eds) *The relevance of social science for medicine*, Dordrecht and Boston, MA: Reidel.

Cabinet Office (2000) *Adding it up,* London: Policy Innovation Unit, Cabinet Office.

Davies, B. and Challis, D. (1986) *Matching resources to needs in community care*, Aldershot: Gower.

Doyal, L. and Gough, I. (1991) *A theory of human need*, Basingstoke: Macmillan.

DSS (Department of Social Security) (1999) *Opportunity for all: Tackling poverty and social exclusion*, Cm 4445, London: The Stationery Office.

Duncan, A., Giles, C. and Webb, S. (1995) *The impact of subsidising childcare*, Manchester: Equal Opportunities Commission.

Florio, M. (1990) 'Cost–benefit analysis and the control of public expenditure: an assessment of British experience in the 1980s', *Journal of Public Policy,* vol 10, no 2, pp 103-31.

HM Treasury (1991) *Economic appraisal in central government*, London: HMSO.

HM Treasury (2000) *Tackling poverty and making work pay – Tax credits for the 21st century*, The Modernisation of Britain's Tax and Benefit System, No 6, London: HM Treasury.

Howarth, C., Kenway, P., Palmer, G. and Miorelli, R. (1999) *Monitoring poverty and social exclusion 1999*, York: Joseph Rowntree Foundation.

Kelman, S. (1981) 'Cost–benefit analysis: an ethical critique', *Regulation*, vol 5, no 1, pp 33-40.

Nash, C. (1997) 'The benefits of costing', *New Economy*, vol 4, no 3, pp 193-9.

Neuburger, H. and Fraser, N. (1993) *Economic policy analysis: A rights-based approach,* Aldershot: Avebury.

OECD (1993) 'Active labour market policies: assessing macroeconomic and microeconomic effects', *OECD Employment Outlook*, pp 39-80.

Piachaud, D. (1999) 'Progress on poverty', *New Economy*, vol 6, no 3, pp 154-60.

Piachaud, D. and Sutherland, H. (2000) *How effective is the British government's attempt to reduce child poverty?*, CASEpaper 38, Centre for Analysis of Social Exclusion, London: LSE.

Rowthorn, B. and Ward, T. (1979) 'How to run a company and run down the economy: the effects of closing down steel-making in Corby', *Cambridge Journal of Economics*, vol 3, pp 327-40.

Sen, A. (1984) *Resources, values and development*, Oxford: Blackwell.

Sen, A. (1999) *Development as freedom*, Oxford: Oxford University Press.

Sugden, R. and Williams, A. (1978) *The principles of practical cost–benefit analysis*, Oxford, Oxford University Press.

UNIDO (1972) *Guidelines for project evaluation*, New York, NY: United Nations.

Waldfogel, J. (1999) *Early childhood interventions and outcomes*, CASEpaper 21, Centre for Analysis of Social Exclusion, London: LSE.

Walker, R. (ed) (1999) *Ending child poverty: Popular welfare for the 21st century*, Bristol: The Policy Press.

Williams, A. (1993) 'Cost–benefit analysis: applied welfare economics or general decision aid?', in A. Williams and E. Giardina (eds) *Efficiency in the public sector*, Aldershot: Edward Elgar.

FIVE

The price of parenthood and the value of children

Heather Joshi and Hugh Davies[1]

One of Henry Neuburger's pioneering achievements was to have been the first man to take a year's leave from Her Majesty's Treasury to stay at home with his newborn daughter, and to enable his wife to keep up her career. This set a precedent for the advance (slow though it may have been) of employment policies which recognise the family responsibilities of both fathers and mothers. Henry also extended the frontiers of conventional national income accounting in his work on household production, based on time budget data (Murgatroyd and Neuburger, 1997). This chapter offers another example of the potential uses (and pitfalls) of time budgets: an attempt to illustrate the costs of children in both the marketed economy and the time resources of parents.

Our exercise is based on a simulation model of lifetime incomes for hypothetical couples of various levels of earning power and various numbers of children. We take data on paid work and rates of pay from the 1994 British Household Panel Survey (BHPS), and simulate net earnings over ages 16-65. We generate lifetime incomes in a 'timewarp', frozen in this case in 1998, from which prices and tax rates are set in perpetuity. The method is described in full elsewhere (Davies and Joshi, 1995, 1999).

The cash costs of children can be derived from this model. Direct expenditure on children is assumed to be related to the child's age and family income (see Davies and Joshi, 1995). It also includes a component of childcare expenditure if mothers are employed when they have children under school age or if they have full-time employment once their children are over school age. Indirect costs are the earnings forgone by mothers with given numbers of children compared with those who remain childless. This involves a simplifying but generally realistic assumption that, unlike

Henry Neuburger, fathers do not (or cannot) adjust their earnings downward in response to parenthood.

It is mothers' earnings which tend to be forgone, but the 'sacrifice' is not necessarily borne by them alone. This depends on the fathers' role as 'providers', about which we make a range of assumptions. Another question is whether the cash costs fully cover all the time costs of child rearing. Here, the inputs of the mother and father may also be compared, to the extent that they can be reliably measured.

The lack of information about whether the costs of children are pooled, and indeed how long the parents' partnership may last, raises the question of which parent 'pays for the kids?' (Folbre, 1994). Forgone earnings are 'more than mothers' business', if they affect partners supporting them. But, if such support becomes less certain or complete, the balance of time use becomes relevant. Domestic specialisation becomes less attractive, mothers may seek to earn their own cash and protect their own earning power, particularly if the workload does not adjust in some way. One way might be to cut fertility, but another could be increasing fathers' involvement in unpaid childcare. This would be a direct way of sharing the costs – as well as the joys – of parenthood.

This chapter presents an attempt to add parents' foregone free time into the account of the costs of children and their distribution between mothers and fathers. We do this by splicing on to some simulated biographies estimates of father's and mother's unpaid time. The distinction between time cost and jointly enjoyed family life is difficult to draw. Indeed, as we go on to argue, we prefer to think of the resource flows we have estimated as being investments in the children as much as charges on their parents. We conclude that policy for equal opportunity among men and women also involves policy aimed at the wellbeing of children. In the 'productive enabling state' envisaged by Henry (see John Hills, Chapter Eight), policies, including those involving public expenditure, may contribute to more than one policy objective (for other examples, see Neil Fraser, Chapter Four).

Costs of parenthood within the production boundary

We consider here illustrative earnings streams for three hypothetical British couples, with low, medium and high levels of education, where the wives have alternative childbearing histories: one, two or four births, or none[2]. Because the evidence on domestic work used below only applies to persons under pension age, these 'lifetimes' are only projected up to the husbands'

65th birthdays. Rather unrealistically, the children are assumed to fend for themselves once they are 16. In both the low and medium skilled cases childbearing starts relatively young (23 and 25 respectively) and there is a break in earnings. In the high education case there is more attachment to the labour market and a (near) continuous record of fulltime employment is maintained even when the first child is an infant, that is no greater interruption than paid maternity leave. This sort of pattern has been becoming increasingly common among highly skilled people in the 1990s, also among the mid-skilled particularly if they have deferred childbearing beyond the age assumed here (25). For people with a high level of education, the earnings costs of children are minor, nil if they only have one. For the less educated cases the marginal earnings costs of children after the first tend to diminish, reflecting the 'scale economies' of having more than one child in the care of mothers staying at home. Those who are highly skilled keep their earnings costs down by purchasing childcare. The less skilled provide more of their own.

For the low skilled couple with two children, earnings foregone (undiscounted up to the father's 65th year) are: £245,000 gross; £188,000 net of taxes and pension contributions. Total direct expenditure costs are £119,000. For the mid-skilled couple where the mother interrupts earning less, but earns more per hour, the losses are almost the same: £245,000 gross, £178,000 net – direct expenditure £138,000. A small amount of childcare expenditure is imputed (£4,000), partly to support her return to the labour market part-time when her youngest child is two. For the high-skilled couple, direct costs – of £221,000 – play a larger absolute and relative role both because earnings are hardly interrupted and because the sums allocated to expenditure rise with the family income level. Table 5.1 shows these figures and the corresponding estimates for families with one or four children.

Another assumption to be made is how far these couples pool their incomes. This will determine how far the net costs are shared between mothers and fathers. We make the following assumptions:

(a) The couples pool all incomings perfectly: each takes a half share of the 'kitty' however much or little was contributed. This means that expenditure costs including childcare, and forgone earnings are equally divided between partners in every year from the first child's birth.

(b) Pooling all costs except childcare: as (a), but childcare expenditure is regarded as a first charge against wives' earnings. They then contribute their earnings net of tax and childcare cost to the pool.

Table 5.1: Labour market, care and consumption (expenditure) costs

Earning power of couple		One child	Two children	Four children
		£'000 over ages to retirement, 1998 prices[a]		
High	Gross forgone earnings of mother[b]	0	39	169
	Mother's forgone net earnings[c]	0	25	113
	Childcare expenditure	35	45	39
	Other expenditure	121	221	358
	Total net expenditure	156	291	510
Mid	Gross forgone earnings[b]	139	245	436
	Mother's forgone net income[c]	101	178	324
	Childcare expenditure	4	4	0
	Other expenditure	82	138	225
	Total net expenditure	187	320	550
Low	Gross forgone earnings[b]	170	245	387
	Mother's forgone net income[c]	128	188	305
	Childcare expenditure	1	0	0
	Other expenditure	74	119	195
	Total net expenditure	203	307	500

[a] The simulations cover all ages from marriage to man's age 65: the highly skilled marry when the man is aged 26, the medium skilled at 24 and the low skilled at 22.

[b] Gross earnings forgone are in the pre-retirement period, they do not include effects on pay deferred as pension.

[c] Net forgone income is the difference in earnings, net of taxes and pension contributions, between a mother and a woman who remains childless.

(c) Only outgoings pooled: the expenditure costs are shared between the parents equally (that is each one foregoes 50p of own consumption or saving for every pound spent on the children). Husbands make no compensation for marginal changes in the wives' labour market income, so that direct costs are shared, indirect costs are not[3,4].

The result of applying these assumptions to income and expenditure flows while both partners are alive is a foregone conclusion on assumption (a), the wife and husband splitting the costs 50:50. On assumption (b) there is not much of a departure from the equal split where, as for the low- and mid-skilled couples, there is not much purchased childcare. For the highly educated couple the wife's share rises to 58% with two children. On the more extreme sharing assumption (c), for the least- and mid-skilled couples the wives would be responsible for around 80% of the costs whatever the number of children, but the graduate wife for just over 60%. We return to the graduates (in Table 5.3) below. In other words, fathers who contribute only to the outgoings for children would pay about one fifth of the total costs of children in families where mothers take a large amount of time away from paid work, and two fifths in highly paid dual-earner families. Comparing (a) and (c) illustrates that the cost to mothers of providing their own childcare depends in part on how much access they have to their partners' income.

Beyond the boundary: time costs

How do children affect the lifetime allocation of time to market work, domestic work and leisure? The earnings cost of children considered above represents time diverted to childrearing by mothers, along with the loss of wages entailed by interrupting employment and working part-time. This is not the only way to measure the time costs of children. Time may be diverted from activities other than employment, and it may be diverted by other people. Although we have assumed that men's paid work is not affected by fatherhood, their use of unpaid time may be. How children affect mothers' and fathers' time budgets is important if the different ways of spending time – childcare, housework, leisure or sleep – generate value in themselves besides the income that time may generate.

As the limited information on unpaid work in BHPS does not include childcare, evidence on domestic work time has been taken from a different data set – the time budgets in the 1987 Social Change and Economic Life Survey. Jenkins and O'Leary (1996) estimated regressions to predict time classified as domestic work by age, number of children, presence of a pre-school child, own and spouse's paid work time, separately by sex and marital status. Davies (1995) used these coefficients to add hours of unpaid time to the simulation model for couples under retirement age.

It may be helpful to review the technical and operational definitions of work used in economic theory and time budget analysis. Hawrylyshyn (1977) defines work as, 'an activity of an individual which may be done by a third person (generally hired at a market price) without affecting the utility value returned to the individual'. This creates a problem in classifying certain activities like commuting, studying and some of the time that parents spend with their children. Supervision of children while engaged in activities, such as eating a meal or watching television, tends to be classified as leisure. So would some active parenting like reading with a child. There is also the time when a parent is 'on call', although they may be asleep, which tends to limit their freedom while not counting as work. Indeed specifically identified childcare tasks absorb relatively little measured housework time compared to the extra housework associated with children. Treating activity as a dichotomy – work or not – is not well suited to multi-tasking. It also overlooks the intrinsic enjoyability of much work, be it paid or unpaid, as well as the instrumental value of its results. If parents and children enjoy the time they spend together, valuable results tend to follow.

Table 5.2 shows the results of imputing unpaid domestic work, conditional on employment and other sociodemographic characteristics, into our simulation model. We start from assumptions about how many hours of paid work these illustrative British couples do, and how these hours are affected, in the case of women, by parenthood.

Even before considering the impact of children, we should note that the men are doing more paid work over a lifetime than their wives, consistent with BHPS data. This can be seen even among the childless, where hours of paid work between spouses diverge, particularly at low skill levels (see columns headed 'Base' in Table 5.2). Mid-skilled mothers of two children cut theirs by 28 thousand hours, their less skilled counterparts by 38 thousand. These totals rise to 56 and 66 thousand for four children, and are cut, but not halved, by having one instead of two children. Graduate mothers again show a contrasting story. If they have just one child, and if we count whatever time they have for maternity leave as employment, not a single hour of paid work is foregone. There are 10 thousand hours of foregone paid work per mother if they have four children. By construction, fathers' paid hours are unchanged by the presence of children.

The second line of each panel deals with lifetime hours in domestic activities. Again the baseline couple with no children displays a traditional division of labour with women doing more unpaid work than men, but the two sexes show roughly equal total work times. This is apparent in the roughly similar entries for men and women (in these couples) under 'Other unpaid time'. This represents the difference between total work (paid and unpaid) and a daily quota of 16 waking hours. This balance of time includes leisure, and dubious categories like commuting and being in attendance, or 'on call' whether for a paid job, childcare or other caring activity. These entries will also carry the errors created by splicing the two data sets, and the arbitrary assumption about sleep.

Table 5.2: Estimated effect of children on time allocation

	Lifetime thousands of hours from marriage to man's age 65: paid and unpaid activities							
	Women[a]				Men[b]			
		Effect of:				Effect of:		
	Base				Base			
Couple type	**0 children**	**1 child**	**2 children**	**4 children**	**0 children**	**1 child**	**2 children**	**4 children**
High								
Paid work	79.1	0	–1.8	–10.1	81.1	0	0	0
Unpaid work[c]	46.5	3.4	7.3	16.6	32.0	2.9	5.0	7.5
Other unpaid time[d]	101.5	–3.4	–5.5	–6.6	114.0	–2.9	–5.0	–7.5
Mid								
Paid work	81.0	–15.8	–27.7	–56.1	93.8	0	0	0
Unpaid work[c]	51.0	12.4	22.2	42.5	36.3	0.9	1.6	1.5
Other unpaid time[d]	106.7	3.4	5.6	13.6	108.7	–0.9	–1.6	–1.5
Low								
Paid work	83.3	–25.9	–38.1	–66.3	98.4	0	0	0
Unpaid work[c]	54.6	17.9	27.3	47.3	37.7	–0.5	0.7	0.0
Other unpaid time[d]	112.3	8.0	10.8	19.0	114.4	0.5	–0.7	0.0

[a] Impact on women's paid time is taken from simulations based on BHPS data.

[b] Impact on man's paid time is set at zero by construction.

[c] Unpaid (domestic) work imputed using estimates by Jenkins and O'Leary (1996).

[d] Other unpaid time includes leisure, and discrepancies, after fixing a daily quota of 8 hours' sleep.

How is mothers' time diverted from the labour market spent? The estimates also show a larger increase in the time devoted to unpaid work than from the fathers' (the high-skilled couple with one child excepted). This increase rises with the number of children but does not generally account for the whole time withdrawn from the labour market. For example, in the case of the mid-skilled wife the forgeone 28 thousand hours with two children are not quite matched by the extra 22 thousand hours of unpaid work. The balance of time could be leisure, but it is likely to be spent with children, and is therefore likely to fall into the hard-to-classify category of not-quite-free time, which may be all the leisure some mothers get. The graduate families are again an exception, mothers not even appearing to gain leisure. These 'work-rich time-poor' women come out as having less free time than their spouses, even without children.

Fathers are shown as gaining a few thousand hours of domestic work, which necessarily entails the corresponding loss of some man-hours of non-work (paid hours being held constant by assumption). In the mid-skilled couple the father with two children contributes 1,600 extra domestic work hours in a lifetime. In some cases children are associated with minor reductions in fathers' domestic input, an intensification of mothers' specialisation when they stay at home with their children. In the ever-contrasting case of the graduates, unpaid inputs from husbands are higher especially if there are children: graduate fathers of two raise their lifetime hours of unpaid work by 5 thousand each. Fathers may also have their leisure modified by responsibility for children when not recorded as 'working'. Thus the increase in fathers' unpaid work may understate their direct time contribution to parenting.

The proportion of total work that is unpaid is greater in the years of childrearing. These are the years when spouses specialise most and mothers appear to have more non-work time. The graduates are, as usual, an exception. The division of work between home and the labour market is almost the same for men and women, whether or not their children are present. The labour market behaviour of highly and less qualified women involves a polarisation in their domestic life-styles as well. It is becoming difficult to generalise about a 'typical' British family.

If there are costs of foregone free time to add to the total cash estimates presented in Table 5.1, the negative terms in the 'Other Unpaid time' rows of Table 5.2 can be used as a rough starting point. Besides the uncertainty about how the quantity is measured, there is also uncertainty about how it should be valued. We have valued these terms at two alternative experimental prices. One applies a global constant price to everyone's free time, of £6 – this was approximately the average net hourly pay of a childless woman in our model. This assumption resembles the first variant used by Murgatroyd and Neuburger (1997) to estimate the aggregate value of unpaid work for the Household Satellite Account, being related to a general wage level, the same for men and women, except that this is net of taxes. Our alternative assumption values each person's unpaid time at their own average net wage. This would reflect the value of these activities at the margin, but has the debatable feature that it values the time of men and women, and of the skilled and unskilled, differently. This resembles Murgatroyd and Neuburger's last variant, disaggregating by gender and industry, though here we use skill level instead of industry, and we only cover illustrative individuals not the whole economy. In each of our two variants the price of unpaid time is constant over the years.

Adding these valuations of unpaid time committed to children to the account given in Table 5.1 made little difference in the case of the low- and mid-skilled. Table 5.3 therefore concentrates on the highly skilled, showing the total costs including the value of non-market time committed by both parents, on both bases, and also on the basis that it has zero value, as in Table 5.1.

Even at the higher set of prices, the estimated loss of 'leisure' for this dual career couple is no more than 28% of total costs in the case of one child, and 21% in the case of four. With the man's time being valued about 10% more than the woman's, and the woman committing about 10% more unpaid time where there are two children, the contributions of both spouses happen to balance (£51,000 each). For one child, the totals are also close, but the man's is just below the woman's. For four children, the man's longer hours are valued at £77,000, and the woman's at £61,000, though in this case she diverts more time from paid work (worth £113,000 as reported in the bottom panel).

Where the unpaid time is uniformly valued at £6, the total value comes down. The gender difference in time allocation can be seen more clearly: for one child, around £20,000, with more from mother than father; for two children, around £30,000, again slightly more from the mother; in the family of four, the father has more unpaid time – worth around £45,000.

Adding these items into total costs also affects the calculations of their division between men and women. This commitment of time cannot be pooled. Hence the share of the woman on the perfect pooling scenario no longer has to be 50%, though it is where the valuations of each parent's

Table 5.3: Distribution of net costs of childrearing between mother and father

Various assumptions about non-market time and degree of pooling	High skill couple One child	High skill couple Two children	High skill couple Four children
i) non-market time valued at own wage			
Total net costs up to 65 (£ '000)	217.4	392.7	648.3
including non-market time foregone:			
unpaid time man @£10.30	30.0	51.2	77.3
unpaid time woman @£9.28	31.5	51.2	61.0
Share of net costs borne by woman (%)			
a) perfect pooling	50.4	50.0	48.7
b) pooling except for childcare	58.4	55.7	51.8
c) only direct expenditure pooled	58.4	58.9	60.5
ii) non-market time valued at common wage			
Total net costs up to 65 (£ '000)	193.8	353.2	594.4
including non-market time foregone:			
unpaid time man @ £6.00	17.5	29.8	45.1
unpaid time woman @£6.00	20.4	33.1	39.5
Share of net costs borne by woman (%)			
a) perfect pooling	50.8	50.5	49.5
b) pooling except for childcare	59.7	56.8	52.8
c) only direct expenditure pooled	59.7	60.3	62.3
iii) non-market time not counted			
Total net costs up to 65 excluding non-market time (£'000)	155.9	290.3	509.9
woman's foregone earnings	0.0	25.1	113.3
Share of net costs borne by woman (%)			
a) perfect pooling	50.0	50.0	50.0
b) pooling except for childcare	61.2	57.7	53.8
c) only direct expenditure pooled	61.2	62.0	64.9

time contribution is the same: two children, own prices. The woman's share dips (slightly) below 50% where the value of the man's time is the greater – in cases with four children.

On the other two assumptions about splitting, the woman's share is a little lower than if the time element is neglected, as shown in the bottom panel. Although the father's share is almost everywhere under a half, it is greater where his time is given a greater weight. This truism underlines the unresolved problem of how unpaid time should be valued.

Burden or blessings?

Any balance sheet of parenthood runs into many sources of joy and grief which neither we, nor National Accountants, attempt to take into account. Beyond the production frontier are also considerations of health and social interaction, for example, as well as unpaid time. Time devoted to children which is not simultaneously classified as domestic work may not be free time. As argued above, it may itself be enjoyable because of, not despite, the presence of children. If we take into account the pleasures and rewards of time spent with our children, parenthood can be seen in a more positive perspective than as the endlessly costly venture depicted above. This notion suggests children benefit from some moments of undivided and relaxed parental company. But we have not been able to differentiate 'quality' time from other time spent with children.

If the quality of time can vary, so can the 'quality' of children, which may well vary according to the amount of money, as well as the amount and quality of time, devoted to them. 'Paying for the kids' is not without benefit to any parent concerned for the child's wellbeing. There is a flourishing US literature which describes the resources flowing to children as investments in their lifetime wellbeing (for example Haveman and Wolfe, 1995; Duncan and Brooks-Gunn, 1997). Parental 'inputs' include the material goods which our simulations allow for; parental attention and interest in education (which take time we may or may not have measured); and, to some degree, stable parental relationships.

Among such studies now being replicated in Britain, Joshi et al (1999) find only minor effects of family structure on child development, but strong positive effects of mother's education and family income. Children seem to thrive from cash coming into the family, whichever parent earns it (McCulloch and Joshi, 1999; Joshi and Verropoulou, 2000). Hence another perspective on our cost estimates is not just whether a family can afford the costs of an extra child, but whether the expenditure plan envisaged is an adequate investment in its human capital.

Apart from the graduates' offspring, the children in this exercise are attributed less in direct expenditure than the value of the mothers' forgone earnings. Their parents observe a fairly strict division of labour, and there appears to be relatively little time input from their fathers. In the graduate couple, the mother foregoes little (or no) employment, childcare is purchased, along with more market goods than in poorer households. Parental time at home is scarce, but more equally divided between mother and father. For this to be a recipe for successful childrearing, the parents may need to substitute quality for quantity in the time available to children. Their attempts to balance paid work and family life are more likely to be successful if the workplace can accommodate a range of options for flexible practices.

Pointing towards policy

This chapter has taken the 'costs of children' beyond a focus on reasons why people might want to avoid parenthood. It has not elaborated on why those who do have children may choose alternative packages of direct and indirect cash costs. Spending time and money on children has its benefits in the ensuing wellbeing and prospects of children. We have asked how costs may be experienced differently by men and women. This is relevant to the understanding of fertility behaviour, of relations between genders and generations, and of policies to support the quality of children's lives. Low fertility may not have been perceived as a problem to policy makers in Britain in the late 20th century, but it may become one in the 21st, if the balancing of parenthood and the rest of life are seen as a problem by too many people.

The presumption that fathers' role is confined to that of breadwinner and giver of family discipline is being eroded. Some fathers, at least, want to be involved in the more intimate, nurturing activities of parenting, traditionally allocated to mothers. The transformation of motherhood entails a redefinition of fatherhood (for instance Burgess and Ruxton, 1996; Joshi, 1998). The present estimates of fathers' involvement in the time costs of children are small but not invisible, particularly in dual career households. Sharing the time, rather than dividing time and dividing cash, may be an emerging form of family organisation better suited to gender equity and to successful reproduction. The next thing to look out for is how fathers may be adjusting hours of paid work as well as their non-market time where our simulation has allowed them freedom. It is here that employment practices such as parental leave, flexible and reduced hours at decent rates of pay, curbs on long hours, which have been pioneered by HM Treasury itself, may be needed to break a constraint (Hewitt, 1993). Another constraint is the unequal rates of pay of men and women, which still provide a disincentive to role sharing, particularly among the less skilled.

At the other end of the emerging polarity in parental employment patterns, low-skilled parents may have less employment and thus have more abundant time, but not income. Child poverty is at least as serious a problem as any 'birth dearth' caused by the 'costs of children'. Directing resources towards poor families should raise their quality of life immediately and also help raise the productivity of the next generation. Appropriate measures could take the form of early education, subsidised daycare, or, again, family-friendly employment practices. The latter two would cut the foregone earnings which, in this study, loom large for the least advantaged. An alternative would be higher cash benefit available to caring parents whether or not they stay at home, in recognition of their valuable work. Henry would have applauded the steps that the New Labour government is taking in these directions, and he would have shown a keen interest in taking them further.

Notes

[1] The authors are grateful for comments on an earlier draft by Sue Himmelweit and from other participants in the seminar held at CASE to discuss this collection.

[2] The four-child case is a reasonable upper limit; the three-child family is not shown but is roughly between the two- and four-child examples.

[3] On our crude assumptions wives foot half the bill for expenditure on children whatever their own current resources, thus we assume they make an intertemporal transfer of cash if necessary, although we have not otherwise made any allowance for saving and borrowing.

[4] Another possibility, not pursued here, would be to treat Child Benefit as belonging totally to the wife, rather than, as assumed here, being pooled in the family kitty.

References

Burgess, A. and Ruxton, S. (1996) *Men and their children; proposals for public policy*, London: IPPR.

Davies, H. (1995) 'Domestic production, the lifecycle and full income', Typescript, London: Birkbeck College.

Davies, H. and Joshi, H. (1995) 'Social and family security in the redress of unequal opportunities', in J. Humphreys and J. Rubery (eds) *The economics of equal opportunities*, Manchester: EOC.

Davies, H. and Joshi, H. (1999) *Who bears the cost of Britain's children in the 1990s?*, Discussion Paper in Economics 27/99, London, Birkbeck College.

Duncan, G.J. and Brooks-Gunn, J. (eds) (1997) *Consequences of growing up poor*, New York, NY: Russell Sage Foundation.

Folbre, N. (1994) *Who pays for the kids? Gender and the structures of constraint*, London: Routledge.

Haveman, R. and Wolfe, B. (1995) *Succeeding generations: On the effects of investments in children*, New York, NY: Russell Sage Foundation.

Hawrylyshyn, O. (1977) 'Towards a definition of non-market activities', *Review of Income and Wealth*, vol 23, no 1, pp 78-96.

Hewitt, P. (1993) *About time: The revolution in work and family life*, London: IPPR/Oram Rivers Press.

Jenkins, S.P. and O'Leary, N.C. (1996) 'Modelling domestic work time', *Journal of Population Economics*, vol 8, no 3, pp 265-80.

Joshi, H. (1998) 'The opportunity cost of children: more than mothers' business', *Journal of Population Economics*, vol 11, no 2, pp 161-83.

Joshi, H. and Verropoulou, G. (2000) *Maternal employment and child outcomes*, London: The Smith Institute.

Joshi, H., Cooksey, E., Wiggins, R.D., McCulloch, A.A., Verropoulou, G. and Clarke, L. (1999) 'Diverse family living situations and child development', *International Journal of Law, Policy and the Family*, vol 13, pp 292-314.

McCulloch, A. and Joshi, H. (1999) *Child development and family resources*, ISER Working Paper, 99-15, Colchester: University of Essex.

Murgatroyd, L. and Neuburger, H. (1997) 'A household satellite account for the UK', *Economic Trends*, vol 527, pp 63-71.

SIX

Well being or wel fare?

Meghnad Desai

Introduction

There is a paradox at the heart of Left politics. In the European Union, 11 out of 15 governments are Left of Centre and members of the Socialist International. Yet the Left feels beleaguered. It is searching for new ways to deal with the many problems of globalisation, welfare reform, law and order, people's perception of health risks, child abuse and so on. Socialists have been revisionists ever since they started but after the end of a century during which the fortunes of Socialist parties waxed and waned, there is much searching for new ways, not to say third ways.

The biggest battle has been about the reform of the welfare state. It is intimately connected with the room for manoeuvre a government thinks it has left to fashion its economic policies given the facts of globalisation. Welfare is central to the vision of a society that a Left movement strives for – how egalitarian, how libertarian, how much choice, how much compulsion? These perennial questions have all crystalised around the debate on welfare.

In this chapter I wish to take a completely different approach to the welfare issue from that which has been hitherto articulated in the debate. I do this not to evade the difficult issues of redistribution. On that subject I have already written strongly in support of a Basic Income and my solution at one level to the reform of the welfare state remains a basic income (Desai, 1998). Thus what is being raised here is not a substitute for the debate on redistributive egalitarianism but a new approach to the rationale for a welfare state.

Many arguments are intertwined with this debate. We have for example heard that the Lloyd George/Beveridge welfare state (and similar arrangements elsewhere in Europe) have replaced and in some sense eliminated or at least enfeebled the older tradition of self help and mutual help – the old friendly societies and so on. We have heard that the welfare state has undermined the family and that we need a new policy on the family. Welfare dependency among able-bodied people has raised the ire of many and the present UK government is wedded to a policy of work for those who can and welfare for those who cannot. There is a perennial discussion on means testing versus universality.

Rethinking welfare

Starkly put, there has until now been a dichotomy between 'inside' and 'outside' in the economic sphere and this dichotomy has to be overcome. We think of the economy, money, Gross National Product (GNP) hours worked, business, productivity, budget deficits, exchange rates, financing the welfare state as the 'outside', that is important relevant political issues. Our perception of the problems of the welfare state and the proposed solutions is concerned with income entitlements and (politically) affordable taxation, the need to find paid work rather than benefits for the people claiming. In this context the very word 'benefits' comes to signify its opposite – a bad thing to be eliminated if possible. We worry about rather than welcome the prospect of people living a longer life since to the outside view an extra year of life represents costs to the Exchequer rather than a boon to the person living longer. Thus ageing becomes a problem where formerly longevity was for a long time a desirable goal.

The 'inside' is a whole host of invisible, and by the criterion of the politician and the policy makers, unimportant, or certainly uneconomic, things. These are things which involve living rather than working – eating, sleeping, childbearing and rearing, parties, friendships, caring. This is the private domain which is not of any immediate concern to politics unless, as in the BSE case, it becomes a public issue. Inside is a matter of private (consumer/citizen) choice; it is the domain of the individual. The reform of the welfare state and even the rethinking of socialism is unconcerned with this domain[1].

This, I want to argue, is a central and cardinal error of thinking on the Left. I am not the first to think that. Feminists have been telling us from the rooftops, as it were, that the economy has to be rethought. But the point has been there, though hidden, since the origin of the critique of existing capitalism one hundred and fifty years ago (see Rowbotham, 1998). Work outside may be pleasurable or it may be dull, but it is not its own reward. Its principal purpose is to enhance life inside. Indeed work inside – unpaid work mainly done by women – is central to our wellbeing, even though the welfare state concerns itself with paid work and the consequent entitlements outside. Living which happens inside is about wellbeing. I want to argue that in ignoring the inside, the welfare state neglects issues of wellbeing and highlights the means (for instance, paid work) rather than the end – wellbeing.

Is this more than a cliché? Can one talk about wellbeing rather than welfare and does that mean there are no resource constraints or no need to compete globally and so on? "Yes", "Yes" and "No" are my immediate answers respectively to these three questions, and in what follows I wish to put together an argument in justification.

Let me start with another (related) dichotomy – people and things. The outside is about things – about goods and services. But it is about a subset, a large subset no doubt, but yet a subset of things. Thus private goods and services are what the economists mainly study. The production and purchase of private goods generate incomes and expenditure. Public goods are also within the domain of economics and we study them more and more. These are also outside. They differ from private goods/services in well known ways but they are subject to a monetary calculus. There is another category hitherto ignored or at least not distinctly studied, which I shall call *social goods*. (In each of these three cases, goods include services.) These are the inside goods; they are what we actually consume though we purchase private goods. They are often but not always produced within the household/family and are studied as household production using rules of (outside) economics. But the social goods are more than goods produced within the household. They are the truly private goods since they are privately produced in small settings of two or a few individuals. As I argue further below social goods and their provision ought to be the central concern of all societies.

But we also have problems about people. There was a time when we used class categories and the Left thought it had a monopoly over working-class loyalty. The welfare state was constructed with a stylised picture of the working class in mind – male, unskilled, manual and so on. As the class structure has altered, there is a tendency to deny its salience. We are often told that we are all middle class and we are consumers who have choice. This homogenisation of the citizenry is a tactic to contain and shape its demands as well as to construct a response that will be cost-effective (that is money-saving) for the state. But, at the same time, identities of gender, ethnicity/race, religion are multiplying. To respond to the demands of 'concrete' citizens rather than 'abstract' consumers is time consuming and expensive for the state. Denying these multiple identities, at least as far as the outside sphere of the welfare state is concerned, is a deliberate political response of the new revisionism. But precisely for that reason, it leaves the citizens unhappy and feeling manipulated by the public authorities who they see only spin their way out of difficulties.

Wellbeing is not expensive. Indeed it may be cost effective to aim for it and would be more satisfying for citizens. It does, however, require a quite complex way of looking at people and things. In fact, it requires a major conceptual effort to design and implement new ways of doing things and not just ways of cutting public expenditure. It is worth making an effort to go through the hoops of rethinking welfare as wellbeing, and inside as being as important as outside. It will rejig the private/public divide in more than one sense; it will restate the subject of our efforts as well as its objective. It is an invitation to think as much as to rethink.

Poverty and wellbeing

The main activity men and women have is living. This means not just eating and drinking and sleeping and lovemaking and procreating and childrearing but also friendships, caring for each other and friends, working productively and if possible creatively, earning enough to get by and more, learning and teaching, communicating, participating in family and broader social activities, taking part in politics and other social activities, reading, watching TV, playing or watching sports. Wellbeing is a complex subjective feeling that comes out of all these activities or 'functionings' as Amartya Sen, the Nobel Laureate, calls them. The standard of living is a product of the number and variety of functionings enjoyed by individuals and wellbeing, at least the way I would like to define here, is the subjective sense of satisfaction and fulfilment from these functionings (Sen, 1987).

The aim of any society and of the state as one of its active principals should be to promote the wellbeing of its citizens. Many of the activities, you will have noticed, are joint with other people; they are social. Even eating is better in company than alone, even if you could eat more on your own but may have to share with another. If you give a party and no one comes, your per capita supply of food and drinks is very large, but you are hardly likely to enjoy it. Thus the picture of the lonely individual consumer maximising satisfaction/utility may be all right for economic pedagogy, but it is not how citizens' wellbeing is defined or should be measured. Thus GNP per capita or consumption (that is consumers' expenditure) per capita is not a sufficient measure of wellbeing even if we ignore the problem that per capita income/consumption is always badly distributed.

The individual almost always operates actively not in isolation but in a group. We are born of and with a mother, and often in a family. We die leaving family and friends behind. Across the life cycle of individuals, it is friendships and joint activities which enhance wellbeing. For individuals wellbeing arises from many such social activities. It is this quite elementary fact which has been ignored in the 'outside' approach to welfare. It is this ignoring of the social of the 'inside' which has made the welfare state a failure. Let me illustrate.

Take poverty. Its measurement[2] has raised perennial debates – absolute versus relative, universal definition or culture-bound ones, lifetime or instant, static or dynamic and so on. But eventually all measures of poverty come down to measuring the adequacy of money available to purchase certain quantities of goods and services. Whether these are necessities or comforts and luxuries often leads to disputes about the poverty measure. But poverty measures, important as they are, measure purchases not functionings. Yes you can have so many calories or so much clothing or shelter or cigarettes and booze plus television or whatever. But it is not about how you live, who your friends are, whether you are threatened by your neighbours because of who you are, whether you are happy, or well. Poverty measures deal with the material aspects of purchasing goods and services. Hence these measures and the very notion of poverty underlying such measures remain outside and are inadequate for studying wellbeing.

Being commodity expenditure based, the usual definition of poverty is fetishistic; indeed it is sometimes foodist because it is the calories count that looms large. It is dominated by a notion of adequate calories. There have been attempts at getting out of these individualistic and fetishistic measures of poverty. Two are of interest to us here.

First is Booth's original attempt to identify the London poor. What sparked his initial curiosity was truancy by primary school pupils. Primary education in the 1870s and 1880s was not free, but required a payment of 4d. Some families kept their children away from school because of lack of cash. Then the argument was made that a family's income be gauged for adequacy to answer the query of whether it had the wherewithal to send a child to school but was not doing so wilfully, or whether poverty was the cause (Gillie, 1996). Here poverty is related directly to self exclusion and is related to a social activity – going to school. Peter Townsend's (1979) monumental work on UK poverty took a similar view in which some of the questions related to a family's inability to reciprocate certain activities – a birthday party for their school-going child who is invited to other such parties in friends' houses, party invitations, eating out with friends and so on – due to inadequate income. Here again living is seen as a social activity and the quality of living depends not so much on how much one consumes but who one consumes it with. If you have to eat alone, you are deprived though you may or may not be poor in material income. (You may of course like to eat alone by choice but that is another matter.) So poverty can be thought of according to living in the community, eating what are thought to be normal dishes, joining in communal activities – watching soaps on TV and so on.

The other strand takes us to Sen's notion of capabilities. If we could define living as the capabilities we wish everyone to have then it is quite possible, if not inevitable, that the cost of providing those capabilities may cost different amounts in different societies across space and time, but they all relate to a notion of a minimally adequate standard of living. Capabilities are, for Sen, combinations of functionings from which an individual can choose. Poverty then would be having a limited capability set in terms of the number of functionings to choose from, that is, the poor cannot do very much in their lives.

Capabilities and functionings

Capabilities encompass political and social life as well as life within the family. These capabilities are taken to be 'co-realisable'. They all have to be achieved to represent a minimal base from which living can start. One may have higher levels of living via a greater and more diverse number of functionings, but non-achievement of these capabilities permits hardly any functioning. Thus to have knowledge may mean merely literacy or it may mean being a literate articulate writer; the first is necessary, the latter enjoyable. We seek for everyone to have the minimum, and the more they can have, the higher their wellbeing will be.

The virtue of speaking of capabilities or a community-oriented concept of poverty, as Peter Townsend does, is to point to the importance of more than material goods and services. But even if we confine ourselves to food, it is not calories which count but edible food which is acceptable. A Muslim will not be happy with a bacon sandwich even if it is nutritious nor will a vegetarian with a hamburger. Thus it is not only the income required to buy the calories, but the choice to buy what you want to eat that is important, as far as wellbeing is concerned. Thus a part of our functionings is the idea of doing things together or doing them in ways which are socially/culturally satisfying.

But beyond consumption of goods and services purchased are public goods which are essential – clean air and clean water and a healthy surrounding, crime-free living area, schools which are accessible, libraries, a legal framework that prohibits discrimination on any ground, sound money and so forth. And yet, even as such a list could be extended, it will never be enough. This is because any language of goods and services which are purchased, or indeed provided, leaves the argument outside. It is important to turn the argument for wellbeing and how the state can facilitate its provision inside. This is what I will do next.

Social goods

The welfare state has concentrated on a minimum guarantee of resources to enable citizens to cover what the state considers is the cost of living. In calculating this cost of living the state is, of course, mean and fetishistic; it restricts rather than extends choice, often providing specific goods as laid down administratively. But the important point is that it is unequipped to think about wellbeing in any way and hence fails to promote it. The living, whose cost the state pays, is unconnected with what people in their daily lives ordinarily consider living. Of course, in its other expenditures the state may pay for health and education. But it is in paying the various 'entitlements' that the narrow view is taken. Let us first put that in the centre and then think of the cost of that living.

Economists have a twofold distinction about goods – private goods and public goods. Private goods are things which are bought and sold which a person can exclusively consume and which, if one has, someone else cannot have. The so-called laws of demand and supply relate to private goods. Scarcity, value and price are notions relating to private goods, which are the stuff of markets. Public goods are by contrast non-excludable. Public goods are not bought and sold by items but their provision has to be financed through taxes, subsidies and so on. For private goods we have the notion of externalities whereby one person's consumption involuntarily affects someone else – for example smoke, noise. In public goods it is the joint demand of many which determines supply. Joint consumption is part and parcel of public goods.

In the course of living we do use private – that is, purchased – goods and public goods but they are inputs to our activities and not directly relevant. I propose the concept of *social goods* as the bread and butter of living. Social goods are neither private nor public but we may use those public or private goods as inputs in the production of social goods. All living consists of the production and consumption of social goods. What are social goods?

Social goods are neither bought nor sold (although market substitutes are available). Their production is joint within a household or a group, large or small. They are produced on non-profit-making criteria, and cost minimisation is not directly an issue in their production. They are produced using private and public goods as inputs. But it is social goods that we most often consume, not private or public goods. (There are extreme cases where a solitary individual buys and consumes a private good in an unmediated fashion, but these are exceptions which need not concern us.)

But if externalities and interdependence are exceptional peculiarities about private and public goods, they are the essence of social goods. Social goods are produced to be consumed *jointly*, and indeed the whole point of producing them is to consume them jointly. The pleasure of the partner consumer is of the primary importance in the social good being consumed and supplied.

Take caring for example. It is not only caring for disabled, infirm or elderly people but caring for an able bodied person who is sick or the baby who has to be nurtured and looked after that is at issue. Storytelling to the children before bedtime is a social good produced by the busy parent in 'quality time'. It is meant to give pleasure to both parties in the process. The material inputs to this process would be books bought as private goods or borrowed from public libraries (which are a sort of public good). But time is the most crucial input, the joint availability of the parent and the child at the latter's bedtime. Time at other hours is not substitutable for this joint time.

Social goods are thus produced using private goods and public goods, plus the time of the producers who are part of the closely knit group. Time spent on the production of social goods has both utility and disutility aspects but it is not leisure. (Leisure can be defined as time spent entirely on oneself – grooming for instance.) In the production of social goods, like caring, cooking and serving meals, women do the disproportionately large amount of work, and this has to be factored into any discussion of wellbeing. Nevertheless, often the time spent on production of some social goods (say cooking) is not entirely tedious but can be pleasure-giving.

In the consumption of social goods, jointness is most important. There is utility derived by consumers from their own consumption but also from the consumption of the other person. Thus social goods are shared in the sense that individual consumers derive more utility from joint consumption than they would from consuming alone. In a meal shared by two, it is possible that one party may be completely selfish and derive no pleasure from the other person's satisfaction, but this is unlikely and not enough to rule the notion of social goods out of hand.

Many other examples of social goods could be given – parties, trips taken together, meetings of voluntary groups; indeed, almost any sort of social relationship. Time is the prime ingredient, along with private and public goods, but the time is used in transforming the public and private goods into social goods. Thus a meal is made from bought ingredients but the transformation from the bought inputs into a meal takes time and it is eating it together which makes it into a social good. A meal cooked by a single person eaten alone is a household production but it is not a social good. A meal eaten out in company of someone is a social good, but it is commercially produced.

Wellbeing consists of the consumption and production of social goods. It is time spent on the consumption and production of social goods which is time most valued ('quality time'). Time spent on paid work including going to and from the place of paid work is of secondary and instrumental importance. Of course, even at the place of paid work, camaraderie among workers may lead to social goods being produced and consumed. There are friendships at work and extracurricular office life adds much fun to a dull work routine. But it is the consumption and production of social goods which is what occupies the most valued time and the greater that time, the better people feel. Wellbeing is thus generated by these social goods-oriented activities. There are some social bads of course, produced within the household, non-marketed. Domestic violence is a social bad, for example.

It is best to regard paid work as entirely instrumental and done only to get money to be able to buy the private goods required to produce and consume social goods. Thus private time spent on consumption of social goods gives pleasure and work time (including getting to work time) is barren but useful to earn the money. Much work is done in the production of social goods but it is not paid work. There is a tendency to regard only paid work as work and think of the producers of social goods as not working (as the debate on single parents has shown recently). This is false. It is merely the case that paid work is necessary as an indirect input to the generation of wellbeing which consists of the consumption of social goods. The priority is well-being via the consumption and production of social goods.

Most of what Sen calls functionings are the consumption and production of social goods. Even political activities, which are voluntary and unpaid and collective, are social goods. Without the notion of social goods at our disposal such activities can be classified only as leisure time activities, but as many who have been to political meetings will testify, they are hardly leisure.

Time and wellbeing

The time spent on the consumption and production of social goods is a measure of wellbeing; it is not wellbeing as such but it is a good proxy for it. It is simply the time spent living. Time spent doing paid work is necessary, of course, but it is not part of wellbeing; it is only indirectly instrumental to it. (There will be exceptions for people who are engaged in paid creative work, but for the bulk of the population we may ignore this.) Thus the value of things produced in the private and public goods sector – the outside economy as it were – is an indirect and imperfect measure of wellbeing. The expenditure on buying consumption goods – which are private goods by definition – is also an imperfect measure of wellbeing, although it is most generally used in measures of standards of living. Thus neither Gross Domestic Product (GDP) nor consumers' expenditure are good measures of wellbeing. It is the time spent on the production and consumption of social goods which is the real key to wellbeing. It is this time which must be enhanced as a result of public policy.

Consider a poor household. Typically the household members spend too much time doing paid work which still leaves them insufficient money to buy the private goods with which to produce social goods and consume them. To the extent that social goods can be produced with time alone (chatting, socialising) their wellbeing is enhanced. Indeed in poor societies people find many such activities which do not need bought goods but time (conversation, gossip), or which stretch out the bought goods over a long time (card playing, boules). Lack of private goods diminishes wellbeing by restricting the quantity and quality of social goods consumed. But time spent on the consumption of social goods is a measure of wellbeing and in the production and consumption of social goods time is a good substitute for money/resources. This is partly why bygone societies, though materially poorer than us, managed to sustain a high level of wellbeing. Our incomes are much higher but less than proportionately to our levels of wellbeing by comparison.

This is again frequently asserted and seems to be an anti-progress sentiment. Obviously with the range of private and public goods available, we can do today what previous generations, especially those before the Industrial Revolution, could not do. Labour productivity is higher today and real wages have, over the long run, kept up with the rising productivity. We live longer than they did and so our life cycle is longer. In what sense could they be said to be better off than we are?

One way to think of this is that in everyday life we have just as many hours as they did. Each hour of work brings us many more goods. Another way of putting this is the well known measure of prosperity which asks us how many minutes of paid work it takes on average to buy a loaf of bread, or a car, or a washing machine. In all these measures there is progress. Thus we work fewer hours than previous generations and can buy more. But we still feel harried. Economists such as Tibor Scitovsky (1992) and Stefan Linder (1970) have pointed out the pervasiveness of a feeling of being harried or joyless as the consumers of a modern economy. These critiques are reflected in popular literature all the time, but especially in the notion of quality time that well-paid, two-worker households find they are most deprived of.

It is possible to make sense of all this within the social goods framework. Out of the fixed amount of daily time of 24 hours if we net out the hours for sleep for example, which are physically necessary, we have left what I will call Gross Total Time (GTT). Now paid work takes not only the standard eight-hour work time (in a stylised case), but the time of getting there and back plus getting ready for work. Call this gross hours of paid work (GHW). The time for living is the difference between the two: Net Living Time is equal to GTT minus GHW. Thus if you sleep 8 hours, say, then GTT is 16 hours and if for an 8-hour working day you have to spend 2 extra hours travelling, GHW is 10 hours. This leaves 6 hours for Net Living Time (NLT). For women involved in unpaid housework, whether they are doing paid work or not, adjustments have to be made before we can compute NLT.

Now my contention is that wellbeing depends on the number and kinds of things we can do in our Net Living Time. If, as is the case, different members of a household have different work times then the common NLT hours may be indeed smaller. Thus it can easily be that the *intersection* of a husband and wife's NLTs may be very small indeed. *This intersection of the two NLTs is quality time.* This is why holidays are so valuable because all time becomes living time and everyone in the family has free time simultaneously. The worth of every hour spent in paid work increases in terms of purchasing power over private goods as real wages rise, but the trade-off between NLT and money gets worse as we get more prosperous. Thus wellbeing 'bought' by each hour of paid work or each pound of income gets smaller since the net living time gets squeezed out.

Of course different people will have different trade-offs. Private goods and NLT are substitutes for each other; you can have a take-away rather than cook. You can also choose that set of functionings which economise on NLT; do by a quick e-mail or telephone call what would be more enjoyable in face-to-face conversation and so on. But at both ends there are absolute and irreducible minima; you must have some money to buy private goods, no amount of time would at that level of income compensate for lack of private goods. And by the same token no amount of money will compensate for lack of interactive social time; I cannot hire someone to make love on my behalf even if I could pay him a fortune, or even take part in my child's birthday celebration as my substitute.

The upshot of this is that in terms of standard economic calculus, one hour of paid work – despite the higher productivity and hence higher real wage – buys less social goods than it used to. In other words, wellbeing is getting expensive even as private and public goods are getting cheaper. This is, of course, a secular tendency originating at the beginning of the industrial revolution. But the recent trends in the squeezing of NLT are not just an illusion. Two sorts of obvious economistic trends are at the root of this:

(1) Each hour of paid work requires an extra overhead of travel and preparation time so an eight-hour day becomes a ten- or eleven-hour day; thus wage per gross hour is lower than wage per actual working hour;
(2) Each hourly wage has to be adjusted downwards for direct and indirect taxes.

Of these two, the most visible and politically unpopular are the direct taxes, but indirect taxes also enter prices of private goods and lower net purchasing power. But the first effect, the overhead loading in paid work while noticed – as commuter complaints and so on – is not directly seen as shrinkage of purchasing power of an hour of paid work. But the effect is nevertheless there. Thus paid work is worth less in terms of what it buys of living time. The more NLT shrinks, the higher is the price, in terms of the amount of private goods which will compensate for the lost NLT[3].

Now the reaction to this on the part of many citizens is to blame the politicians for their feeling of being harassed. They also resent the people they think are scroungers, that is, getting paid without working. These people have what the busy paid employed people do not have – free time. And they also seem to have for free (without spending any gross or net time) what the busy people have to pay for from their paid, working time, in other words, money. So it is easy to think that those on benefits are better off than those who are materially richer but feel acutely the lack of living time. However, those on the dole are not necessarily better off. Their set of functionings is restricted by lack of money, since money and NLT are not perfect substitutes. Also, in some sense we have forgotten those things which our forebears could do, without money but with time. So the free time is less productive of wellbeing since the set of functionings is restricted.

Wellbeing and reform of the welfare state

Now the reactions of politicians in reforming the welfare state have been perverse if you agree with the analysis so far. Far from releasing the NLT of paid employed people – say by reducing commuting time, encouraging working at home or in the neighbourhood, making travel more congenial so that it can be combined with other activities, such as reading or conversation – they are set upon making the unemployed work so that they too can experience the squeezing of living time.

The classic case of this is the approach to single mothers. The state has decided that rather than 'sit at home', these women ought to go out to work. It has decided that every hour spent not working is worthless and every hour spent doing paid work is worth every penny that is earned. Both of these are fallacies. Let us take the second consideration first. As I argued above, every hour of paid work is loaded with extra overhead time for getting to and from work. Thus the hourly wage is less than what it seems. Then there is the matter of taxes. The state gains by the fact that single mothers give up benefit and contribute to direct tax as well as the extra indirect tax they pay on the difference between pay and benefit. So it is a definite benefit for the state that single mothers work. But for these women their net purchasing power is enhanced by much less than it appears from looking at gross pay and may in many cases of low wage payment be less.

In terms of NLT and wellbeing there is hardly any chance that such women will be better off. They will have to buy childcare and for their children the bought care may not be as good as their mothers' time. But the mothers' spending power, net of bought childcare as well as all other deductions, buys less NLT than it did before. Like many other employed people they too will feel harassed since their wellbeing is not increased by this exercise.

The reduction of NLT is costly for the state too. The main cost is in children's wellbeing. The increase in child abuse, child violence and children's crime are in some sense functions of the lack of time that the parents suffer. It is not so much the breakdown of the traditional family. It is the changed circumstances in which the traditional family does not have the NLT to do what it used to be able to do and the gadgets it can buy for its children are no substitutes. What they need is time and time is one thing the parents do not have. It takes time to know that your children have arrived at the school they set out to reach and time to look after them when they return to the home. Yes one can have after-school hours activities and other substitutes but they are shoddy in quality and expensive of cash. They are designed to keep parents at work primarily and only secondarily to keep pupils engaged away from home. So parents hire baby minders and au pairs and nannies.

So what?

The shrinkage of NLT and the extra money each hour of such time costs, mean that in terms of wellbeing we are less well off than we are in cash income *per se*. This conclusion is in line with other attempts to measure wellbeing or welfare in terms of indicators other than income. But the focus here is different. It is not macroeconomic and nor is it about pollution, important though these matters are. The emphasis is explicitly on wellbeing measured by individual time, the kind of social goods a person can acquire with that time and the consequent wellbeing they enjoy. There follows from this analysis a critique of the welfare reforms and indeed the notion of welfare state as such. So what policy conclusions can we derive from this analysis?

Nothing I have said should be taken to imply that we do not need to do paid work. The compulsions of competitive economy, the need to generate paid work by providing a stable economic framework and so on, are there. It also does not say that there are no budget constraints on governments. What it does say is that we should look carefully at the price we are paying for what we get from the welfare state and rethink our policies from the viewpoint of wellbeing. Thus:

(a) We should calculate the real cost of welfare policies taking into account NLT. Given the above analysis, the real wage per gross working hour is clearly less than the hourly wage, and the net purchasing power of the pound earned net of direct and indirect taxes is also less than meets the eye. These two steps ought to lead us to calculate what each hour of NLT costs in terms of each hour of gross working time and in terms of net purchasing power of the hour worked.
(b) We should be able to calculate the extra cost of buying services or goods which could be made with unpaid time especially if we can allow for quality. We know in the case of carers that the state is saved an immense amount of money by the availability of unpaid or low-paid carers. The same is true of childcare.
(c) The switch from public provision which was unpriced or subsidised to fully priced private provision may have benefited the state financially but it may have cost the citizens extra gross working time and reduced their wellbeing. It may emerge that in many cases the financial saving for the state is illusory and even if the money sums saved were positive, the trade-off in terms of wellbeing may suggest that this move was harmful. Transport is a case in point. The switch from public to private buses, urban transport and railways has everywhere increased the price paid and often increased the congestion and travel time. This is not true of many other privatisations, for example telecommunications, so this is not an anti-privatisation point but a matter of the correct economic calculus. If we add the value of extra time spent in reaching the destination – waiting time plus travel time – it may turn out that privatisation of public transport was a bad bargain. By contrast free public transport may prove economically sound if individual time was valued properly.

Conclusion

The welfare state is not an arrangement that necessarily enhances wellbeing. Historically it has been much more concerned with the world of paid work and with providing a safety net in terms of money to buy private goods. The ways in which it does these things undervalues citizens' living time and overvalues its own financial savings. Recent reforms have worsened this tendency by stressing paid work at the cost of reduced wellbeing. The result has been a feeling of harassment and reduced wellbeing.

There are other and wider lessons which could be drawn from this analysis. Thus it says something about building new houses in brownfield sites and near places of work rather than in remote rural areas. It says that crowded urban settlements may be beneficial and locating shopping nearby rather than far away is also beneficial[4]. But above all, this analysis wishes to bring to the forefront living and caring as major concerns of citizens whose wellbeing is promoted by availability of living time. Welfare states need to focus their attention on living and wellbeing and away from paid work and welfare benefits. A new calculus is required which assesses programmes in terms of time saved for living rather than just money saved for the Exchequer.

Notes

[1] But see Anne Harrison, Chapter 3 and Heather Joshi and Hugh Davies, Chapter Five for discussion of moving analysis more in this direction. On caring, see Bubeck (1995).

[2] Measurement of poverty is a problem that has two main aspects. The first one is the calculation of the money value of income which defines the poverty line. The second problem, having got the line defined, is calculating how many people are poor, and how poor are the poor. I am concerned here with the first question.

[3] Note that these issues are different from the usually discussed ones of tapers and the high rate of taxation at the bottom.

[4] See the contribution by Jenny Neuburger in Chapter Twelve of this volume.

References

Bubeck, D. (1995) *Care, gender and justice*, Oxford: Clarendon Press.

Desai, M. (1998) 'A basic income proposal', in R. Skidelsky (ed) *The state of the future*, London: Social Market Foundation.

Gillie, A. (1996) 'The origin of the poverty line', *Economic History Review*, vol XILX, no 4, pp 715-30.

Linder, S.B. (1970) *The harried leisure class*, New York, NY: Columbia University Press.

Rowbotham, S. (1998) 'Dear Mr Marx: a letter from a socialist feminist', in L. Panitch and C. Leys (eds) *The Communist Manifesto now: Socialist Register 1998*, Rendelsham: The Merlin Press.

Scitovsky, T. (1992) *The joyless economy: The psychology of human satisfaction*, Oxford: Oxford University Press.

Sen, A. (1987) *The standard of living: The Tanner Lectures*, Cambridge: Cambridge University Press.

Townsend, P. (1979) *Poverty in the UK*, Harmondsworth: Penguin.

Part Two: The economy as a whole

SEVEN

Four decades of changing macroeconomic policy

Christopher Allsopp

Introduction

Contributing to a volume such as this, marking one economist's career and looking to the future, is an excuse to indulge in generalisations about the changing framework of UK macroeconomic policy since the 1950s – that is, about five decades of economic history. Such a perspective is more usually the province of major policy makers, such as Chancellors of the Exchequer or Central Bank Governors where, typically, the present is viewed favourably in the light of the unaccountable errors of the past.

My objective is more modest: to give a highly selective account of some of the major things that have changed and of some of the major things that have not changed (or that have changed less than commonly supposed). If, in the course of such an account, some misperceptions can be laid to rest, that would be a bonus. And, if the account were to have some bearing on UK policy issues at the beginning of the new millennium, that would be even better.

The account is divided into three sections. The next section focuses on the enormous changes in policy 'regime' or framework that have occurred: *Plus ça change ….*; the following section looks at some of the things that have not changed (especially the need for an overall framework for policy that provides a credible commitment that inflation will be controlled in the medium term): *plus c'est la meme chose*; the final section draws some of the threads together with an eye on present concerns and possible future problems.

Plus ça change ...

From the standpoint of the year 2000, nothing could seem more obvious than that UK macroeconomic policy has changed out of recognition. The Keynesian consensus of the 1950s and 1960s gave way to the turmoil and irresponsibility of the 1970s which ushered in 'monetarism' and the Medium Term Financial Strategy (MTFS). That failed with the inflation of the late 1980s, as did the brief experiment with the Exchange Rate Mechanism (ERM) of the European Monetary System (EMS). When that system broke down, there was yet another regime change with the adoption of *inflation targeting* – which led (in 1997) to the setting up of a new Monetary Policy Committee (MPC) within an 'instrument independent' Bank of England.

Meanwhile, the world has altered. The Bretton Woods system of fixed-but-adjustable exchange rates broke down at the end of the 1960s. Oil price shocks – two up and one down (in 1985) – punctuated the 1970s and the 1980s. The end of the Cold War and especially German reunification delivered a shock, across Europe, at the beginning of the 1990s. Eleven European countries irrevocably adopted a common currency at the beginning of 1999, with the UK, so far, outside, looking in. Financial liberalisation over several decades has, domestically, altered the way the economy works and, internationally, altered the constraints and the rules of the game.

Economic theory and econometric practice have also changed. The Phillips curve relationship between inflation and unemployment was tied down and emasculated in the late 1960s to be replaced with the 'natural rate of unemployment' (NRU)/NAIRU[1] framework – still the dominant paradigm for macroeconomic analysis. Forward-looking 'rational' expectations, monetary policy games and 'credibility' have altered the rhetoric of political/economic debate. Macroeconometric modelling frameworks for forecasting and policy analysis are now incomparably more sophisticated than the equivalents of spreadsheets available to 1960s policy makers (see Simon Wren-Lewis's chapter). Despite this, forecasting errors are still a potent source of mistaken policies – as in the late 1980s Lawson boom when the excessive strength of consumer demand was seriously underestimated.

A blow-by-blow discussion of all the twists and turns would clearly not be helpful. The following is a selective account of some of the major changes and milestones along the way.

The control of inflation

The current conventional wisdom has it that a typical policy maker of the Keynesian consensus years was more or less exclusively concerned with maintaining growth and full employment and had little concern with, and no theory of, inflation. This is a travesty. The control of inflation was, from the beginning, always recognised as a *necessary* condition for the use of demand management to maintain high employment (as was an acceptable balance of payments position)[2]. The simple Phillips curve never fitted well with such a framework and, arguably, trade-off ideas were not very influential in policy circles until reimported from the US in the mid 1960s with the influential study *Britain's economic prospects* by Caves (1968). The policy *reaction function* (to use the modern terminology) was closely tied down by the commitment to very narrow bands for the exchange rate *target* under the Bretton Woods system. The exchange rate commitment also dictated the assignment of fiscal policy as the main instrument of stabilisation policy[3].

It is also not true that the so-called Keynesian policy makers had no idea of what to do about inflation. In fact they had two potential remedies, neither of which appeared particularly palatable: general monetary and fiscal deflation (the oldest remedy in the book), and 'incomes policy', which was always recognised as costly and difficult to sustain. It was pessimism about the heavy costs of monetary and fiscal deflation that led to the search for a less costly alternative – a debate that continued into the 1980s[4]. The way in which the issues were perceived is well illustrated by an international report for the Organisation for Economic Co-operation and Development (OECD), the Fellner Report (1964), which was written at the beginning of the 1960s looking forward to the problems likely to emerge later in the decade. Increasing inflationary pressure was foreseen, with (at that time) the majority arguing with reluctance that policy needed to be extended into control over the wage–price formation system and the minority (including Fellner himself) suggesting that inflation was inevitable unless unemployment was allowed to rise.

Much has been written about the late 1960s, prior to the shocks of the 1970s. The period is defining in terms of the grand narrative about what comes after in the 1970s, the 1980s and even the 1990s. It was a time of increasing inflationary pressure. There was excess demand in the US due to the Vietnam War and increased social expenditure (Johnson's Program for a Great Society) combined with grass-roots militancy and political protest. In Europe too, high employment was threatened by cost-push pressure manifest in political protest, labour militancy and wage explosions. This is the time when inflationary pressure came to be described as originating in competing claims (obviously, but not only, between organised labour and firms[5]) with unemployment *functional* in reconciling the competing claims in equilibrium with steady inflation (the non-accelerating inflation rate of unemployment, or NAIRU). The notions were formalised by Rowthorn (1977) and used empirically by Layard and Nickell (1985) in their account of the rise in unemployment in the UK[6].

Suppose one adopts this 'competing claims' or NAIRU-type framework and considers the problem of stabilising inflation at some low rate: what would be the options looking forward? There are basically three:

(1) **Non-accommodating demand management policies**. Ultimately this involves leaving the parties to fight it out in real terms – with unemployment (perhaps heavy unemployment) functional as the 'disciplinary device' in reconciling the competing claims.
(2) **Incomes policies**. These come in different guises, ranging from cooperation to coercion. But their rationale is to substitute for unemployment in the competing claims equilibrium. Given a non-accommodating policy against inflation, a successful incomes policy would lower equilibrium unemployment.
(3) **Supply-side reforms**. This 'third way' seeks to abolish or mitigate the power structures and imperfections that would otherwise need to be contained by unemployment or incomes policies. More positively, improvements in (for example) institutions or training, may also seek to lower the 'natural' rate of unemployment[7].

Much of the history of macroeconomic policy making in the OECD countries since the 1960s can be seen from the perspective of these three paradigm cases. Thus, in the UK, incomes policies under the 1964-70 Labour government gave way to the deflation (1) and supply-side reforms (3) of the Heath administration. Famously, as the pain rose, there was a U-turn towards incomes policies (2) – which, politically, were traded for more expansionary policy (the Barber boom)[8]. Skipping the details, reliance on the incomes policy route gave way more and more to the policy of non-accommodating demand policies. The phrase 'There is no alternative' (or Tina), which is usually applied to Thatcher's 'monetarism', actually referred not to monetarism but to the alternative of incomes policy. The Thatcher government swept away the remnants of incomes policy, unashamedly adopting the rhetoric of supply-side reform (3). Monetary targets and the (1980) MTFS were designed to deliver a non-accommodating nominal framework (1). After the failures of the Lawson boom in the second half of the 1980s and a move to a different form of non-accommodation – entry into the ERM – policy since 1993 has again been firmly based on the twin planks of non-accommodation (1) – now in the form of inflation targeting and, since 1997, with delegation of monetary policy to the MPC – and supply-side reform (3). What Nigel Lawson termed his 'abiding legacy' (Lawson, 1992) – a non-accommodating macroeconomic policy framework to control inflation with accent on the supply side to deal with unemployment and growth – appears to be just that.

Experience in other countries has been more diverse. Thus, for example, Scandinavia until the 1990s adopted the incomes policy route with some success. Cooperative agreements, effectively forms of incomes policies, are still a feature of some successful countries – notably Austria, the Netherlands and Ireland. In most of continental Europe, however, non-accommodation has been accompanied by persistently high unemployment (still about 10% of the labour force in the year 2000). Not surprisingly, perhaps, the conventional wisdom increasingly ascribes this major failure within Europe to insufficient attention being given to supply-side reforms and 'flexibility' – that is, to (3).

The management of nominal demand

The developing consensus that a major aim of macroeconomic policy should be to set up a stable non-accommodating and credible nominal framework against inflation begs the crucial set of questions about how this should be delivered. One of the most startling features of the past decades in the UK is the number of different frameworks that have been tried, all with the avowed aim of delivering stability. And all but the one in place at the moment have ended in failure.

The focus of the original, broadly Keynesian, framework of the 1950s and 1960s was on a notion of potential output at 'full employment'. It involved the avoidance of excess or deficient demand. With an exchange rate commitment under Bretton Woods, fiscal policy was actively used as the main instrument for stabilisation (though credit controls were also important). Short- and longer-term disequilibria tended to express themselves most obviously as balance of payments crises and the developing conflict between internal and external objectives was one of the main reasons for the so-called 'stop–go' cycle. After devaluation in 1967, inflation became more overtly an issue. The regime collapsed at the beginning of the 1970s in line with the international breakdown of the fixed-but-adjustable exchange rate system.

With the inflationary shocks of the early 1970s and the move to floating currencies, the regime had to change. Passing over the muddled British response to the first oil crisis (basically to try to avoid excess demand but otherwise to rely on incomes policy and a competitive exchange rate), monetary targets were adopted (for 'M3' and then 'Sterling £M3'), effectively from 1976, and targets for public borrowing (in the form of the Public Sector Borrowing Requirement, the PSBR) were announced[9]. This period requires two comments.

First, the main reason for the adoption of monetary targets appears to have been as an operating basis for monetary policy: that is, as a substitute for the exchange rate commitment of the Bretton Woods era. The monetary target could be seen as an alternative 'nominal anchor' appropriate to a floating exchange rate regime. The German 'demonstration effect' was also important[10]. The developing academic framework of Friedman-type 'monetarism' seemed less influential at the time – though it does seem to have been important in the unfortunate choice of broad money (M3/£M3) as the target[11].

Second, though the macroeconomic framework in this late 1970s period looks, superficially, similar to the policy of the Thatcher government, it was in fact very different. The key point is that the main thrust of inflation reduction and control in the 1970s was still reliance on incomes policy. The monetary and fiscal framework was designed to be consistent with this rather than, so to speak, doing the work itself (although it is true that relatively high unemployment levels were increasingly tolerated). With the breakdown of incomes policy in the 'winter of discontent' (1978/9) the policy framework was effectively in ruins.

The Thatcher experiment has to be seen as a decisive break – but it remains, even now, difficult to disentangle reality from rhetoric. The early rhetoric was avowedly 'gradualist monetarist', based on Friedman (1968) rather than New-Classical ideology (Laidler, 1985). Politically, monetarism was sold as a quickish fix which would lower and control inflation and lead to lower unemployment. (Recall that the election slogan was 'Labour isn't working' with a picture of a seemingly endless dole queue.) To the extent that recession was envisaged in response to changing monetary policy, it was a relatively mild, Friedman-type, adjustment over about two years. The toughness came later when the combination of high interest rates, a tight fiscal policy and the effects of the second oil shock (which were coming through in 1979) led to major recession and an unprecedented rise in unemployment that needed, in political terms, to be positively connoted.

The MTFS, introduced in 1980, formalised the declining ranges for the monetary target and presented what were termed 'consistent forecasts' for the PSBR. The fiscal aspects of the MTFS came to be seen as important as the 'monetarist' aspects. The intellectual background to this specifically British version of monetarism was obscure, with the fiscal targets (or consistent forecasts) being presented as necessary in order to control money, in order to control nominal spending. Perhaps it is best to follow the view expressed by John Fforde (1983), at the time an executive director at the Bank of England, that the MTFS allowed a larger downward management of demand than would otherwise have been politically feasible.

The MTFS ran into problems more or less from the start. It proved difficult to meet the monetary targets with the instruments available – basically the short-term interest rate[12]. And the fiscal framework was not set up in cyclically adjusted form (though there was some recognition that PSBR reduction would be quicker in boom than in slump). An evaluation of this period of economic history is not appropriate here (but see Allsopp, Jenkinson and Morris, 1991). Two rather general points are, however, worth stressing. The first is that the *instruments* of policy (especially the short-term interest rate) had to be used extremely *actively* to try to meet the targets. This also meant large movements in the exchange rate. The second is that the medium-term framework certainly did not ensure stability – indeed, the formulation of the fiscal rules in particular was destabilising. The nice but simplistic presumption of monetarist theory that a simple rule for the development of a monetary aggregate would provide a stable nominal framework turned out to be very far from the truth.

The second half of the 1980s was very different from the first. It is tempting to suggest that it marked a return to something not unlike 1960s pragmatism in demand management, though there was continuing search for an appropriate nominal anchor (for example, shadowing the Deutschmark). What did occur was, in intellectual terms, rather boring: namely a large forecasting error, especially about the strength of consumer demand, an error which is widely blamed for the excesses of the late 1980s 'Lawson boom' (see Burns, 1995 and Simon Wren-Lewis, Chapter Two of this volume). Presumably, if demand had been forecast more correctly, monetary and fiscal policy would have been tighter in 1988[13]. While it is certainly true that forecast errors were made, some of the blame must surely lie with the MTFS: the budget surpluses (debt repayments) were heralded as indicating extraordinary success and fiscal responsibility, whereas they were actually a sign of a *private sector* out of control.

The return of demand management was even more apparent in the response to the boom. This was the period when interest rates were used as almost the only instrument to curtail demand with, in qualitative terms, predictable effects on the exchange rate. The 'one club policy' was widely regarded at the time as damaging, largely because of the effects, via the exchange rate, on traded goods sectors and especially on manufacturing.

As so often, if domestic monetary and fiscal indicators and targets do not establish stability, the tendency is to reach for external discipline instead – this time with entry into the ERM. There was an added reason at this time: academic debate suggested the importance of the 'credibility' of the government's commitment to low inflation and the difficulty of establishing it, and there was the tempting prospect of buying into some of the Bundesbank's reputation for non-accommodation of inflation. This short regime also ended in political disaster with Britain's forced ejection from the ERM in 1992.

So, back to domestic targets to ensure stability – this time in the form of inflation targets. Experience since 1993 has, in fact, been remarkable, with steady low inflation and steady growth averaging about 2.8%. Unemployment has fallen steadily but dramatically. And public borrowing, which appeared briefly out of control in the early 1990s recession, is back well under control. The debt to Gross Domestic Product (GDP) ratio is falling (see John Hills, Chapter Eight). So are inflation targets plus fiscal 'prudence' the elusive philosopher's stone that delivers stability?

... plus c'est la meme chose

But has macroeconomic policy really changed? It has certainly swung about. But at a deeper level the history illustrates the difficulty of reconciling the use of macroeconomic policy to stabilise prices and inflation with other objectives such as the stabilisation of output or the promotion of international competitiveness via manipulation of the exchange rate.

Consider, first, the role of macroeconomic policy. In many text book expositions, an exogenously given money supply controls the price level, whilst the real economy looks after itself – generating potential growth. The policy analogue of this simple scheme would be a version of 'monetarism' with the primary task of the authorities being to control the money supply in order to control the price level and inflation in the medium term. With nominal price and wage rigidities and with the system subject to shocks of various kinds, the authorities would also have a role in stabilisation: they would want to control inflation in the medium term with minimum cost in terms of output and price fluctuations along the way.

The first part of this scheme, linking prices mechanistically to the money supply, is blatantly unrealistic, though perhaps there may have been an approximation to it during the gold standard era. In the Keynesian era, as Hicks (1974) argued, prices were determined in a different way. There was, for a time, a period when countries seemed to be on a 'nominal wage standard' – which allowed macroeconomic policy to concentrate on the stabilisation of output and the avoidance of slumps. (In the UK, macro policy was also increasingly constrained by the exchange rate commitment – requiring policy to be directed towards the maintenance of external equilibrium and competitiveness.) Internationally and in the UK the wage standard broke down – most obviously with the wage explosions and other inflationary pressures of the late 1960s[14]. And the exchange rate anchor (an anchor only relative to other countries, such as the US) disappeared with the move to floating exchange rates and the rise in world inflation. Putting aside the attempts to re-impose the wage standard via incomes policies and the misguided attempts to reintroduce an approximation to simple (or so-called 'technical') monetarism, this meant, as outlined above, that demand management policy had to focus more and more on the control of inflation. If there is a general message from the 1970s and 1980s it is that the loss of control over inflation and inflation expectations is extremely costly.

Today there is an answer to the question of what determines the price level and what determines the rate of inflation. Ultimately, that answer is macroeconomic policy through the authorities' policy reaction function – or, more straightforwardly, policy. At this level of generality the question of whether policy is directed towards an intermediate nominal target, such as one or other measure of the money supply or the exchange rate[15], or more directly towards the control of inflation itself, is of second order. What is important is that the perceived commitment to stable inflation in the medium term be sufficiently credible to stabilise inflation expectations.

The conceptual scheme is extremely simple if attention is confined, for the moment, to the single macroeconomic policy instrument of the short-term interest rate. Then, the job of the authorities is to move the interest rate up or down as prices and inflation seem likely to diverge from some norm or target. That is, inflation is contained by some feedback system – applied by the monetary authorities. A simple version is the so-called 'Taylor Rule' (Taylor, 1993) which in fact fits experience in a number of developed countries reasonably well since the mid 1980s[16]. More complicated versions of policy reaction functions are possible, but something can be said about the characteristics of 'reasonable' feedback rules that would do the job (Clarida et al, 1999). One essential characteristic is that *real* interest rates should react positively to deviations of inflation from target. The present regime of inflation targeting in the UK can be seen as an institutional version of such a feedback system[17].

A feedback system needs to be tied to something. In the 1960s in the UK, interest rates (and much other policy as well) were tied to the exchange rate. This was sufficient to ensure that inflation did not get far out of line with inflation in other countries, but conflicts with other objectives such as high employment and international competitiveness mounted, culminating in the decision to devalue in 1967. The gyrations of the 1970s and 1980s can be seen as the search for some other framework or basis for policy: substituting for the simplicities of the monetarist model or nominal exchange rate commitment. The present system of an explicit inflation target is, arguably, much better than the regimes that have been tried before – it certainly has more explicit theoretical justification – but it is not different in kind. Interest rates, via changes in nominal demand, control the economy and ultimately the price level and inflation.

The present system

Inflation targets were adopted after the UK was forcibly ejected from the ERM in 1992. The present system was set up soon after the election of the Labour government in 1997, when the Chancellor announced the delegation of monetary policy to a new MPC at the Bank of England charged with meeting an inflation target set by the Chancellor. The target was set initially at 2.5% for Retail Prices excluding the mortgage interest rate component (RPIX) and has not, at the time of writing, been changed since. In the jargon, the Bank became 'instrument independent', responsible for the operation of monetary policy to meet the externally given target, but not 'goal independent'. The nine members of the MPC (five internal and four external) are individually responsible, under the 1998 Bank of England Act, for their own votes which are recorded in the minutes of MPC meetings, and they may need to justify their position – for example before the Treasury Select Committee. The system is, arguably, one of the most transparent and accountable in the world (see, for example, King, 1997, 1999).

In practice, the MPC sets the short-term interest rate each month with an eye on current developments and future expected inflation (with a forecast horizon of about two years – to allow for lags in the transmission of monetary policy to output and inflation). An important feature of the system is that it is symmetrical in the sense that deviations of inflation from target, which is a single number (not a range), either up or down are treated symmetrically, equally requiring policy action to return the inflation rate towards the target. The system is set up so that the committee has some discretion about how to offset shocks in the short term and about how quickly it seeks to return inflation to the target, but (in principle) no discretion about its commitment to meet the inflation target in the medium term[18]. The idea of such 'constrained discretion' is to allow monetary policy makers to try to minimise the costs of fluctuations in output and in inflation as the economy is buffeted about by various 'shocks' while the longer-term commitment to the control of inflation is maintained[19]. Such a system does not remove potential short-term conflicts between inflation control and stabilisation, but without the discretion aspect of 'constrained discretion' the conflicts would be considerably worse, perhaps threatening the credibility of the system as a whole.

Two reasons are usually put forward for the delegation of monetary policy. The first is that it may be hard for the political authorities to commit credibly to low and stable inflation if they are tempted to cheat by going for lower unemployment in the short term and if private sector agents anticipate this. This could lead to an inflation bias. Delegation could be expected to remove any such bias – basically by removing any temptation to cheat (Bean, 1998a). The second is that an institution specifically charged with inflation control may be better able to develop a reputation for competence and facilitate the establishment of a sensible and transparent 'reaction function'. More generally, it seems right that the democratically elected authorities should be responsible for setting the overall goals of monetary policy while its operation should be delegated to professionals.

The policy reaction function of the authorities – the way in which policy reacts to information as it accrues – should become fairly predictable in such a system, in which case, if markets have much the same information as is available to the authorities, there should be relatively little 'news' in interest rate decisions (King, 1997). (It may also become relatively predictable in less explicit systems, such as that in the USA.) The likely reactions depend, however, on what kind of disturbances are under consideration. To use the well known example, starting from steady growth at potential output and at target inflation, shocks to demand (which would tend to raise or lower inflation depending on whether they were positive or negative) should be offset as far as possible, whereas shocks to the price level and inflation involve trade-offs in the short term between output deviations and deviations of inflation from target. The case of demand shocks illustrates clearly the point, made in the historical discussion above, that the provision of a stable macroeconomic framework may involve the active use of policy and considerable fluctuations in the interest rate.

Interaction with other policy instruments

The new system in the UK specifically assigns responsibility for the control of inflation to the MPC and to monetary policy. Discretion is highly constrained, and the instruments of monetary policy – in practice the short-term interest rate – must be used to meet the target set by the government. The institutional set-up and the monetary reaction function provide the commitment that inflation will be controlled.

But this clearly does not mean that other instruments of policy, such as fiscal policy, are irrelevant to inflation control. Quite the contrary: it remains the overall stance of macroeconomic policy that is relevant to prospects for inflation. A tighter fiscal policy, for example, to the extent that it bears down on the prospects for demand and for inflation, would naturally lead, via the monetary policy reaction function, to lower interest rates. And one could even argue – to forge a link with the policy framework of the 1960s and 1970s – that were a credible incomes policy to be put in place, this too would lead through to lower interest rates (however unlikely such a policy might seem under current conditions). What is different is that the system as a whole contains a credible commitment to control inflation, with a clear delineation of where the responsibility ultimately lies. Clearly too, supply-side improvements, such as reductions in the equilibrium rate of unemployment (the NAIRU) should lead through to lower interest rates than otherwise and, in effect, to the upward management of demand to take advantage of the improvement on the supply side.

As Bean (1998b) and others have noted, the fiscal authority, or more broadly, the Treasury, is in the position of a Stackleberg leader. In formulating its policy, it needs to take into account the likely reactions of the monetary authority, which should be predictable. As an example, if the Treasury were to wish to lower interest rates with a view to lowering the exchange rate, it would do well to contemplate a tighter fiscal policy or measures designed to increase private sector savings.

It is not only discretionary fiscal policy that should feed through to monetary policy. The properties of the fiscal system should affect the monetary policy reaction function. If fiscal policy is set for the medium term, 'over the cycle' – which is current policy – it implies that the fiscal stabilisers are allowed to operate as shocks occur and as fluctuations in GDP arise. These stabilisers are large: a 1% change in output would feed through to about 0.5% of GDP change in the government's budget position. This degree of built-in fiscal stabilisation implies that interest rates need to fluctuate less than otherwise. And if government expenditure totals are fixed in nominal terms, price shocks would translate through to real expenditure reductions, also serving to take some of the weight off the monetary policy reaction function.

The new monetary arrangements look like a major change to one aspect of macroeconomic policy. But their significance is much greater than that. The commitment of monetary policy to the control of inflation in effect commits the whole of macroeconomic policy to the objective of price stability. Within this framework, traditional questions of (for example) the appropriate mix of monetary and fiscal policy still arise, and are as important as ever.

Lessons from the past for the future

The breakdown of inflation control from the late 1960s proved extremely costly. Though much of the breakdown is understandable in terms of increasing pressures on the system and major conflicts between objectives, the trade-offs were not improved, except perhaps in the short term, by inflation: on the contrary they appeared to get worse. So the broadest lesson is that there is little gain in giving up on inflation control and considerable costs.

To be sure, the breakdown was not confined to the UK. There was an extremely unfavourable combination of rising cost-push pressures interacting with very large oil and other commodity price shocks which would have tested any macroeconomic framework. But the UK's experience was relatively poor. Incomes policies, which were undoubtedly helpful in some countries, failed to provide a durable solution in the UK. But the move to non-accommodating demand management policies linked to monetary targets or exchange rate commitments, also failed to provide the desirable combination of anti-inflation commitment with stability.

The new arrangements have got off to a good start. Inflation has been close to target and growth has been relatively rapid. Unemployment has fallen. And there are signs that inflation expectations are stabilising. But the history of the UK warns against complacency. The system has not yet been tested in adversity.

The commitment of monetary policy to the goal of price stability commits macroeconomic policy as a whole to the same goal. For example, an overexpansionary fiscal policy tending to produce excess demand would have to be offset, via the monetary policy reaction function, by higher interest rates than otherwise. The flip side of this obvious point is that the new monetary arrangements increase, rather than diminish, the importance of getting the other elements of policy right. Supply-side policies and, for example, measures to get the savings/investment balance of the economy right – whether by fiscal policy or perhaps by measures to stimulate and stabilise private sector saving behaviour – are as important as ever.

The paradox of the new monetary arrangements is that they are likely to shine the spotlight on the *overall* design of macroeconomic policy to achieve the goal of stable non-inflationary growth.

Notes

[1] Non-accelerating inflation rate of unemployment.

[2] Demand management, following Keynes's influential pamphlet *How to pay for the war*, was introduced during wartime to reduce demand and the likelihood of inflation, not to support employment.

[3] Dow (1964) showed that fiscal policy in the UK was destabilising – too much and too late. As he subsequently made clear, his intention was to argue for better stabilisation policy not the abandonment of the project.

[4] By the 1980s, the role of incomes policies had been 'reframed' as a possible way of reducing the NAIRU given non-accommodating policies against inflation.

[5] The OECD in particular put heavy emphasis on the influence of increasing claims by the government – often called tax-push inflation at the time (OECD, 1970). See also McCracken et al (1977).

[6] Pessimists such as Hayek (1944) had long argued that the postwar project to maintain high employment and growth would break down in turmoil. (From that perspective, the interesting question is why this did not happen for two enormously successful decades.) By the late 1960s, it was not only the pessimists who were questioning whether the existing order could be maintained.

[7] Conceptually, there is a distinction to be made between unemployment which is functional in 'disciplining' the wage–price formation process (competing claims pressure or, for example, unemployment which is functional in stopping 'leap-frogging' in some efficiency wage models) and unemployment due to (say) mis-match, or other imperfections, which have no countervailing function within the macro system. Supply-side reforms may be directed at either or both.

[8] Similar U-turns occurred in a number of other countries, including the USA. In the USA the deflationary response of 1969 was followed by monetary and fiscal relaxation and a brief experiment with wage and price control.

[9] A focus on targets for the PSBR was actually introduced by the 1964-70 Labour government – one of Nicholas Kaldor's abiding legacies.

[10] The German economy weathered the first oil crisis well which many ascribed, in part, to the use of monetary targets.

[11] Variations in broad money, £M3, appeared to lead the economy with something like the famous two-year lag of Friedman's monetary framework. This observation owed much to the fact that oil and other commodity price-induced inflation in 1973/4 followed the explosion of M3 which occurred after the monetary reforms of Competition and Credit Control in 1971.

[12] How anyone ever thought that one could control broad money, most of which pays interest, with the instrument of the short-term interest rates remains a mystery. At the least, it is an indication of the yawning gulf between practical policy and academic economics and, in this case, the perverse influence of academic thought on policy.

[13] The 1988 budget is frequently seen as adding fuel to the excessive boom. In conventional terms, however, it was probably more or less neutral in fiscal impact. The apparent implication under the MTFS that taxes could be greatly cut due to the budget surpluses of the time was, in fact, largely resisted. Hindsight tells us that even larger surpluses should have been aimed for – to compensate for the sharply falling household savings ratio.

[14] For contemporary and near contemporary accounts of the rise in inflation in the late 1960s see OECD (1970) and McCracken et al (1977).

[15] With the caveat that an exchange rate target or commitment is only an anchor relative to inflation in some other country, such as in practice, the US or Germany.

[16] The original Taylor Rule, intended to mimic the behaviour of the central bank in the US, linked the short-term real interest rate to deviations of inflation from target and to deviations of output from potential, both with coefficients of 0.5.

[17] An observed absence of 'sensible' interest rate reaction function in some past period would not imply that policy as a whole was perverse. It could simply reflect a situation in which other instruments of policy were being directed against inflation. And the maintenance of a high real interest rate, as in the first half of the 1980s, even if interest rates were not reacting to variations in inflation, could well be regarded as an anti-inflationary monetary strategy.

[18] There is a 'safety valve' in the 'open letter' system whereby the Governor is required to write an open letter to the Chancellor if inflation deviates from target by one percentage point or more detailing the reasons for the divergence and plans for returning the inflation rate to the target.

[19] A simple analogy to the set-up might go as follows. Consider delegating the urgent delivery of a package (to some distant destination) to a professional courier. The prime commitment necessary is the commitment of the driver to deliver the package to the right address. But it is also important that the delivery is effected as quickly as possible. For that, the driver needs discretion and skill, to avoid hazards such as traffic jams. The set-up leaves the driver with constrained discretion.

References

Allsopp, C.J., Jenkinson, T. and Morris, D.J. (1991) 'Macroeconomic policy in the 1980s', *Oxford Review of Economic Policy*, vol 7, no 3, pp 68-80.

Bean, C.R. (1998a) 'The new UK monetary arrangements: a view from the literature', *Economic Journal*, vol 108, no 451, pp 1795-809.

Bean, C.R. (1998b) 'Monetary policy under EMU', *Oxford Review of Economic Policy*, vol 14, no 3, pp 41-53.

Burns, T. (1995) 'Managing the nation's economy – the conduct of monetary and fiscal policy', South Bank Business School Annual Lecture (text from HM Treasury, January 1996).

Caves, R.E. (ed) (1968) *Britain's economic prospects*, London: George Allen and Unwin.

Clarida, R., Gali, J. and Gertler, M. (1999) 'The science of monetary policy: a new Keynesian perspective', *Journal of Economic Literature*, vol 37, no 4, pp 1661-707.

Dow, J.C.R. (1964) *The management of the British economy, 1945-60*, Cambridge: Cambridge University Press.

Fellner, W., Gilbert, M., Hansen, B., Kahn, R., Lutz, F. and de Wolff, P. (1964) *The problem of rising prices*, Paris: OECD (a report of a group of experts to the OEEC, originally published in 1961).

Fforde, J. (1983) 'Setting monetary objectives', *Bank of England Quarterly Bulletin*, vol 23, no 2, pp 200-8.

Friedman, M. (1968) *Dollars and deficits: Living with America's economic problems*, Englewood Cliffs, NJ: Prentice-Hall.

Hayek, F.A. von (1944) *The road to serfdom*, Chicago, IL: University of Chicago Press.

Hicks, J. (1974) *The crisis in Keynesian economics*, Oxford: Basil Blackwell.

King, M. (1997) 'The inflation target five years on', *Bank of England Quarterly Bulletin*, vol 37, no 4, pp 434-42.

King, M. (1999) 'The monetary policy committee 2 years on', *Bank of England Quarterly Bulletin*, vol 39, no 3, pp 297-303.

Laidler, D. (1985) 'Monetary policy in Britain: successes and shortcomings', *Oxford Review of Economic Policy*, vol 1, no 1, pp 35-43.

Lawson, N. (1992) *The view from No 11*, London: Bantam Press.

Layard, R. and Nickell, S.J. (1985) 'The causes of British unemployment', *National Institute Economic Review*, vol 111, pp 62-85.

McCracken, P., Carli, G., Giersch, H., Karaosmanoglu, A., Korniya, R., Lindbeck, A., Marjolin, R. and Matthews, R. (1997) *Towards full employment and price stability: A report to the OECD by a group of independent experts*, Paris: OECD.

OECD (1970) '*Inflation: The present problem*', Paris: OECD.

Rowthorn, R. E. (1977) 'Conflict, inflation and money', *Cambridge Journal of Economics*, vol 1, no 3, pp 215-39.

Taylor, J.B. (1993) 'Discretion versus policy rules in practice', *Carnegie-Rochester Series on Public Policy*, vol 39, pp 195-214.

EIGHT

Taxation for the enabling state

John Hills[1]

In economic management and in politics, there is little escape from the discussion of tax. Tax revenue has represented between one third and two fifths of total national income over the last 20 years, so its scale and design has major effects on the economy. Decisions on how much tax should be levied on different kinds of activity or individuals is one of the central decisions of British politics – hardly surprising with £10,000 to be raised every second. But much of this discussion treats tax as if it was simply a loss to those who pay it and to the economy as a whole, rather than as a vital mechanism to ensure that collective aims can be met and for ends which the market would fail to achieve. As Henry Neuburger put it in a paper for the Fabian Society Taxation Review,

> ... we have to promote the idea of tax as a contribution to the maintenance of the welfare state and not as a deadweight burden.... A modern democratic state requires adequate levels of taxation. The most consistent poll finding we have about tax is that a large majority of people agree with this analysis.... They believe in the productive enabling state and the means to finance it. (1989, pp 1 and 5)

The tax system is not there only – or indeed, mainly – as a redistributive mechanism. Its role is also to finance the provision of goods and services from which everyone benefits. To understand its function and effects, we have to look at spending at the same time. The overall level of taxation is largely determined by the amount of government spending required, while the effect of government on distribution can only be understood by looking at tax and spending together. Analysing their joint impact is becoming even more important as the government increasingly uses the tax system – through a widening use of 'tax credits' – instead of what were formerly social security benefits.

This chapter sets out the background against which decisions on the

Figure 8.1: Tax ratio 1978-79 to 1999-00

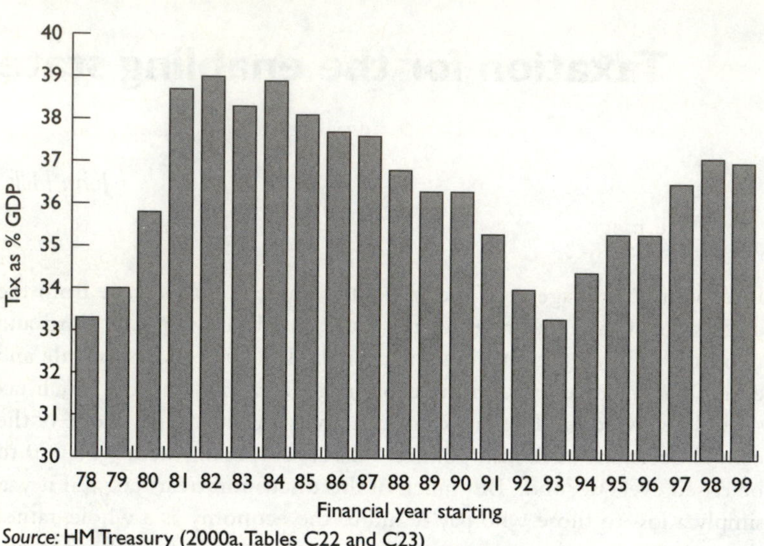

Source: HM Treasury (2000a, Tables C22 and C23)

tax system are taken, looking at trends in taxation and spending over the last 20 years, at their impact on distribution, and at what we know of public preferences for them. It then considers the impact of recent changes in tax policy since the 1997 change of government.

The level of taxation and public spending

Figure 8.1 shows how the tax ratio (total tax and National Insurance Contributions as a share of national income) has varied since 1978-79. A first point to note is how narrow in some ways the variation is. From an inherited level of just over 33%, the Thatcher government took tax to 39% of Gross Domestic Product (GDP) in 1982, near the lowest point of the recession. It then fell back through both the recovery of the late 1980s and the recession of the early 1990s, reaching a low point in 1993-94 back at 33%, before rising again through the recovery of the later 1990s to reach 37% by the end of the decade.

There is little clear trend over the period (or indeed, looking further back to the start of the 1970s), despite the political sound and fury. Some of the movements relate to the economic cycle, with a tendency for the ratio to fall in economic booms as the denominator, national income, grows rapidly (for instance, 1973, 1979 and the late 1980s) and to rise in recessions (notably the mid 1970s and early 1980s). But politics or the driving force of the public finances can buck such trends, as with the tax-cutting policies set in the run up to the 1992 election and the subsequent rise to cut back public borrowing afterwards.

One result of this comparative stability over the last quarter century is that the UK has moved from being a country with a fairly typical level of taxation amongst industrialised countries to being firmly in the low tax half of the range. By 1996, Britain's tax ratio (in this case, measured in relation to GNP) put it fourteenth out of twenty-one Organisation for Economic Co-operation and Development (OECD) countries. A similar ranking in 1986 would have put the UK above three countries it is now below, Spain, Canada and Italy; back in 1975 its ratio was just above the mid point of the international range[2]. The scale of variations between countries is far greater than the range over time in the UK. Only two other countries, Spain and Iceland, had ratios in 1996 within the range in which British tax revenues have been confined for the last quarter century. Whatever it is that has constrained this measure of the state in Britain, it is clearly not an iron law of the economics of modern economies. Other countries – some more successful economically, other less so – have made very different choices.

One of the drivers behind the trends here has of course been the level of public spending. Figure 8.2 shows the evolution over the same period of two measures of public spending. General government expenditure combines central and local government current and capital spending (with proceeds from privatisation counted as a negative item, significantly reducing it in the second half of the 1980s). Total Managed Expenditure (TME) – the total on which policy now tends to focus – includes spending by publicly owned corporations beyond their trading revenues as well (a much smaller part of the economy now than in the past).

For most of the period, tax revenues have been well below either measure of public spending, with particularly wide gaps at the start of the period shown and in the early 1990s. In contrast to the stability of the tax ratio, there has been a trend towards lower public spending as a share of GDP since 1975-76, when TME reached a peak of nearly 50% of GDP. Alongside this, there are clear swings with the economic cycle, with spending on some items like social security rising in recession (and with the denominator, national income, shrinking in the worst recessions).

Notably, however, the experience of different items within the public spending total has been very different, as can be seen for recent years in

Figure 8.2: Tax and public spending 1978-79 to 1999-00

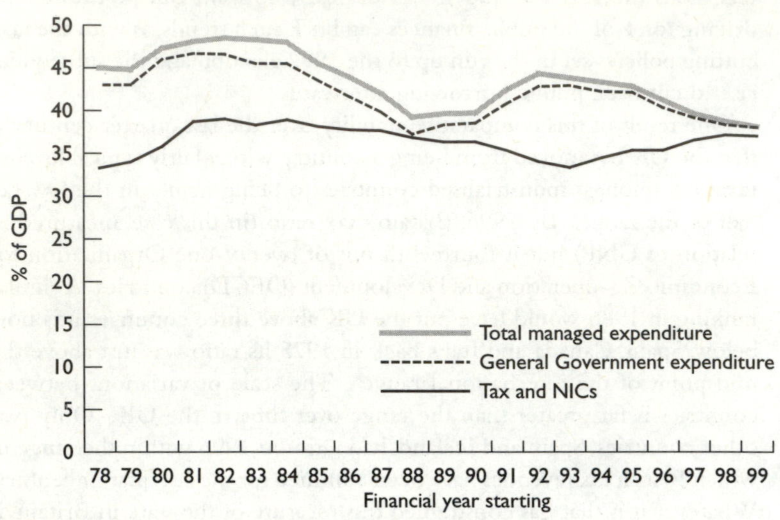

Source: HM Treasury (2000a, Tables C22 and C23)

Figure 8.3. In 1983-84, the three largest elements of the welfare state, health, education and social security, totalled about 22% of national income, or 46% of public spending (TME). By 1999-00 they still represented 21.5% of national income, but this was 56% of public spending[3]. This is part of a longer-term pattern of stability – spending on the welfare state as a whole (including housing and personal social services) has fluctuated around a quarter of national income for the whole of the period since 1975[4]. When people talk about the 'inexorable growth of the welfare state', they are talking about a period which ended a generation ago, at the time of the oil crisis and the International Monetary Fund (IMF) visit to the UK, predating Mrs Thatcher's election.

By contrast, one of the big losers has been defence spending – halved as a share of national income between 1984-85 and 1997-98 – while there were also notable falls in spending on housing, transport, trade and industry, and debt interest. But perhaps the most striking change has been the 'enormous fall in public investment' highlighted by Corry and Neuburger (1997, p 80). The high levels of net public sector borrowing in earlier periods and their more recent falls have to be seen against the background of what was once substantial new public investment. Figure 8.4 shows the longer-term pattern for both public sector net

Figure 8.3: Government spending as % of GDP 1983-84 to 1999-00

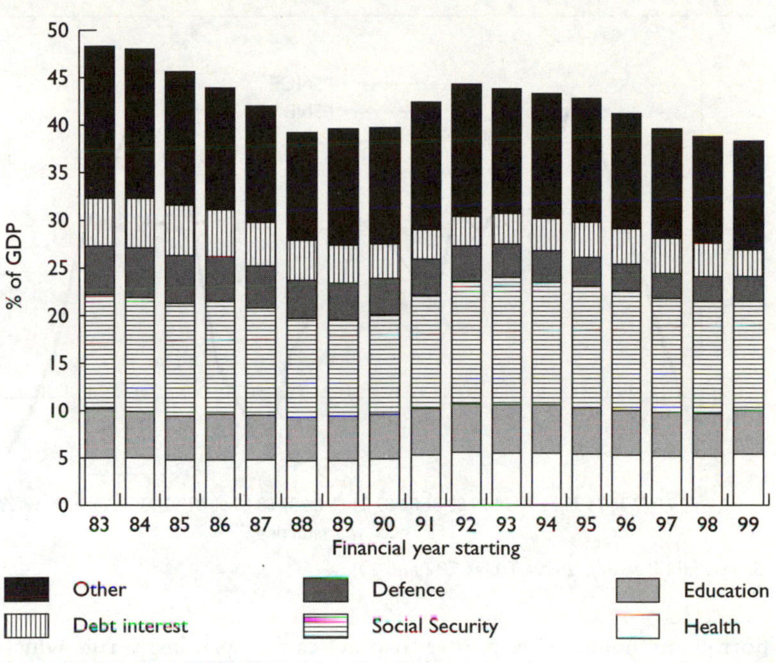

Source: HM Treasury (2000b, Table 4.4, and earlier equivalents)

borrowing, and net capital expenditure (PSNCE) (net of depreciation of existing assets).

What this figure makes plain is the contrast between two periods of high borrowing, the mid 1970s and the mid 1990s. In the earlier period high public borrowing was mainly to finance high public investment. After 1975-76, both fell rapidly, with net borrowing briefly negative in the late 1980s, while net investment fell to near zero – gross investment was barely above depreciation. The huge increase in net borrowing, nearly reaching 8% of GDP in 1992-93 and 1993-94, did not correspond, however, to a surge in investment, but rather to the effects of current spending rising as recession bit, combined with taxes cut ahead of the 1992 election on the strength of what turned out to be wildly optimistic revenue forecasts[5].

The relationship between these two totals has been given much greater importance by the current government through its adoption of the 'Golden Rule' in designing its fiscal policies – that over the economic cycle net

Figure 8.4: Public sector net borrowing and capital spending 1970-71 to 1999-00

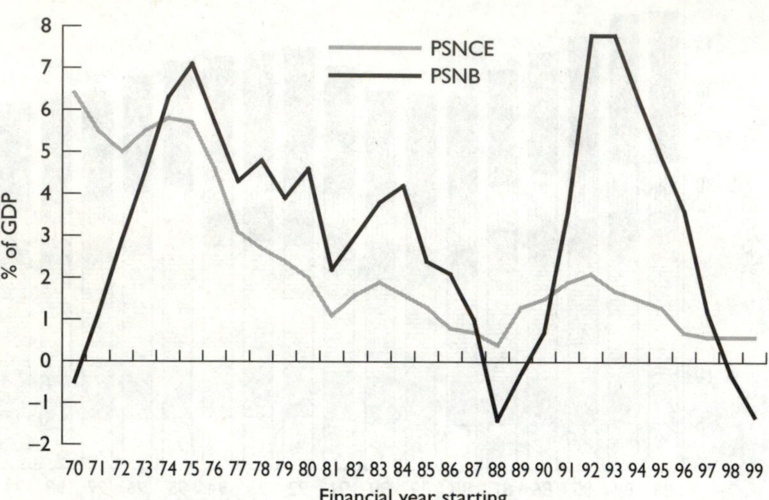

Source: HM Treasury (2000a, Tables C22 and 23)

borrowing should be no greater than net capital spending, a rule which appeared to be being met in its early years in government for the first time since the early 1970s.

The balance of taxation

When people talk about what is happening to tax, they often focus on income tax, and particularly on the *rates* of income tax – for instance, the 22% 'basic rate' which most people pay on any additional income, or the 40% paid at the margin by people with taxable income (after allowances) of more than £28,400 (2000-01 system). The Thatcher government is thought to have been 'tax cutting' principally because it reduced income tax rates, even though, as Figure 8.1 showed, the total tax ratio rose thanks to increases in other tax rates such as those of Value Added Tax (VAT) and National Insurance Contributions (NICs). The Blair government's pledge before the 1997 election was, similarly, not to increase income tax *rates* – indeed, the basic rate was cut in April 2000. This did not prevent a rise in the tax ratio in its early years, nor some people paying more income tax,

Table 8.1 Taxes and National Insurance Contributions 1999-00

	£ billion	% total
Income tax (net)	92.3	27.7
NICs	56.4	16.9
Corporation tax (excluding North Sea)	32.9	9.9
North Sea	2.5	0.7
Capital taxes	11.0	3.3
VAT	56.7	17.0
Fuel and VED	27.2	8.2
Alcohol and tobacco	12.0	3.6
Other indirect	6.2	1.9
Council tax and business rates	28.3	8.5
Other	8.0	2.4
Total	333.6	100.0

Source: HM Treasury (2000a, Table C9)

as allowances like mortgage interest relief or the Married Couples' Allowance were abolished.

Yet, as Table 8.1 shows, income tax is responsible for only 28% of all tax revenues. The rest comes from a variety of somewhat less politically visible sources – notably VAT and NICs (each one sixth of the total) and Corporation Tax (a tenth). Conventionally, the first five items in the table are often described as *direct* taxes – individuals and businesses pay them according to the amounts of income they receive – while taxes like VAT or those on fuel, cars, alcohol and tobacco are described as *indirect* taxes – tax is collected by businesses as they sell goods and services, and the amounts people pay do not depend on their incomes. As a country, Britain makes greater use of indirect taxes than most. Most other industrialised countries raise much more from social security contributions, the equivalent of our National Insurance Contributions.

Over the Conservative years from 1979 to 1997, direct taxes became less and indirect taxes more important. This was mostly, as Table 8.2 shows, because VAT rose from 9 to 17% of the total, coincidentally mirroring the increase in the main *rate* of VAT from 8 to 17.5%. As Neuburger (1989) discusses, Labour has traditionally been linked to preference for direct taxes and Conservatives to indirect taxes, while the greater visibility of the former has worked to Labour's political disadvantage. As he goes on to argue, these preferences reflect the assumed greater progressivity of direct taxes on the one side, and the idea that

Table 8.2 Tax composition 1978-79 and 1999-00

	Share of total tax revenue (%)	
	1978-79	1999-00
Income tax[1]	32.9	27.7
National Insurance Contributions[2]	21.1	16.9
Corporation Tax[3]	6.9	9.9
Capital taxes[4]	2.0	3.3
VAT	8.6	17.0
Other indirect	17.6	13.7
Rates/Council tax	10.1	8.5
North Sea	0.9	0.7
Other[5]	–	2.4
All	100	100

[1] Net of tax credits in 1999-00 (would be 28.3% if measured gross)
[2] Includes NI surcharge in 1978-79
[3] Includes Advance Corporation Tax. Excludes North Sea revenues
[4] Includes Development Land Tax in 1978-79
[5] Includes National Lottery 'good causes'

Source: Kay and King (1980, Table 1); HM Treasury (2000a, Table C9)

indirect taxes interfere less with freedom on the other. He suggests that both ideas are spurious. The second certainly is. Any tax, whatever it is called and however it is collected, puts a 'wedge' between people's income and the (pre-tax) value of the goods and services they purchase. It does not really matter very much in the end whether someone has an income of £100, pays £20 income tax, and then buys £80-worth of VAT-free goods or alternatively has a tax-free income of £100 and buys goods for £100, including £20 of VAT. Both kinds of tax mean that people can consume less from the market than otherwise (in return for which they receive the services provided through the state). Both change the pattern of returns to and costs of different kinds of behaviour.

It is also true that indirect taxes are not necessarily regressive (forming a greater share of income of the poor) and direct taxes are not necessarily progressive (forming a greater share of the income of the rich). The Poll Tax was effectively a direct tax, but was highly regressive. Certain kinds of consumption – 'luxuries' – do represent a greater share of income for the rich than the poor. In his analysis of this Henry Neuburger identified items like meals out, car purchase, recreation, holidays and financial services – including saving – which would be more progressive to tax than income.

However, in practice, indirect taxes clearly are much less progressive than direct taxes. Figure 8.5 shows figures derived from the Office for

Figure 8.5: Tax by income group 1998-99

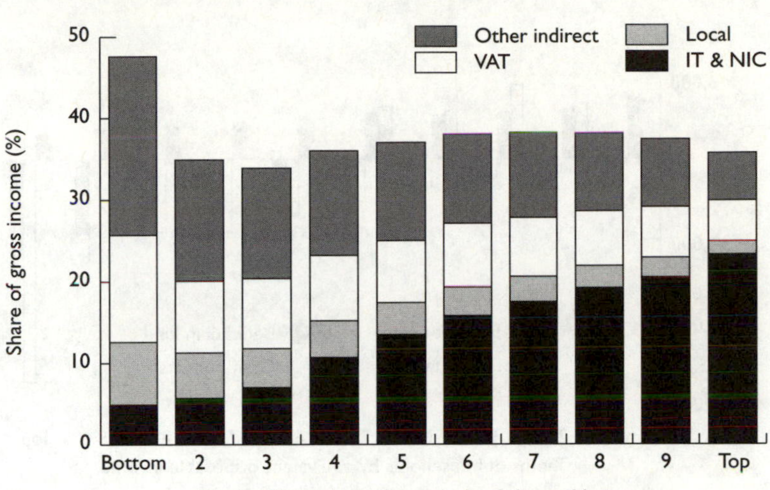

Source: Harris (2000, Table 2a, Appendix 1)

National Statistics'(ONS) analysis of the impact of different kinds of taxation by income in 1998-99. The most striking finding from this is that the British tax system is not, on this analysis, progressive. Overall the taxes allocated by ONS represent 37.1% of household gross income (including income from cash benefits as well as from market sources). But for the richest tenth of households they are below this, and for the poorest tenth they are much higher[6]. In particular, indirect taxes represent 35% of gross income for the poorest, but only 11% for the richest. As is well known, taxes on tobacco are strikingly regressive but taxes on fuel and on cars are also regressive.

It is hard to make such analyses definitive – to do so, one has to have a clear idea of the *incidence* of a tax – who is really worse off compared with what would have happened without the tax? Allowing for such uncertainty, for instance in how to allocate employer NICs, the clearest conclusion is that for most of the income range the British tax system is roughly *proportional* – one way or another, most income groups pay about the same share of income in tax. But it is only so because of the contribution of direct taxes. Three factors drive the regressivity of indirect taxes:

Figure 8.6: Distribution of taxes and benefits 1998-99

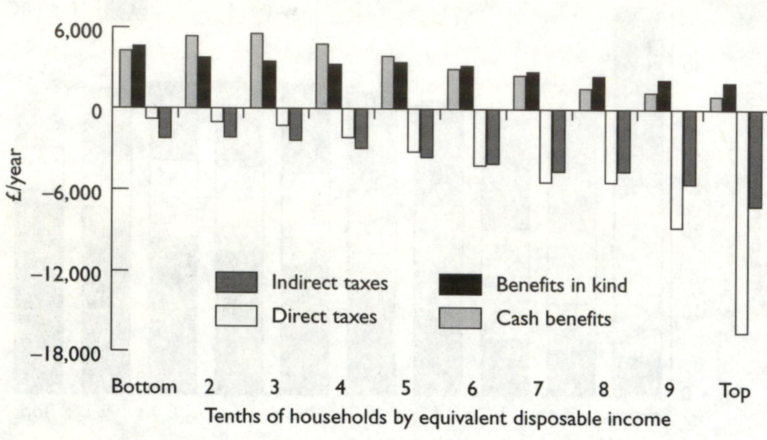

Source: Harris (2000)

(1) People with higher incomes save more (and savings are not subject to indirect taxes – and are not likely to be);
(2) More of the consumption of those with lower incomes goes on heavily taxed items like tobacco (despite the VAT exemption of necessities like food and lower rates on domestic fuel); and
(3) Many indirect taxes are set as lump sum amounts (such as vehicle licences or the part of tax on wine which is a fixed amount per bottle whether cheap or expensive).

Again, however, it is important not to look at the impact of taxation in isolation and assume, for instance, that this means that the state does not have a redistributive effect. The tax system may not be progressive in itself, but what it finances certainly is. Figure 8.6 shows from the same source the ONS's allocation of both taxes and the benefits of most parts of public spending between income groups. The poorest tenth may pay most tax as a share of its income, but this amount – about £3,000 per household in 1998-99 – is much lower than the amounts allocated to it from social security and from benefits in kind from public services like the NHS and state education, totalling nearly £9,000 per household. The net gain averages nearly £6,000. The same favourable balance holds for the next four tenths of the distribution, although to a declining extent.

At the top, tax may be a smaller share of gross income, but the absolute amount – averaging nearly £24,000 – is much greater than the benefits allocated of around £3,000. As with the allocation of the impact of taxation, the precise way the benefits of public spending are allocated here can be questioned[7], but the overall effect is clear: the *combination* of taxation and the spending it finances is redistributive.

What do people want?

Conventional political wisdom has been that voters want lower taxes and will vote for parties that promise them. In the run-up to the 1997 election, Labour's pledge on income tax rates was backed up with a promise to hold to the Conservatives' very tight spending plans for the following two years. As a result, and helped by a strong economy and falling unemployment, spending (TME) fell from 41.2% of GDP in 1996-97 to 37.7% in 1999-2000[8].

This belief appears to conflict with what remains one of the consistent findings from the long-running *British Social Attitudes* survey (and from other polls). Since the late 1980s there has been a large majority for *increased* public spending on 'health, education and social benefits', even if this means higher taxes, and only a tiny proportion of the population opts for lower taxes and lower spending on these items. Nearly two thirds of respondents continued to choose the increased tax and spending option in 1998 during Labour's first two years of spending restraint[9]. People do indeed seem to support taxation to finance the 'enabling state'.

However, simply wanting *more* tax and spending does not necessarily mean *much* more. Heath and Curtice (1998) show that until 1994 a majority saw Labour as being to their Left on the balance between tax and spending: people wanted more spending, but feared Labour would go too far. After then, opinion became much more balanced between those who thought Labour would do too much or too little. Second, different items have higher or lower priority, particularly if the personal consequences of higher taxes are spelt out. Brook, Hall and Preston (1996) show in their analysis of the 1995 *BSA* (*British Social Attitudes*) survey that majorities remain in favour of higher health and education spending when people are given specific tax consequences for themselves, but not for other items like the police, the environment and defence. It is little coincidence that health and education have been Labour's spending priorities in office, with Labour now committed to increasing health spending rapidly in the next four years – with plans which would take

NHS spending to 6.3% of national income by 2003-04[10] compared to 5.3% in 1996-97 and 5.2% in 1998-99, the second of the two years of fiscal restraint. Nor is it a surprise that Conservative politicians have committed themselves to match these figures.

But what of the more explicitly redistributive part of public spending – the social security budget? First, inequality is unpopular[11]. Four fifths of respondents to the 1998 *BSA* survey say that the gap between those with high incomes and those with low incomes in Britain today is too large. Furthermore, three quarters say it is 'definitely' or 'probably' government's responsibility to do something about it, against only a sixth who say it is not. When tax is specified as an instrument, more than half say that 'government should increase taxes on the better-off to spend more on the poor', and only a sixth prefer the statement that 'the better-off pay too much tax already'. However, if the instruments are more closely specified, the scale of agreement reduces, for instance if 'welfare benefits' or 'redistribution' are mentioned.

Looking at attitudes to the benefit system in more detail reveals a conflict in people's minds. On the one hand, a large majority believes that unemployment benefits are too little to live on (and this reaches 80% when the amounts of benefit are actually specified). On the other, there are increasing concerns about the extent to which benefits for the unemployed cause disincentives and are open to fraud. Until 1996, when asked to choose between the two propositions, that unemployment benefits are too low and cause hardship or are too high and discourage work, the larger group of respondents chose the former[12]. However, the gap had been narrowing and in 1998, the larger group chose the 'too high and discourage work' option.

These competing concerns about inequality, the low level of benefits, disincentives and fraud mean that people react differently to options for different kinds of benefits, as Table 8.3 shows. In line with the preference for higher spending on 'health, education and social benefits' described above, people generally say they want higher spending on social security benefits. More than two thirds say they want higher spending on benefits for those who care for people who are sick and disabled, disabled people who cannot work, retired people, and parents who work on very low incomes. Very few call for lower benefits for these groups. When it comes to single parents the largest group opts for the *status quo*, although more respondents still opt for extra spending than for lower on benefits within this group. By contrast, while the largest group again goes for the

Table 8.3: Would you like to see more or less government spending on benefits for ...

	Spend more	Spend the same as now	Spend less
People who care for sick or disabled	82	15	1
Disabled people who cannot work	72	23	2
Retired people	71	25	2
Parents who work on very low incomes	68	26	3
Single parents	34	41	21
Unemployed people	22	40	35

Base: 3,146

Source: Hills and Lelkes (1999) based on *British Social Attitudes* survey.

status quo for benefits for unemployed people, in this case more say they would like to see lower than higher spending on them.

These responses have two important implications. First, as with health and education spending, public preferences are clearly for increases in spending on the bulk of the items making up social security, even if this means higher taxes, rather than the reverse. What is often not realised is that social security spending is overwhelmingly on the groups which are favoured in the table. Only 21% of the 1998-99 social security budget was spent on the non-disabled population of working age; only 6% directly on the unemployed[13].

But second, policies based on across-the-board benefit increases would not necessarily be popular if benefits aimed at the unemployed were included. This does not necessarily reflect lack of concern about unemployment, poverty or inequality. It may be as much a judgement about appropriate instruments. Two thirds of the 1998 *BSA* survey respondents agreed that, 'it should be the government's responsibility to provide a job for everyone who wants one' – a policy going well beyond the measures included in the 'New Deal' (against a quarter who said it should not be). 'Jobs not higher benefits' would best summarise public attitudes to the unemployed in general. Again, it is perhaps unsurprising that the government's welfare reform slogan has been 'work for those who can, security for those who cannot'.

Recent developments in taxation

Some of the key developments in policy under the Labour government since 1997 have been described above, notably the adoption of the 'Golden

Rule' for the public finances, the election pledge not to raise income tax rates, the tight constraints on public spending in 1997-98 and 1998-99, and the rapid increases in health and education spending planned from 2000-01. But another central part of policy has been in its agenda on work and poverty. First, the centre piece of its initial policies was the 'New Deal' for the unemployed, with a series of measures designed to support people – focusing initially on the young unemployed but extended to other groups without work – into jobs. Second, early in 1999, Tony Blair promised to 'end child poverty' within 20 years, and a series of measures in the budgets between 1998 and 2000 channelled extra resources to families with children in particular, but also to others with low incomes.

A key innovation to serve both the aim of promoting work (by ensuring that 'work pays') and of attacking child poverty has been the replacement since October 1999 of what was a social security benefit for low paid families with children, Family Credit, with a new Working Families Tax Credit (WFTC). This is more generous than its predecessor, is withdrawn more slowly as earnings rise, and is intended to be administered differently – through the tax system and the pay packet, rather than paid out as a benefit. It remains to be seen whether the change in payment system has the psychological effects which are hoped for it – reducing stigma and linking the payment to work rather than being seen as a hand-out – and whether the administrative systems cope as people move between jobs and in and out of work. Initial analysis suggests that the impact of increased incentives to work on employment will be positive, but relatively modest[14]. However, the distributional effects are clear and substantial.

Figure 8.7 illustrates how the credit works, showing the relationship between gross and net income resulting from the interaction between direct taxes, benefits and the WFTC for a one-earner couple with two children. The figures are shown in 2000-01 prices, but incorporate the effect on income tax (and hence take-home pay) of the Child Tax Credit which was announced in the 1999 and 2000 budgets, but will start only in April 2001. Several effects of the WFTC are apparent:

- It makes a sizeable contribution to those with low earnings – up to £104 per week for those with the lowest earnings, and more for those working over 30 hours per week[15]. As the government is keen to stress, someone working full-time at only the minimum wage would have take-home pay and WFTC of at least £208 per week, compared to benefit income out of work for this family of £158 per week (although allowing for housing and council tax benefits the gap is smaller).

Figure 8.7: Gross and net income, under Budget 2000 system

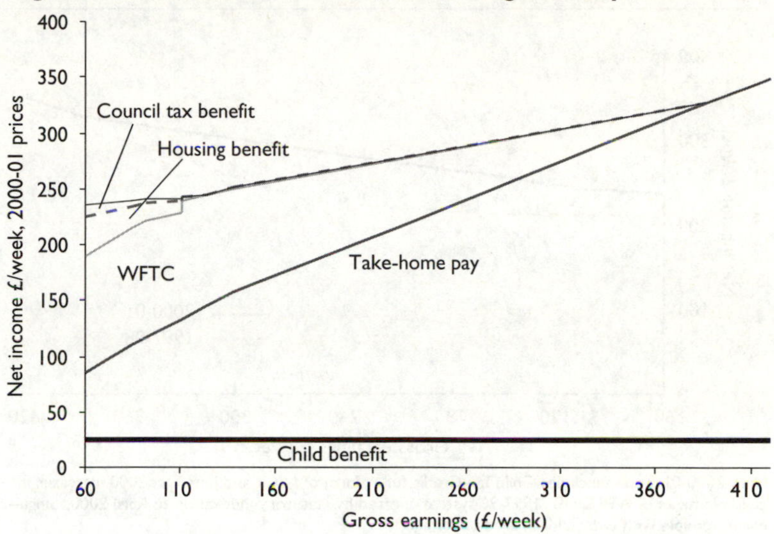

Note: Includes Child tax Credit, full reform of NICs and June/Oct 2000 increases in child elements of WTFC and HB/CTB. Rent assumed to be £50 per week, and Council Tax £14 per week. Single-earner couple with two children aged under 11.

- Its effect is to carry most working families, except those with very low pay, off Housing Benefit and Council Tax Benefit (unless rent is much higher than the typical council rent used here).
- This, in combination with the lower, 55%, WFTC withdrawal rate as income rises means that the most severe aspects of the 'poverty trap' – where higher gross earnings have little effect on net incomes – have been reduced.
- Entitlement to the credit extends well up the earnings scale, nearly to average earnings in this case. As a corollary of the reduced *depth* of the poverty trap, a milder version of it affects more people.

Figure 8.8 compares the relationship between gross earnings and net income under the system created by the 1997-2000 budgets with what the situation would have looked like if the tax structure and benefit rates of April 1997 had simply been adjusted by the rules for 'statutory indexation' for inflation up to April 2000. The difference between the two reflects not only the introduction of the WFTC, but also a number of other important changes, including:

Figure 8.8: Net incomes, 1997-98 and Budget 2000 systems

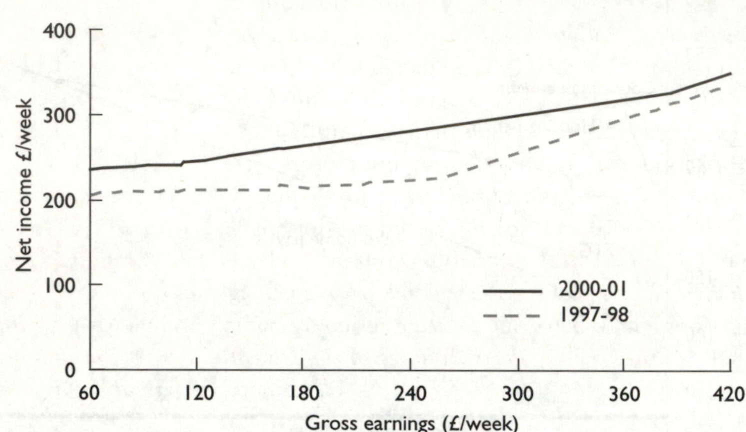

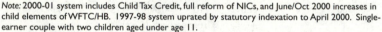

Note: 2000-01 system includes Child Tax Credit, full reform of NICs, and June/Oct 2000 increases in child elements of WFTC/HB. 1997-98 system uprated by statutory indexation to April 2000. Single-earner couple with two children aged under age 11.

- Reduction in NICs for the low paid (taking account of the reforms to be finalised in April 2001).
- Abolition of the Married Couples Allowance in income tax and its replacement by higher rates of universal Child Benefit and the Child Tax Credit (the latter actually in effect in April 2001).
- Higher elements for children in means-tested benefit rates.
- Replacement of the old initial 20% rate of income tax with a 10% band.

Taken together the budget measures mean significantly higher net incomes for this kind of family over a wide range of below-average earnings – more than £25 per week at the lowest levels, rising to a maximum of nearly £60 at the point where Family Credit would previously have run out.

This kind of example suggests that the reforms to the tax and benefit system since May 1997 have significantly helped low-paid families with children. However, what is in effect a single family type (a one-earner couple with two children aged under 11) represents a small minority of the population as a whole, and it is this group which has been most favoured by the reforms. The impact of the reforms on the population as a whole might look very different. To establish this one needs to look at

Figure 8.9: Impact of Labour Budgets 1997-00 (compared to statutory indexation)

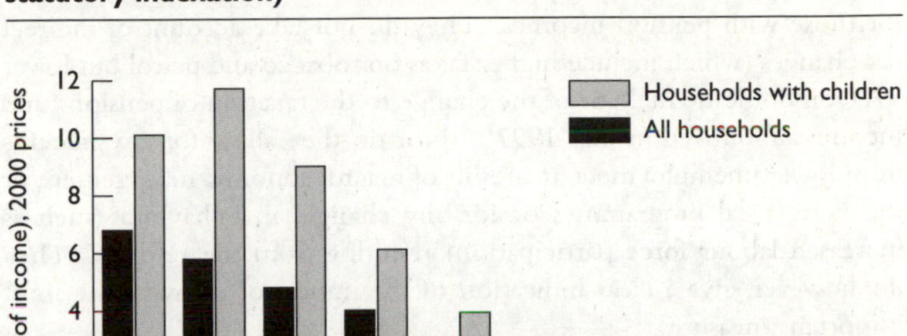

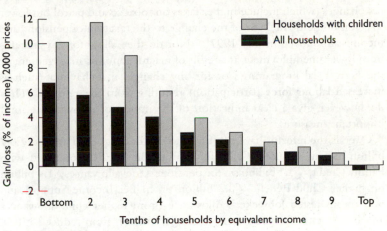

Source: POLIMOD

their effects on a representative sample, and to compare the net incomes generated by the tax and benefit system resulting from the reforms with calculations of what they would have been in the absence of reform. The results of such an exercise, carried out on the Cambridge University Microsimulation Unit model, POLIMOD, are shown in Figure 8.9. This compares the results for the whole population of the system created by the budgets between 1997 and 2000 with an 'unchanged' system, as it was in April 1997 (but with benefit rates and tax thresholds adjusted for inflation according to the rules for 'statutory indexation'). They update estimates of the impact of the budgets up to 1999 given in Piachaud and Sutherland (2000). The columns show the difference in net incomes (adjusted for family size, or 'equivalised') for each successive tenth of the income distribution, with the poorest tenth on the left. Results are shown for all households and for just those with children in each tenth.

The reforms analysed include those described above to NICs, benefits for children, the WFTC, abolition of the Married Couples Allowance and introduction of the Child Tax Credit, the basic rate cut to 22% and replacement of the 20% income tax band with the 10% band. They also include: introduction of the minimum wage; the winter fuel allowance for pensioners (at £150 per year); the more generous rates of Income Support for pensioners (the 'minimum income guarantee'); the real increase in the upper limit for NICs; abolition of mortgage interest relief; abolition of special benefits for lone parents; and reduction in Incapacity Benefit for those with pension incomes. They do not take account of indirect tax changes (which include higher taxes on tobacco and petrol but lower VAT on domestic fuel), or of the change to the taxation of pension fund income announced in July 1997[16]. Nor do they allow for any benefits from lower unemployment as a result of macroeconomic management or the New Deal programmes or for any changes in behaviour (such as increased labour force participation) resulting from the reforms. They do, however, give a clear indication of the impact of many of the most important measures.

Overall, the reforms have a net cost to the Exchequer of around £6.7 billion[17]. This includes £1.2 billion from the WFTC compared with Family Credit, £1.1 billion on the pensioners fuel allowance, £1.4 billion on higher Child Benefit, £2.2 billion on higher Income Support and non-means-tested Jobseeker's Allowance (from higher child allowances and higher rates for pensioners), and £1.9 billion from reduced NICs. The income tax changes (excluding the WFTC) largely cancel one another out, and other measures raise a little over £1 billion net.

Allowing for a £1.3 billion increase in gross earnings from the minimum wage, households gain £8.1 billion overall – an increase in average household income (adjusted for household size) of 1.7%. As Figure 8.9 shows, however, gains are much larger than this for lower income groups on average, particularly those with children. The poorest tenth gain nearly 7% (10% for those with children), and the next tenth nearly 6% (12% for those with children). In percentage terms these gains fall as one goes up the distribution, while the richest tenth is 0.4% worse off than it would have been in the 'indexed' 1997-98 system. On this comparison, the four Budgets since 1997 have clearly had a progressive effect, with significant gains at the bottom and small losses at the top[18]. Allowing for indirect tax changes the gains at the bottom would be somewhat smaller, and if one could take account of pension fund taxation the losses at the top would be larger, giving a more clearly redistributive picture. It should also be noted that the changes have varying effects *within* income groups, so that even for families with children in the poorest tenth, 25% are 'losers' under the changes (for instance, some lone parents with older children), while 75% are 'gainers'.

One of the main controversies around New Labour's policies has been what one can call its 'selective universalism' – increasing some social security benefits, but not others, and spending on some services like health and education but not others. Critics on the Left have called for increases in *all* social security benefits beyond the rate of inflation – for instance for the basic state pension to be increased with earnings rather than just with prices. Without this, the *relative* living standards of those dependent on benefits will fall.

It should also be noted that 'statutory indexation' of the benefit and tax systems actually delivers a gain, other things being equal, to the public finances. First, if benefits are only price-linked, and incomes are growing in real terms, the cost of social security falls in relation to national income and to taxes taking a constant share of it (other things being equal). Second, if features of the direct tax system like the personal allowance or threshold for higher rate tax are *only* uprated for price inflation, rising real incomes pull taxpayers higher up the schedule. This 'fiscal drag' means that tax rises as a share of income. Chancellors can 'index the system' but still benefit from a rising direct tax ratio.

For both these reasons, it is interesting to compare the results of New Labour's fiscal policies with an alternative 'neutral' policy. What would have happened if all benefit rates and all the features of the direct tax system which are set in cash terms had been increased not just in line with price indexation, but in line with income growth? After all, other things (such as changes in unemployment or demography) being equal, this kind of uprating would be consistent with a constant tax ratio and constant social security spending as a share of GDP (and thus with continued fiscal stability if this had been achieved to start with). It can be argued that this is a more appropriate 'steady state' benchmark than price indexation.

The Treasury forecasts that between 1997-98 and 2000-01 money GDP will have grown by 16%[19]. Figure 8.10 shows the distributional effects, again by comparison with statutory indexation, if all benefit rates and direct tax thresholds had been uprated by this amount. First, instead of the net cost to the public finances of £6.7 billion compared to indexation from actual policies, this alternative would have had a net cost of £9.2 billion. Uprating with incomes would have meant £6.4 billion in higher benefits, compared to the £4.8 billion under actual policies (including the WFTC as a benefit for these purposes). The government has indeed spent less than it would have done under an 'Old Labour' policy of uprating all benefits with incomes. At the same time, uprating with incomes would have meant £2.7 billion *lower* direct taxes (mainly income tax) than under statutory indexation. This gives the measure of the fiscal drag from which the Chancellor has benefited – more than the £1.9 billion he has 'given

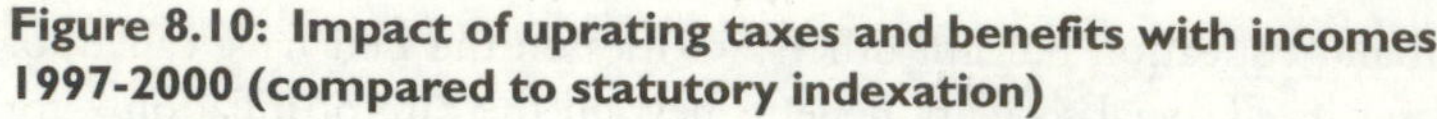

Figure 8.10: Impact of uprating taxes and benefits with incomes 1997-2000 (compared to statutory indexation)

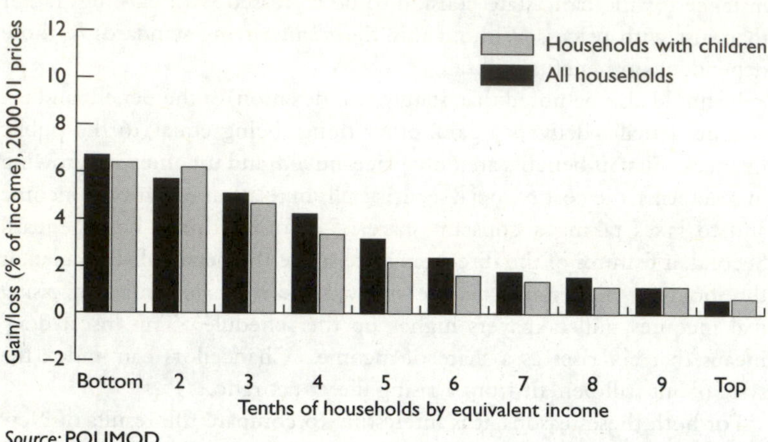

Source: POLIMOD

away' in his reforms to NICs, which explains one of the ways in which the tax ratio has risen despite the tax cuts.

Overall, household incomes would be 2.1% higher under this 'neutral' policy than under statutory indexation. As benefits are the most important part of this, the largest 'gains' are at the bottom – nearly 7% for the poorest tenth, and 6% for the second group. Effectively, this is the increase in real benefit rates needed to keep up with rising overall living standards. The top tenth would have gained 0.7% (mainly through the elimination of fiscal drag). The comparison with Figure 8.9 is instructive. Overall, the bottom four tenths do almost exactly as well under New Labour's policies as they would have done if all benefits had been linked to incomes without any change in structure. This is despite the £2.5 billion lower net cost to the public finances of actual policies. About half of this lower cost reflects the gains coming from outside government through the minimum wage. The other half is because the higher income groups do slightly worse under actual policies, and the top tenth is 1% worse off under them. Within the lower income groups families with children do better than under straight income indexation, so other groups do worse[20].

One assessment of the government's record would thus be that it has simultaneously delivered as much to low income groups as more expensive 'Old Labour' policies would have done, while generally going with the grain of the progressive parts of public opinion described earlier, reforming the structure of the system to improve work incentives overall[21], and delivering the improvement in the public finances charted in the first section. In these terms, it is a very impressive achievement.

Alternatively, one could say that the tax and benefit reforms have only barely delivered enough to the lowest income groups as a whole to prevent inequality rising: any actual catching up of relative living standards at the bottom will have to come from the improved labour market and rising numbers in work and off benefits. By themselves the measures may stem the tide of rising inequality, but not reverse it. And even to continue standing still in these terms will require a flow of new measures benefiting the poor. This may be hard if the case for financing them has not been made through positive promotion of what is needed as well as what has been achieved.

Official calculations suggest that the measures taken so far 'will lift 1.2 million children out of poverty'[22], using a poverty line of half average income. Independent analysis confirms this order of magnitude for the reduction in the numbers *compared to those if no changes had been made*[23]. However, it is still too early to tell whether child poverty will actually fall by this amount, and indeed whether inequality and poverty as a whole will fall. This is for three reasons. First, tax and benefit changes are only part of the picture. What happens to unemployment and the distribution of market income also matters. Second, inequality and relative poverty measures like half average income set government a moving target: real income increases at the bottom are needed just to keep up with rising living standards. Without them, inequality and relative poverty will rise. We will not know how all these factors play out until we see analysis of the actual income distribution, rather than just the simulations of the kind shown in Figure 8.9.

But there is a third problem, highlighted by the latest official income distribution figures published in April 2000, shown in Figure 8.11. This shows the Gini coefficient measure of household income inequality over the period from 1977 to 1998-99, Labour's second year in office. It shows inequality of four measures of income, reflecting the impact of the tax and benefit system as described in the second section: market income; gross income (which includes cash benefits); disposable income (which deducts direct taxes from this); and post-tax income (which deducts the ONS's estimates of indirect taxes as well). The picture in earlier periods shown will be familiar to those who have followed the story: market income inequality grew almost continuously from 1978 to the early 1990s; the other measures grew less in the early 1980s, but very rapidly in the

Figure 8.11: Effects of taxes and benefits on inequality 1977 to 1997-98

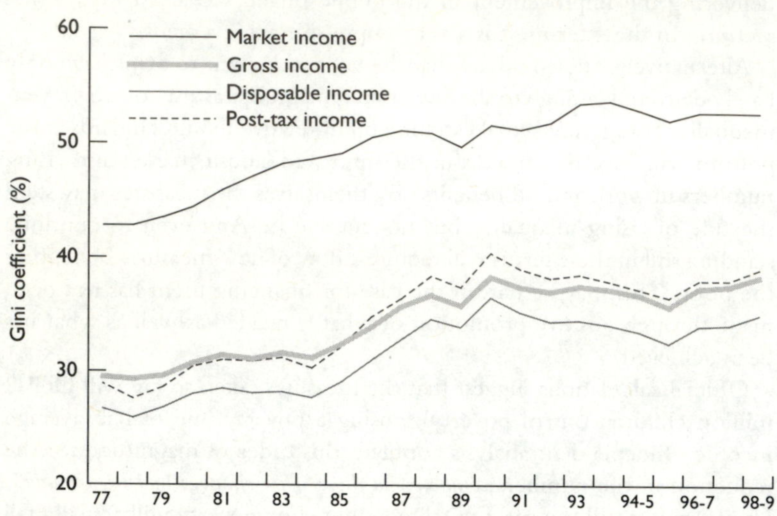

Source: Harris (2000). Figures are for inequality of household incomes.

second half of the decade; under the Major government there was first a fall and then a rise in inequality.

What is new in these figures is the picture it gives of changes between 1996-97, the Conservative's last year in office, and 1998-99, Labour's second year. While market income inequality did not change, the other measures each *rose* by one percentage point. As most of this occurred between 1997-98 and 1998-99, inequality clearly rose at the start of Labour's time in office. What was happening was that gross incomes at the bottom – largely driven by benefits, which remained price-linked – were falling behind rising real incomes higher up the distribution. As a result the total numbers with incomes below half the average – the nearest measurement we have to a poverty line – rose between 1996-97 and 1998–99[24].

How can this be reconciled with the picture given in Figure 8.9? The answer is the time-lag effect, summarised in Table 8.4. Few of the reforms discussed above were announced until March 1998 or later, while one of the features of tax policy under New Labour has been the gap between announcement of policies and their implementation. By 1998-99, *none* of the reforms benefiting the bottom of the distribution analysed in Figure 8.9 was in place; the WFTC will only have its full effect in 2000-01;

Table 8.4: Tax and Benefit reform implementation lags

Measure	Announcement	Start	Full effect	Visible in distribution statistics
New Deal	July 97	Jan 98	1998-99	2000
Minimum Wage	Manifesto	Apr 99	1999-00	2001
NIC reform (1)	March 98	Apr 99	1999-00	2001
WFTC	March 98	Oct 99	2000-01	2002
Child Benefit, children's benefit rates	March 98	Apr 99	2000-01	2002
NIC reform (2)	March 99	Apr 01	2001-02	2003
Child Tax Credit	March 99	Apr 01	2001-02	2003
Integrated Child Credit	March 00	2003?	2003-04	2005

some measures will not have their full effect until 2001-02. While in some cases this kind of delay is inevitable given the administrative reforms required, it does mean that it is too early to judge whether New Labour's strategy for tackling poverty and inequality is a success. Indeed, for those not directly affected by the measures themselves it will be some time before we can gauge their impact from official analysis of the income distribution. This takes time. For instance, on previous patterns, it will be 2002 before we see either the ONS analysis of the household income distribution for 2000-01 or the key DSS figures for *Households below average income*, which will give us a clear picture of the impact of the WFTC, a reform announced in March 1998.

Conclusion

Writing in 2000, an analysis of the kind presented in this paper shows a better balance in the public finances than would have been the picture at almost any point in the last quarter century. This is not just a matter of steady economic growth, fiscal stability and the 'Golden Rule'. It is also that the balance of tax and spending changes announced since 1998 has real prospects of helping growth in living standards for the poor, while carrying the weight of public opinion behind the measures used to do this and to improve public services. At the same time, if progress is going to be made towards the abolition of child poverty in 20 years as promised by the Prime Minister, the measures described above will have to be added to every year. Otherwise, incomes at the bottom will slip behind again, as they did up to 1998-99. This will not be possible if taxation is thought of by politicians and the public as simply a 'burden', and if the positive, enabling results of what it finances are left unconnected to it.

Notes

[1] The author is particularly grateful to Holly Sutherland for great assistance with the POLIMOD simulation results shown in Figures 8.9 and 8.10 and for helpful comments to her, Andrew Glyn, and participants in the seminar at LSE in April 2000 when a draft of the chapter was presented. POLIMOD uses micro-data from the Family Expenditure Survey which are Crown Copyright and are kindly made available by the Office for National Statistics through the Data Archive. The author is grateful to ESRC for support of CASE at LSE, where the chapter was written.

[2] Fugeman (1999), table 1; Hills (1996), figure 4.3.

[3] The plans in the 2000 Spending Review (HM Treasury, 2000c, tables A1 and A2) imply health spending rising by about 0.9% of GDP between 1999-2000 and 2003-04, and education spending by 0.8% of GDP, while social security falls by 0.4% of GDP, giving a total of just under 23%.

[4] Glennerster and Hills (1998).

[5] Hills (1996), table 4.4.

[6] Part of this stems from the high expenditure of households in the poorest tenth in relation to their reported income. To the extent that this reflects misreported or temporary and atypically low income, these figures will overstate the tax burdens at the bottom.

[7] See Sefton (1997) for detailed discussion of these issues.

[8] HM Treasury (2000c), table 49 The plans in the 2000 Spending Review would take TME to 40.5% of GDP in 2003-04.

[9] Hills and Lelkes (1999).

[10] HM Treasury (2000a), tables 5.1 and C3.

[11] For further details of these findings see Hills and Lelkes (1999).

[12] Unpublished information kindly supplied by the National Centre for Social Research from the partial survey in 1997 shows this was still true then.

[13] DSS (2000a), chart 1.1.

[14] Blundell et al (2000) suggest an increase in participation of around 30,000 people, with a benefit to the public finances which reduces the net cost of the increased generosity of WFTC by about a seventh.

[15] In the figure it is assumed that earnings of £111 or more represent at least 30 hours' work. In practice, the jump in the WFTC schedule could come at higher earnings levels for those earning more than the minimum wage.

[16] It is hard to establish what the distributional impact of this measure was, given that its effect could be higher employee contributions than otherwise to occupational pension schemes, lower pensions to be paid out by them in future than otherwise, or lower contributions by firms to their schemes (or fewer 'contribution holidays' for them). The impact – on current contributors to schemes, on future occupational pensioners, or on shareholders – is likely to have been progressive, so that if one could adjust for this the figures shown in Figure 8.9 would become less favourable to those at the top of the distribution.

[17] Not allowing for the cost of raising public sector wages to comply with the minimum wage.

[18] For more detailed analysis of the effects of the first three budgets, see Piachaud and Sutherland (2000).

[19] HM Treasury (2000a), table C3.

[20] For instance, while households with pensioners in the bottom tenth of the overall distribution gain as much – 8% – under both policies, those in the second tenth gain 4.3% under actual policies, but would have gained 6.4% under income indexation.

[21] Although not for all groups, as Piachaud and Sutherland (2000) explain.

[22] HM Treasury (2000a), p 8.

[23] Piachaud and Sutherland (2000).

[24] By 0.5 million measured before housing costs or 0.2 million after housing costs (DSS, 2000b, table H1).

References

Blundell, R., Duncan, A., McCrae, J. and Meghir, C. (2000) 'The labour market impact of the working families' tax credit', *Fiscal Studies*, vol 21, no 1, pp 75-104.

Brook, L., Hall, J. and Preston, I. (1996) 'Public spending and taxation', in R. Jowell, J. Curtice, A. Park, L. Brook and K. Thomson (eds) *British Social Attitudes: The 13th Report*, Aldershot: Dartmouth.

Corry, D. and Neuburger, H. (writing as S. Gray) (1997) 'Recent history of public spending', in D. Corry (ed) *Public expenditure: Effective management and control*, London: Dryden (for IPPR).

DSS (Department of Social Security) (2000a) *The changing welfare state: Social security spending*, London: DSS.

DSS (2000b) *Households below average income 1994/5-1998/9*, Leeds: Corporate Document Services.

Fugeman, D. (1999) 'An international comparison of taxes and social security contributions (1986-1996)', *Economic Trends*, March, pp 49-63.

Glennerster, H. and Hills, J. (eds) (1998) *The state of welfare: The economics of social spending* (2nd edn), Oxford: Oxford University Press.

Harris, T. (2000) 'The effects of taxes and benefits on household income, 1998-99', *Economic Trends*, no 557, April, pp 45-83.

Heath, A. and Curtice, J. (1998) 'New Labour, new voters?', Paper presented to the Political Studies Association Annual Conference, April.

Hills, J. (1996) 'Tax policy: are there still choices?', in D. Halpern, S. Wood, S. White and G. Cameron (eds) *Options for Britain*, Aldershot: Dartmouth.

Hills, J. and Lelkes, O. (1999) 'Social security, selective universalism and patchwork redistribution', in R. Jowell, J. Curtice, A. Park and K. Thomson (eds) *British Social Attitudes, The 16th Report: Who shares New Labour values?*, Aldershot: Ashgate.

HM Treasury (2000a) *Budget 2000: Prudent for a purpose*, HC 346, London: The Stationery Office.

HM Treasury (2000b) *Public expenditure: Statistical analyses, 2000-01*, Cm 4601, London: The Stationery Office.

HM Treasury (2000c) *Spending review 2000*, Cm 4807, London: The Stationery Office.

Kay, J. and King, M. (1980) *The British tax system* (2nd edn), Oxford: Oxford University Press.

Neuburger, H. (1989) *Direct and indirect taxation: A socialist approach*, Fabian Taxation Review Background Paper No 5, London: Fabian Society.

Piachaud, D. and Sutherland, H. (2000) *How effective is the British government's attempt to reduce child poverty?*, CASEpaper 38, Centre for Analysis of Social Exclusion, London: LSE.

Sefton, T. (1997) *The changing distribution of the social wage*, STICERD Occasional Paper 21, London: LSE.

NINE

European integration and its implications for policy making in the 21st century

Iain Begg

In the last 40 years, European integration has significantly changed the institutional and political context of policy making. Eurosceptics might deplore the seemingly inexorable accretion of power by 'Brussels', while Europhiles argue for closer integration, but there are few areas of policy untouched by 'Europe'. In contemplating policy making in the 21st century, therefore, the constraints and opportunities resulting from European Union (EU)[1] membership and the resulting shifts in competence for different areas of policy must be properly understood and taken into account.

Henry Neuburger was well aware of this and his was one of the first voices urging the British Labour Party to rethink its approach to the EU. The subsequent transformation in the party and, indeed, in the topography of British politics, has been remarkable. The Tories have managed to tear themselves apart over Europe and have adopted increasingly extreme views, whereas Labour can present itself as pragmatic. Unions which, fifteen or twenty years ago, saw the EU as an alarming capitalist conspiracy are now actively campaigning for Britain to sign up for the single currency, while the various employers' organisations adopt increasingly intransigent positions for and against closer integration.

This chapter explores the ramifications of closer union in Europe for economic and social policy making. It argues that, for better or worse, a new policy framework has been constructed and that the EU plays a central role in the formulation of policy. Within this framework, however, the member states continue to shape and implement policies, although the EU appears to be increasingly active in coordinating across states. The next section reviews the UK's relationship with the EU. The development of policy coordination since the Treaty of Amsterdam is then discussed and the prospects for different policy areas examined. Concluding remarks complete the chapter.

The UK relationship with Europe

Throughout the postwar period, Britain has been a reluctant European. From doubts about the European Steel and Coal Community in the early 1950s and the formation of the European Economic Community (EEC), through staying out of the exchange rate mechanism of the European Monetary System (EMS) to the delay in agreeing the Social Chapter, and, now the opt-out from monetary union (EMU), Britain has been the laggard. Even today, observers of the UK debate on EMU could be forgiven for thinking that monetary union is a remote contingency rather than a done deal, with eleven EU member states participating from day one, Greece joining at the beginning of 2001, and many of the candidate countries from central and eastern Europe keen to join at the earliest opportunity.

Completion of the single European market (SEM), by contrast, is one of the few major initiatives in European construction[2] that did not see Britain dragging its heels. In part, this is because the deregulatory thrust of the '1992' programme chimed with the market-oriented philosophy of the Thatcher government. The SEM programme also adopted a British approach (the 1985 White Paper can be considered to be a UK device for policy making which mapped out a focused and coherent strategy for making progress towards a single currency) and was led by a Conservative British Commissioner (Lord Cockfield)[3]. The fact that the 1986 Single European Act also opened the way for more rapid decision making by qualified majority voting is, ironically, one of the factors that has accentuated EU influence on policy making.

In a report written for the British Labour group at the European Parliament, Henry Neuburger (1989) produced a careful analysis of '1992' in which he came to the conclusion that 'the Cecchini studies cannot bear the weight being put upon them'. Old EU hands will recall that the Cecchini Report (1988) made extravagant claims about how completion of the internal market would both transform the performance of the EU economy and add up to 6% at a stroke to GDP. Today, these estimates look decidedly zany and it is refreshing to note that more recent studies (for example, the overview by the European Commission published in 1996) of the single market put forward a more circumspect view of what has been achieved. Now, the claim is that EU income is some 1 to 1.5% higher over the period 1987-93, that up to 900,000 more jobs have been created and that inflation rates have abated (Monti, 1996). Given the sharp downturn in the EU economy in the early 1990s, even these figures have a whiff of wishful thinking about them.

This outcome may cast doubt on the effectiveness of the whole single market project, although in the absence of a convincing 'what if?' counterfactual study this would be an exaggeration. The single market programme is often criticised for espousing a 'neo-liberal' agenda too rigidly and failing to provide for the construction of a social dimension to European integration. The playing-field may have been levelled in respect of regulatory matters, but not in the rewards to workers, hence the widespread fears of 'social dumping'[4]. This was a concern that Henry Neuburger repeatedly articulated and tried to address by forging alliances with like-minded policy makers in other EU countries in a debate that continues today. Germany has, on the whole, supported a social dimension to the single market, but it has been strongly resisted by the UK under the Tories. Labour rhetoric is softer and the decision to sign the Social Chapter has undoubtedly shifted the ground, but the UK continues to emphasise flexibility as a key aim and, broadly, to resist further economic integration.

The effects of the EU on policy making

The resignation of the Santer Commission in 1999 and the widespread disenchantment with Brussels can be interpreted as a weakening of the influence of the EU and a reassertion of the primacy of member states. European integration, however, will not go away. On the supply side, the spread of cross-border activity and corporate links is evident not only among large multinationals in the manufacturing sector, but also in services and in supply chains. Monetary union has moved from an ambition to a reality and however much UK politicians pretend that it is still a distant option, its consequences for policy making cannot be ignored. EMU is not just the technical reassignment of competence for monetary policy from, in effect, the Bundesbank to the European Central Bank (ECB), it also recasts the entire policy framework. The ramifications of this are only now being digested. Fiscal policy in the EU has to adapt to the demands of the Stability and Growth Pact[5], while redefining its accommodation with monetary policy. Various supply-side measures have to be rethought to reflect changed expectations of how adjustment is to be achieved[6]. In addition, the EU does not stand still: developments in justice and home affairs can be expected to affect labour mobility, and it is likely that as economic integration intensifies, there will be pressures for a greater degree of integration of social policy.

At present, the policy framework in the EU is a curious hybrid, with the supranational level subservient to the member states in certain respects, while in others there is a more familiar, top-down hierarchy of the sort seen in most countries[7]. Overt federalism (as in the US or Germany) is a distant prospect and there is a marked reluctance in many national capitals to see further powers transferred to the EU. Yet, there are bound to be expectations under EMU that the EU will take at least some responsibility for an integrated macroeconomic policy as well as for dealing with asymmetric shocks. In short, the policy framework is one which lacks an overall coherence, yet political imperatives demand that subsidiarity be respected, especially in relation to social policy. This prompts two further questions:

(1) What degree of autonomy and room for manoeuvre should be retained by national governments?
(2) How should the 'borders' between national and supranational policy action be determined?

Rather than new transfers of formal policy competence, the compromise answer that seems to be emerging is a reinforcement of policy cooperation and the development of new approaches to coordination. Efforts to coordinate economic policy across the EU have, latterly, been enhanced under the various 'processes' named after the European Councils at which they were agreed. The area of policy that is most developed in this regard is the employment strategy. The first steps towards a concerted policy response were taken at the 1994 Essen Council, but it was only following the Amsterdam Treaty, agreed in 1997, that concrete action was taken to establish what is now known as the European Employment Pact.

According to the conclusions of the Cologne Council held in June 1999, the 'Employment Pact embodies a comprehensive overall approach bringing together all the Union's employment policy measures.' Echoing the Maastricht Treaty, the Pact has three pillars that are supposed to be pursued together, implying policy integration. They are:

(1) "Further development and better implementation of the coordinated employment strategy to improve the efficiency of the labour markets".

Now known as the *Luxembourg process*, the aim of this pillar is to enhance the effectiveness of the Member State labour market policies and encourage job creation.

(2) "Comprehensive structural reform and modernisation to improve the innovative capacity and efficiency of the labour market and the markets in goods, services and capital". The *Cardiff process* is geared to improving the supply side of the EU economy by, first, liberalisation of markets and allowing greater sway to competitive forces. In addition, it focuses attention on the apparently inferior performance of the EU in innovation and technological advances. A special Council in Lisbon in March 2000 reinforced the member states' commitment to structural reforms, paying particular emphasis to the need to equip the EU economy to compete more effectively in the 'knowledge' economy.

(3) "Coordination of economic policy and improvement of mutually supportive interaction between wage developments and monetary, budget and fiscal policy through macro economic dialogue". This component of the Pact, to be known as the *Cologne process*, has the objective of keeping the EU on a sustainable path of non-inflationary growth and thus assuring a stable macroeconomic context.

The Employment Pact is to form part of the "broad economic policy guidelines as pursued by the member states and the Community", and is meant to facilitate cooperation between member states in economic governance. The Commission, in particular is given the task of identifying best practice and preparing guidelines. Further evidence of a more 'joined-up' approach to economic policy can be seen in proposals to gear the lending of the European Investment Bank (EIB) and the operation of the EU Structural Funds more towards employment creation, and to review tax policy so that it is more employment friendly. In particular, the scope for extensive employment creation in the service sector is highlighted. The special council at Lisbon in March 2000 sought to take the integration of policy further by setting targets for the activity rates.

The Luxembourg process: a possible model?

Under the Luxembourg process, there is an annual cycle for elaborating, implementing and monitoring national employment policies. The key to this process is the notion of Employment Guidelines based on proposals by the Commission. The Council approves a series of priority areas for action, and these guidelines include concrete objectives. Each country draws up a National Action Plan (NAP) which describes how these guidelines are to be put into practice in the way best suited to that country. This process should involve a wide range of partners: unions, employers, local and regional authorities and so on. The Commission and the Council jointly examine each NAP and present a Joint Employment Report to the European Council. The Council, on the basis of the conclusions by the Heads of State or Government, approves the set of Employment Guidelines for the following year. The Council may issue country-specific recommendations upon proposal by the Commission, although the imperative of respecting subsidiarity is repeatedly emphasised in the various documents.

In this way the Luxembourg process proceeds as a rolling programme of yearly planning, monitoring, examination and readjustment. The guidelines are based on four central ideas or 'pillars' of priority action and set three EU-wide quantitative targets, to be attained within five years. The four pillars of policy revolve around a call on the member states to undertake action to support:

(1) Employability
(2) Entrepreneurship
(3) Flexibility
(4) Equal opportunities.

Even a cursory look at each country's NAP shows that the particular measures introduced under each heading vary considerably, but the process does highlight what appears to work and it is evident that countries are making efforts to 'showcase' the programmes that work well and are innovative. It is also dynamic in the sense that both guidelines and scrutiny evolve. The confrontation of policy styles provides a further twist. Some countries (and, it appears, the Commission) would like to see the introduction of explicit targets (for example, for a reduction in unemployment or a number of jobs created), while others prefer a looser coordinating role for the EU level. Certainly, targets without sanctions risk being rather empty, though it can be argued that no government will feel comfortable being shown to have missed a target. Targets might also lead to ill-judged palliatives aimed at meeting the target, rather than achieving longer-term objectives. A compromise between these approaches might therefore be increased use of benchmarking. League tables which show a country to be in the relegation zone rather than competing for the championship can have a salutary effect.

The institutionalisation of EU influence

The institutionalisation of the 'processes' into member state policy making is plainly a key development, or would be if they were seen to make a difference. As the most developed, the Luxembourg process which, at the time of writing, had been through two full annual cycles, does appear to be achieving results. It has prompted member states – the UK included – to elaborate increasingly coherent and comprehensive plans to stimulate employment creation and there are indications that the scrutiny of NAPs by the Commission, together with the exchanges of 'best practice', has prompted governments to rethink their approaches. At the same time, the fact that it is left to member states to determine the content of policy programmes and their implementation means that subsidiarity in policy making is respected. It also means that the emphasis in policy can be adjusted to reflect national needs, rather than being imposed in a potentially inappropriate top-down manner.

Although the Luxembourg process is apparently being adhered to by the member states, an inevitable question is whether it is just window-dressing for policies that would have been adopted regardless. There is no doubt an element of this and it is too early to attempt any meaningful evaluation of outcomes, but an examination of the NAPs suggests that they do represent a shift in approach that is making a difference. On the one hand, national administrations are putting considerable effort into the elaboration of their plans – strategic documents running to 100 or more pages – and they are plainly attempting to address all four pillars and each of the guidelines. France, for example, was initially very sceptical about the notion of employability, but many of the measures in its current NAP are designed to promote it and thus seem to reflect policy learning. On the other hand, the Commission scrutiny elicited a backlash from some member states, implying – perhaps paradoxically – that the process is having an effect.

The Cardiff process has, thus far, not obviously had much impact. But where it does suggest a new direction for policy making is in what is being called 'policy integration' – the horizontal coordination of policy or, in British terms, joined-up government. The surprise ought to be that such coordination is itself a surprising innovation, but it is only too clear that past policy in the EU and in member states has suffered from a lack of it.

It is difficult to judge to what extent the macroeconomic dialogue initiated under the Cologne process has made a difference to national policy making. For the countries participating in monetary union, one consequence is that there is, at least, formal communication between the parties to monetary and fiscal policy, on the one hand, and the two sides of industry, on the other. The unresolved question, however, is whether the dialogue will make any difference to the interest rate decisions of an ECB subject to a Treaty obligation to assure price stability as its primary objective.

Although both 'Cardiff' and 'Cologne' do not yet have much of a track record, it can be argued that the influence of the EU level through the elaboration of guidelines has become a new form of policy setting in which the contribution of the EU is to provide a framework and a degree of surveillance, without having a direct competence over the policy area. This 'soft' form of Europeanisation is, manifestly, a way of securing additional centralisation of policy making without the formalities of Treaty changes or legally binding Directives. But although it could be portrayed as a form of creeping centralisation, a more charitable view is that it reconciles the inconsistencies in the EU policy framework without provoking a political furore. This does, however, raise issues of legitimacy in policy making and the durability of the arrangements which will need to be addressed before too long.

Whether, or to what degree, this philosophy can be broadened to other domains is an intriguing question for 21st century policy making. An advantage of the EU level is that it can take a more strategic view of objectives and draw on the diverse input coming from member states. Where relevant (as is the case for the macroeconomic dimension of fiscal decisions) inconsistencies between member states can be thrashed out in the development of guidelines or benchmarking. Policy innovation can be stimulated simply by tapping into the wider base of experience provided by the range of countries.

Equally, the EU level has to beware of undue intrusion in national policy debates and to recognise that it will have to confine its role to broad targets, often only qualitative rather than quantitative in nature. Challenges will arise where the needs of some countries clash with others. The EU level in the shape of the European Commission also has limited resources, so that it risks being overstretched if it takes on responsibility for too many policy areas.

An extension of EU influence?

In any reconfiguration of policy competencies, therefore, a variety of influences bear on the optimal involvement of the EU level. These include:

- Accountability and the sensitivity of national interests in the policy domain;
- Institutional capacity;
- The degree to which reconciliation of member state policies is desirable (or a lack of coherence is damaging);
- The benefits of coordination and the scope for policy learning.

For different policy areas, these factors will matter to differing extents and bear on the evolution of the policy-making process. To illustrate the issues, it is instructive to review a range of policy domains from these perspectives.

Fiscal policy highlights many of the dilemmas that arise from the emergence of the EU as a significant policy influence. Clearly, if EMU is to function effectively, there cannot be fiscal anarchy with member states adopting mutually incompatible fiscal stances and no machinery for integrating fiscal and monetary policy. The excessive deficits provisions in the Treaty and the Stability and Growth Pact were designed to counter these risks and, though open to the criticism that they could impart a deflationary bias, should limit the problem[8]. Fiscal policy, however, remains a competence of member states and there are especially strong grounds for believing that any move to diminish national responsibility for underlying decisions about taxation and public expenditure will be resisted. Some also question whether a pan-European fiscal federation would be economically efficient (Fatas, 1998). It has also been argued that a collective monetary policy will penalise countries which succeed in making their economies more flexible because the ECB will be constrained to average out in making its monetary policy decision. Integration could, therefore, have perverse incentives for supply-side policy.

Taxation is at the heart of the relationship between the citizen and the state, and demands robust accountability procedures. In its present state of institutional development, the EU is a long way from offering such accountability. Although the fiscal stance is about the balance between public expenditure and taxation, and thus logically distinct from the financing instruments and spending programmes that make up the two aggregates, public debate on these issues will tend to be conflated.

Taxation also affects the levelness of the business playing-field and thus has implications for the single market. Indirect taxes can distort competition by giving consumers incentives to cross jurisdictions to purchase goods and services. Direct taxes can influence location decisions of companies, while labour taxes may render operating costs uncompetitive in areas where rates are high. The influence of European integration in this regard is twofold. First, there will be pressure on governments from the business sector to avoid tax structures that adversely affect competitiveness. Much of the impetus for reform of social protection in countries with high social charges comes from this fear of competition in the single market. Second, if distortions are to be avoided, then disparities in tax rates have to be limited. Immediately, this second influence comes up against the objection that taxation is a vital national interest that cannot be dictated by 'Brussels'. Yet it is clear that national autonomy will be circumscribed.

Similar considerations apply to regulatory policy. A sizeable part of the '1992' programme, as Henry Neuburger rightly pointed out, was concerned with 'removal of barriers'. But it was by no means exclusively concerned with deregulation, and many of the areas in which single market legislation underpins the regulatory framework can be characterised as a recasting of regulation. Often this is accompanied by the emergence of a new regulatory style that may be rooted in one or other country's tradition, but ultimately takes a form that is unique to the EU[9]. What the single market has done is to strike a balance between liberalisation and the elaboration of rules that prevent a 'race to the bottom' in regulation.

Here again, the message for national policy makers in the 21st century is that new initiatives in regulation have to anticipate and accommodate the balancing of interests across the EU, rather than respond purely to national imperatives. In some of the areas currently subject to review in the single market agenda, such as regulation of utilities or of financial services, the process of mediation between a market-oriented UK approach and the social aims of certain continental countries is fascinating to watch.

Social protection

One area where the EU has feared to tread is social protection. In part, this is because the Treaty does not give it competence, but there are also evident national sensitivities about cherished facets of the welfare state. For many, the social policy system that has evolved since the Second

World War in most Western European countries is an enviable achievement. Security of income is assured by continuity of employment and stability in earnings, and in this regard the rights to employment protection and good working conditions enjoyed by workers are held to be desirable features of European society. Social protection provides for those not active in the labour market and insures workers against temporary unemployment. Together with an expectation that the state will strive to assure a high level of employment and the provision of good public services, these are the essential components of the European social model[10].

There is a strand of thinking now that a social dimension is needed to complement economic integration and the likelihood is that the architects of EU development will see this as a priority for the coming years, over ten years after Henry Neuburger made the case. The economic case for centralisation of social policy rests on two main foundations. First, higher tiers of government are best placed to mediate between competing demands for social expenditure and the logic of fiscal federalism points towards an EU role (Oates, 1991). In the US, it is the federal level which finances the major welfare programmes, even if they are implemented by state and local government, and the same is true of other nations. Second, in a single market, differences in social provision and in the means of financing it can lead to market distortions.

Thus far, it is the regulatory aspects of social policy that have been most developed at European level, particularly those concerning the workplace. There is, however, a groundswell in favour of minimum standards to be applied across the EU to avoid what has come to be known as 'social dumping'. This is usually dressed up as social justice, but a more cynical explanation is that it relates to preservation of jobs in areas at risk because their high standards translate into higher costs.

EMU will affect social policy, directly or indirectly, in various ways. To the extent that the promise of EMU will deliver a more prosperous EU economy that employs more people and generates higher incomes per head, the outlook should be positive. Under this 'Dr Pangloss' scenario, the demands on social protection should be lessened and tax rates should be lower for a given level of social protection. The trials of the transition to EMU do, however, illustrate the down side. Relative stagnation of the EU economy means that the financing of social protection comes under strain and that governments face acute difficulties in maintaining discipline in the public finances.

Evidence from the US, Canada and other federal countries shows the important role played by 'automatic' fiscal stabilisers in dampening shocks

(Bayoumi and Masson, 1995). Whether it is on the tax side or the benefit side that the effect arises depends on the detail of the respective systems, but the aggregate effect can be substantial. Estimates vary markedly on the importance of flows from the federal level in the US, but are agreed in showing that both the stabilising and redistributive effects of the EU level of governance are negligible by comparison even with federations where the federal level is modest in scale. The absence of cross-border social protection could, consequently, be a problem for the coherence of the EMU policy framework.

Concluding remarks

The development of a new EU policy framework has been motivated by shifting political priorities, formal legal agreements (notably the Treaty) and a perceived need for policy integration to tackle common problems. Market integration has been both a cause and a consequence of political decisions to integrate. The UK cannot remain aloof from these trends, even if it continues to stay out of monetary union, and it is clear that EU membership will have a profound impact on policy making in the 21st century.

In recent years, the macroeconomic priorities of the EU have shifted, notably to give greater weight to employment as the fear of inflation has receded, prompting a far-reaching reappraisal of economic governance under EMU. The various steps towards a coherent strategy in the last few years suggest that a comprehensive response is now being put together and should augur well for the EU's economic prospects.

The outcome of the Cologne European Council and the elaboration of the Employment Pact are developments that break new ground in policymaking. On the one hand, the outcome recognises that action to increase employment cannot be confined to the labour market, but must be complemented by appropriate macroeconomic policy and structural reforms. Procedures are in place and seem to have engaged the support of the member states. There also appears to be a willingness on all sides to approach the Pact positively and to make the various processes effective. However, although some EU-wide targets have been set, several member states have resisted attempts to devise explicit targets for NAPs. More use of 'benchmarking' and other forms of quantitative targets might, however, be desirable to motivate policy makers. What these tensions illustrate is the difficulty of deciding where to draw the line between interference and the establishment of common aims and standards.

On the other hand, the policy style that has evolved is one in which the division of labour between the EU and the member states hinges critically on a distinction between rule setting and implementation for many areas of policy. Oates (1999, p 1145) argued that in the last few years, an earlier trend towards centralisation may have reached "some sort of peak with a modest swing back in the direction of devolution of public sector activity". He points to the simultaneous devolution in member states "while the Community develops a set of supranational institutions for governance and economic management". Yet what seems to be happening is more subtle in the EU, with a reshaping of roles along functional lines, not across policy areas. Although it has obviously been assigned new responsibilities in relation to monetary policy to add to its remit for trade and agriculture, the EU level seems to be carving out a new niche in which its strategic function is increasingly a coordinating one.

Doubts remain, nevertheless, about whether the single market and EMU have created a sufficiently coherent policy framework. The profusion of actors involved in economic governance is, arguably, still an obstacle to policy integration and there are confused policy assignments between tiers of government. Moreover, the objectives of the different agencies are not *necessarily* consistent with specific aims such as employment creation. In particular, the ECB mandate to assure price stability must be met before the focus of monetary policy can be the general economic policies of the Union. The distinction may prove to be less onerous in practice than in the formal language of the Treaty, but it nevertheless means that an integrated approach to employment is likely to remain more difficult to secure than in the US where the Fed has the well known 'dual mandate'.

There are echoes in the very fluid EU policy setting of the issues with which Henry Neuburger grappled in his many years of advising on policy. He always stressed the importance of a social dimension to policy, and was forceful over a decade ago in advocating it as a necessary component of the single market. Today, that call is being heeded with the adoption of the European Employment Pact and a determination in many quarters to develop a new and better European social model, rather than, as many on the Right hoped, its dismemberment. For British policy makers in the 21st century, 'Europe' will continue to have a strong influence and will impose constraints or afford opportunities that have to be taken into account in policy choices. To pretend otherwise, as so many do, is to ask for trouble.

Notes

[1] The term EU is used throughout to describe the integrated economic space in Europe, except where specific reference is made to earlier institutional forms.

[2] The recent initiatives towards a common approach to defence might also be mentioned.

[3] One of the ironies of the SEM is that Lord Cockfield and Jacques Delors formed a very effective partnership (for an account of the development of the SEM, see Cockfield, 1994) and it is evident that Cockfield has a high regard for the former Commission President who, in the late 1980s, was at risk of succeeding General Galtieri and Arthur Scargill as British public enemy number one.

[4] The notion that, for competitive reasons, governments will compete to lower social standards, in much the same way as competitive devaluations.

[5] The Stability and Growth Pact, agreed prior to the start of EMU, is designed to restrict government deficits with the aim of making it easier to avoid conflicts between fiscal and monetary policies. The pact sets a limit for public deficits of 3% of GDP under normal circumstances, and has mechanisms for penalising errant member states.

[6] For a summary of adjustment mechanisms, see Begg and Hodson (2000).

[7] According to McKay (2000) Switzerland is the exception that may be most akin to the EU.

[8] Indeed, many economists have argued that overly rigid application of the Pact will have a damaging effect on the EU economy in the short run (see, for example, Eichengreen and Wyplosz, 1998).

[9] See the special issue of the *Journal of European Public Policy*, vol 3:4 on regulation in Europe.

[10] Buti et al (1999) provide a valuable overview.

References

Bayoumi, T. and Masson, P.R. (1995) 'Fiscal flows in the United States and Canada: lessons for monetary union in Europe', *European Economic Review*, vol 39, pp 253-74.

Begg, I. and Hodson, D. (2000) 'Regional adjustment mechanisms under EMU', *Tijdschrift voor Economische en Social Geografie*, vol 94, pp 78-84.

Buti, M., Franco, D. and Pench, L.R. (eds) (1999) *The welfare state in Europe*, Cheltenham: Edward Elgar.

Cecchini, P. (1988) *The European challenge*, Aldershot: Wildwood House.

Cockfield, A. (1994) *The European Union: Creating the single market*, Chichester: Chancery Law Publishing.

Eichengreen, B. and Wyplosz, C. (1998) 'The stability pact: more than a minor nuisance?', *Economic Policy*, no 26, pp 65-113.

Fatas, A. (1998) 'Does EMU need a fiscal federation?', *Economic Policy*, vol 28, pp 165-203.

McKay, D. (2000) 'Political legitimacy and institutional design' *Journal of Common Market Studies*, vol 38, pp 25-44.

Monti, M. (1996) *The single market and tomorrow's Europe*, London: Kogan Page.

Neuburger, H. (1989) *The economics of 1992*, Brussels: Socialist Group of the European Parliament.

Oates, W.E. (1991) *Studies in fiscal federalism*, Cheltenham: Edward Elgar.

Oates, W.E. (1999) 'An essay on fiscal federalism', *Journal of Economic Literature*, vol XXXVII, pp 1120-49.

Part Three: Sectoral issues

TEN

Unions, the national minimum wage and the distribution of pay

David Metcalf[1]

Introduction

For much of the 20th century the distribution of pay in the UK became more compressed. But in the last two decades that distribution widened out again such that by 1998 it was more unequal than at any time during the previous 100 years (LPC, 1998, appendix 3). The growing spread of earnings is attributable to three sets of factors (Machin, 1996). First, the demand for skilled labour increased faster than its supply, mainly because of skill biased technical change. Second, institutions which temper the inequality in earnings either crumbled away (for example collective bargaining coverage) or were axed (for example wage councils)[2]. Third, firms placed more emphasis on contingent pay systems where pay was dependent on the performance of the individual, team or company.

This chapter focuses on the second set of factors – the influence of institutions on the distribution of earnings. This is an important area to study because New Labour's industrial relations policy places great emphasis on resurrecting and nurturing institutions previously left to corrode. There are three main planks to this policy (Metcalf, 1999c). A national minimum wage was introduced in 1999 which will truncate the lower tail of the pay distribution. Next, statutory union recognition procedures came into force in 2000. This too will affect the wage structure because, for example, the distribution of pay among organised workers has a lower variance than that among unorganised employees. Finally, New Labour has embraced the EU Social Chapter which, for example, both promotes more individual rights like maternity leave and collective institutions like works councils. The latter strand is not discussed here.

Rather, the focus is on the impact of the national minimum wage (NMW) and unionisation on the distribution of pay.

Henry Neuburger was acutely interested in, and wrote perceptively about, these issues. In the mid 1980s he analysed (Neuburger, 1984a) the likely consequences of abolition of the wage councils – which occurred in 1993 – and the introduction of a national minimum wage. He anticipated the modest employment effects and minor knock-on consequences on pay differentials for a prudently set NMW. He returned to the link between pay and jobs in his analysis of the 1970s Equal Pay Act (Neuburger, 1984b) where he showed that the Act had resulted in a major narrowing of the gender pay gap but had not resulted in employment losses among female workers. Neuburger was concerned with important issues and used economic analysis to illuminate key policy matters. This chapter follows in that tradition.

National Minimum Wage

The UK's first ever NMW was established in April 1999. The rate was £3.60 per hour for those aged 22 plus and £3 per hour for those aged 18-21. The rate for the NMW was recommended by the LPC (1998), a successful example of the government's social partnership approach to industrial relations (see Metcalf, 1999a).

Choosing the rate for the NMW was a tricky task. The LPC consulted widely across the country and took much written and oral evidence. Its own triangulation exercise involved numbers covered, cost and international comparisons.

Approximately 1.7 million workers were earning below the NMW prior to its introduction, equivalent to 7.3% of employees. There is some uncertainty concerning these numbers, fully discussed in the second report of the LPC (2000), because neither main official data source is wholly suitable to measure the extent of low pay. The employer based New Earnings Survey, in principle a 1% sample of employees, is based on PAYE income tax records and therefore undersamples the low earners who do not pay income tax. By contrast the household based Labour Force Survey overstates low pay in part because 'proxy respondents' – those at home – may not know the true earnings of other household members at work.

The pay of workers newly covered by the NMW rose by an amount equivalent to around 0.4% of the national wage bill. Some of this was offset by lower labour turnover, better work organisation and a repackaging

Table 10.1: International evidence on the national minimum wage

	NMW as % of full-time median earnings[a]	Rate per hour[b] (£)	Rate (PPP) per hour[c]
France	57	3.97	4.10
Australia	54	3.79	4.83
Belgium	50	4.06	4.55
Netherlands	49	4.19	4.56
UK	44	3.60	3.60
Canada	40	2.77	3.74
US	38	3.18	3.38
Spain	32	1.80	2.43
Japan	31	3.74	2.57

[a] Median earnings column refers to late 1997; median earnings includes overtime and bonuses.
[b] Calculated using exchange rates at November 1999.
[c] PPPs are purchasing power parities for final private consumption expenditure for 1998. PPP is the hypothetical rate of currency conversion that eliminates the differences in price levels between countries.

Source: Metcalf (1999b, table 4); LPC (2000, table A7.1)

of various components of compensation. The Monetary Policy Committee (MPC) chose to accommodate this direct wage growth – essentially treating it as a one-off supply-side shock which might modestly influence the price level but not inflation (see Bank of England, 1999).

International evidence was also important to the LPC. The UK had never previously had a NMW so there was a feeling that, at least initially, the UK should set a rate which would put it somewhere around the middle of the international league table. Table 10.1 demonstrates that this is precisely what was achieved, in terms of both the hourly rate (determined either by official exchange rates or purchasing power parity) and the minimum rate as a fraction of median earnings. On this evidence the UK has a lower NMW than Australia, Belgium, France and the Netherlands but a higher rate than Canada, Japan, Spain and the US.

The NMW, even allowing for some non-compliance, has had an important impact on the distribution of earnings. Consider Figure 10.1. It will be seen that the bottom 5% of the pay distribution in April 1998 received substantially higher pay increases between April 1998 and April 1999 (when the NMW came in) than other employees. This contrasts markedly with the period 1993-97 when the lowest 5% of the distribution received the smallest pay increases. Before the NMW was introduced there had been some concern that restoration of wage differentials between

Figure 10.1: Percentile increases in hourly earnings

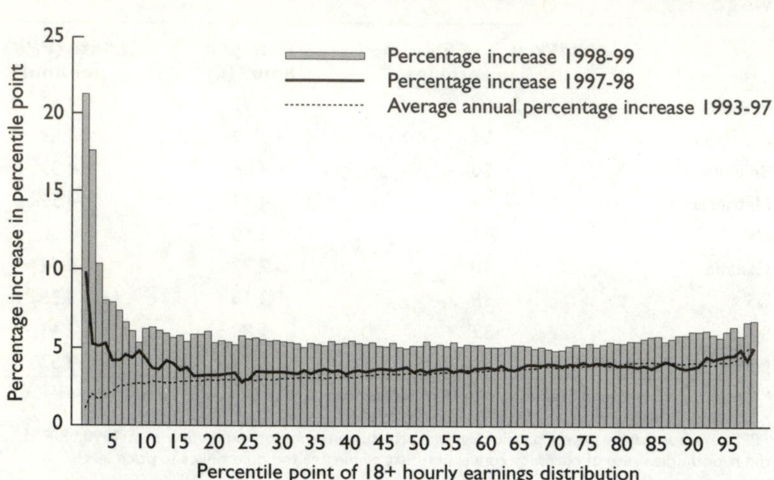

Source: NES, April 1993, 1997, 1998, 1999

the low paid and those somewhat further up the distribution would result in aggregate wage inflation and, consequently, job losses (for example Macrae, 1999). Pay rises for those above the tenth percentile of the pay distribution are remarkably similar and refute the notion that the NMW would have severe knock-on effects. As Neuburger predicted, there was potential to 'squash' the pay distribution. This is a consequence, in part, of the prudent initial rate of the NMW: a higher rate might well have resulted in inflation and unemployment.

Another way to examine the impact of the NMW on the earnings distribution is to analyse panel evidence rather than the cross section evidence of Figure 10.1. Table 10.2 presents such evidence from the New Earnings Survey (NES) matched samples for 1998 and 1999. Of those earning below the NMW figure in 1998, three quarters were receiving at least the NMW amount by April 1999. (The apparent 25% non-compliance in April 1999 needs to be treated with caution. The NES was undertaken only a fortnight after the introduction of the NMW and, in some cases, is based on a March work period. Compliance has increased steadily since April 1999 (see LPC, 2000, appendix 2 for more details). The mean earnings of those in the matched sample rose by almost a third in the year to April 1999 and their median pay by nearly a fifth.

Table 10.2: Increase in hourly earnings for those below minimum wage rates in April 1998

Employee	% receiving at least the NMW in April 1999	% increase in mean earnings 1998-99	% increase in median earnings 1998-99
Female			
full-time	73	42	15
part-time	78	28	13
Male			
full-time	68	37	25
part-time	76	24	22
All	75	31	18

Note: calculated from New Earnings Survey matched sample 1998, 1999.

Source: LPC (2000) table A2.1

Figure 10.2: Hourly earnings distribution

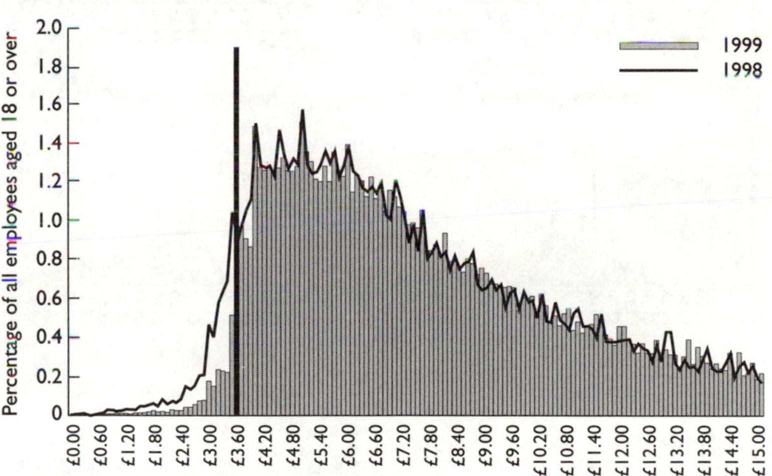

Source: NES, April 1998, 1999

Figures 10.2 and 10.3 summarise the effect of these very substantial pay increases at the bottom of the distribution consequent on the NMW. Overall (Figure 10.2) the lower tail of the distribution moved noticeably to the right with a prominent spike at £3.60. This effect is even more vivid if we consider the pay distributions for low-paying sectors

Figure 10.3: Hourly earnings distribution in low paying sectors

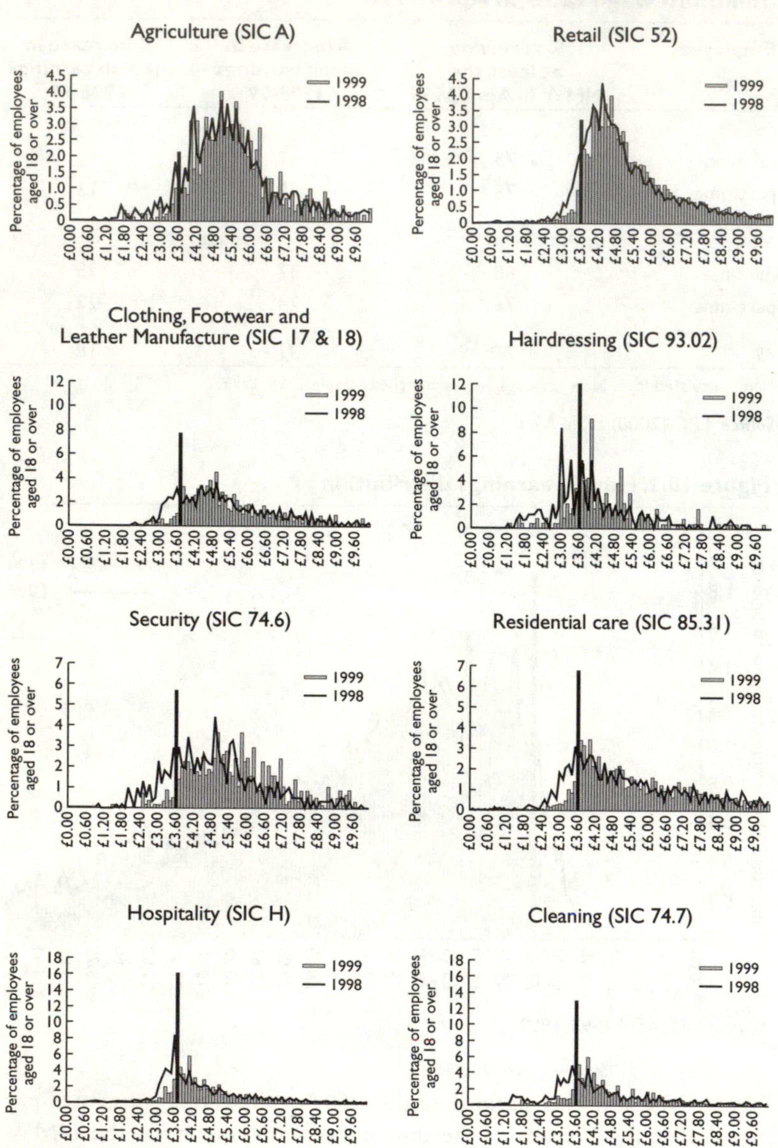

Note: Different scales on each horizontal pair of charts
Source: NES, April 1998, 1999

(Figure 10.3). The spike at £3.60 covers 16% of hospitality and cleaning employees, 12% of workers in hairdressing, 7% in residential care and 6 % in security.

The gender pay differential has also been eroded by the NMW. In the year to April 1999, the gap in the average hourly pay of women relative to men narrowed by a full percentage point, the largest amount for almost a decade. The NES indicates that, of those whose pay was raised to the minimum rates or higher in the year to 1999, over two thirds of the beneficiaries were women, of whom two thirds worked part-time.

It is worth concluding this section by switching attention briefly from the pay to the income distribution. The Institute for Fiscal Studies (IFS) recently concluded that, "the minimum wage will not redistribute income to poorer households" (IFS, 1998). This is true when the sample is all households because so many of those at the bottom of the distribution are non-workers including pensioners, the unemployed or otherwise inactive. But if we confine the sample to working households and ask the very straightforward question, 'how are the aggregate gains from the NMW distributed?', we get a very different picture. Those in the bottom fifth of the household income distribution receive two thirds of the aggregate gains from the NMW whereas those in the top fifth receive only 2.6% of the aggregate gains (see Metcalf, 1999b for more details). The NMW has resulted in the pay distribution becoming more equal. It similarly influences the distribution of working household incomes, an effect which is further strengthened when the Working Family Tax Credit is also taken into account (LPC, 2000, appendix 3); see also John Hills's chapter for analysis of effects of Labour's tax and benefit changes combined with the NMW.

Trade unions and the distribution of pay

A stylised industrial relations fact is that pay dispersion among unionised workers is lower than the spread among their non-union counterparts. For example Machin (1999) states: "Trade unions have traditionally been seen as defenders of egalitarian pay structures. This is reflected in 'equal pay for equal work' notions and the standardisation of pay setting mechanisms, often in the form of rigid pay scales attached to jobs rather than individuals". There are three routes to this greater equality of pay in the organised sector.

First, unions reduce pay dispersion *within* establishments. Unions prefer a single rate of pay for each occupational group whereas in non-union firms with individual pay determination supervisors decide pay levels within a range. Unions also prefer seniority based progression of rates. These preferences stem from unions' desire for objective standards, where pay goes with the job, because of concerns about favouritism, discrimination and the measurement of the 'true' contribution where pay is subjectively related to the 'merit' of the individual. Workers' solidarity is also likely to be greater when workers receive roughly the same pay than when they get different amounts.

Next, union wage policies lead to a narrower wage dispersion in the organised compared with the unorganised sector. However, the strength of this channel, which operates *across* firms and workplaces, has been weakened as collective bargaining has become more decentralised. At the turn of the last century the Webbs (1902) introduced the concept of 'the common rule' into the vocabulary of industrial relations and used it to define trade union objectives. The fixing of a standard rate of pay – the rate for the job – was the pivotal common rule. There are two rationales for the common rule. When firms compete in the same market, both employer and worker interests can be expected to favour a standard rate. The firm does not want a labour contract that is more expensive than its competitors. And for the worker, it takes the wages out of competition – there will be no undercutting. Union solidarity is also more difficult to maintain if some workers are paid markedly more than others for the same job.

The strength of this common rule has ebbed away as the locus of collective bargaining in the private sector has switched from national multi-employer agreements to firm or workplace agreements. Around a quarter of private sector employees are covered by collective agreements of which under a tenth are covered by national agreements. Consequently the dispersion of pay in the organised sector is likely to be higher now than it was two decades ago.

Nevertheless, the organised sector is still likely to have less dispersion, other things equal, than the unorganised. Multi-employer bargaining still exists in parts of printing, textiles, clothing and construction. But even in sectors where national bargaining has disintegrated, unions' own internal organisation permits or encourages pay comparisons across companies. This comes via research support for collective bargaining, the way lay officers are taught to formulate pay claims, industry level forums, and the involvement of fulltime officials in local pay negotiations.

Third, unions operate a *de facto* minimum wage policy via collective bargaining. In local government, for example, the lowest basic rate in the

Table 10.3 Unions and the distribution of pay (dispersion of logarithms of earnings)[a b]

	Union	Non-union
Raw		
Standard deviation	0.457	0.592
90 – 10	1.140	1.470
Variance	0.209	0.351
Residuals[c]		
Standard deviation	0.330	0.439
90 – 10	0.843	1.008
Variance	0.130	0.193

[a] Sample size is 16,730;
[b] standard deviation, 90 – 10, and variance from log earnings;
[c] the residuals are estimated from a regression equation containing the following independent variables: age, qualifications, workplace size, industry, marital status, public/private, fulltime/part-time, permanent/temporary, gender, able-bodied/disabled, ethnicity

Source: Labour Force Survey, Autumn 1998

1997 national agreement was £4.00 per hour. And the Transport and General Union reports a similar lower bound negotiated for some industrial cleaners, knitwear operatives, bar staff and retail workers.

Three measures of the dispersion of log earnings are presented in Table 10.3: the standard deviation, the 90th percentile minus the 10th percentile, and the variance. Consider initially the raw earnings data. On all three measures the union pay distribution is more concentrated than the non-union pay distribution. Now consider the dispersion from the residuals from a regression equation which permits controls for the heterogeneity of people and jobs between the union and non-union sectors. Two strong findings occur. First, considerable pay dispersion remains even when controls are included – the dispersion in the residuals is around two thirds the dispersion in the raw data. Second, it remains the case that, even when we compare essentially homogenous employees in similar workplaces and jobs, the pay dispersion is lower for union members than for non-union employees. Thus union wage policies do matter – the lower dispersion in pay among unionists is not just because they are more similar than non-unionists.

One reason for this lower dispersion in the organised sector is because in unionised firms pay is based more on jobs and less on individual characteristics. Hence the characteristics of workers which raise pay have a smaller effect in unionised workplaces and, in turn, inequality is smaller in union than in non-union workplaces. Consider for example the payoff to extra human capital. The returns to labour market experience indicate that, as compared with those aged under 25, prime age union members earn 37% more while prime age non-union members earn 48% more. Likewise, the returns to higher qualifications are greater and the profile is steeper among the non-union group than for union members. Unions may wish to ponder this finding: it may imply that workers sort themselves, or are sorted by their potential employers, such that the more able prefer to work in non-unionised firms where they can get a higher payoff to their costly investment in human capital.

The 1998 Workplace Employment Relations Survey asked the 2000 respondent workplaces what percentage of employees earned below £3.50, a convenient benchmark as the NMW of £3.60 was introduced a year later. Cross tabulations confirm that union recognition is associated with a lower incidence of low pay:

	% of workplaces with 25% or more employees earning less than £3.50 per hour
No union presence	16
Union present, no recognition	9
Union recognised	2

Thus a mere 1 in 50 workplaces recognising unions had a quarter of their workforces earning below £3.50 per hour but the incidence of such clusters of low pay is eight times greater in non-union workplaces.

These results are confirmed by more sophisticated statistical analysis. The mean percentage earning below £3.50 is 10.5%. Other things equal, union recognition reduces the incidence of low pay by 3.9 percentage points. And where coverage of collective bargaining is above 60% this reduces the incidence of low pay by a further 3.8 percentage points. Thus recognition coupled with extensive coverage reduces the per cent low paid by nearly 8 percentage points or some three quarters of the mean.

The impact of unionisation on the pay structure by gender, ethnicity, health and occupation is set out in Table 10.4. The results are quite remarkable. Unionisation narrows the wage structure for each pair of groups. The fraction of employees who are union members is rather similar for each of the groups, at around a third (column 1). Thus the impact of unionisation on the pay structure comes via the premium associated with union membership (column 2). In each case the lower

Table 10.4: Impact of unionisation on pay structure by gender, race, health and occupation

Group	Fraction unionised	Premium	Union impact
Male	0.330	-0.003	0.026
Female	0.308	0.087	
White	0.320	0.039	0.014
Non-white	0.315	0.084	
Healthy	0.317	0.039	0.006
Health problems	0.336	0.053	
Non-manual	0.321	0.030	0.031
Manual	0.321	0.129	

Notes:

1. Total sample size is 16,489.
2. Hourly pay premium associated with union membership estimated from regression equation with the following controls: age, marital status, qualifications, part-time worker, temporary worker, industry, public sector, workplace size and (as appropriate) gender, ethnicity and health.
3. In all the regressions but one the coefficient on unionisation is significant at better than 1%. Further, in each pairwise comparison the premia are significantly different from one another at 5% or better.

Source: Labour Force Survey, Autumn 1998

paid group – females, non-whites, those with health problems and manuals – receive a higher premium if they are a union member than do their higher paid counterpart groups.

Consequently the average wage structure is narrowed by the following percentages (column 3) compared with what it would be if there were no unions:

Group	If there were no unions wage structure would be wider by %
Male–female	2.6
White–black	1.4
Healthy–health problems	0.6
Non manual–manual	3.1

It should be remembered that many people think of unions as operating to the advantage of able-bodied, white, male workers. Indeed Frances O'Grady, Head of the TUC's New Unionism project, recently described unions as 'male, pale and stale'. If this were the case the wage structures in Table 10.4 would be widened not compressed.

Conclusion

The distribution of pay is influenced by many factors: supply and demand for different types of labour, institutional arrangements in the labour market, and firms' payment systems and methods of organisation. Henry Neuburger believed that institutions matter. He was a passionate advocate of a national minimum wage and aspired to a flourishing trade union movement.

The evidence in this chapter shows just how perceptive Henry was. The national minimum wage promotes greater equality by truncating the lower tail of the pay distribution. It has also resulted in the largest narrowing in the gender pay gap for more than a decade. Likewise trade unions temper the inequality in pay, reduce the incidence of low pay and narrow the pay differentials by race and gender. Thriving labour market institutions are vital if the sword of justice is to be wielded to temper inequalities in the labour market.

Notes

[1] The first section on National Minimum Wage draws on material in the second report of the Low Pay Commission (2000). I am a member of the LPC but I am writing here in a personal capacity: this chapter should not necessarily be interpreted as reflecting the views of LPC members or of the secretariat. The third section on trade unions and the distribution of pay is based on work with two CEP colleagues (Metcalf, Hansen and Charlwood 2000). I am grateful to them for permission to use these research results; and to Sue Fernie for helpful comments on an earlier draft.

[2] Atkinson (1999) adds shifts in pay norms as a further part of the story of the last quarter century.

References

Atkinson, A.B. (1999), *Is rising inequality inevitable? A critique of the transatlantic consensus,* WIDER Annual Lectures 3, Helsinki: UNU World Institute for Development Economics Research.

Bank of England (1999) *Inflation report*, August.

Institute for Fiscal Studies (IFS) (1998) 'Effects of the minimum wage', mimeo, 5 June.

Low Pay Commission (LPC) (2000) *The national minimum wage: The story so far*, Second Report of the LPC, Cm 4571, London: The Stationery Office.

LPC (1998) *The national minimum wage*, First Report of the LPC, Cm 3976, London: The Stationery Office.

Machin, S. (1996) 'Wage inequality in the UK', *Oxford Review of Economic Policy*, vol 12, no 1, Spring, pp 7-22.

Machin, S. (1999) 'Pay inequality in the 1970s, 1980s and 1990s', in P. Gregg and J. Wadsworth (eds) *The state of working Britain*: Manchester, Manchester University Press.

Macrae, N. (1999) 'The minimum wage scandal is a good April Fool's Day joke', *Sunday Business*, 7 March.

Metcalf, D. (1999a) 'The Low Pay Commission and the national minimum wage', *Economic Journal*, vol 109, no 453, pp 44-66.

Metcalf, D. (1999b) 'The British national minimum wage', *British Journal of Industrial Relations*, vol 37, no 2, June, pp 171-201.

Metcalf, D. (1999c) 'New Labor's industrial relations policy', *Perspectives on Work*, vol 3, no 1, pp 12-17.

Metcalf, D., Hansen, K. and Charlwood, A. (2000) 'Unions and the sword of justice', WP 1033, CEP, LSE, January.

Neuburger, H. (1984a) *Unemployment, are wages to blame?*, London: Low Pay Unit, Discussion Series No 4, November.

Neuburger, H. (1984b) *From the dole queue to the sweatshop: Minimum wages and government policy*, London: Low Pay Unit, Pamphlet No 30.

Webb, S. and Webb, B. (1902) *Industrial democracy*, London: Longmans.

ELEVEN

Economic appraisal in transport

Chris Nash and Peter Mackie

Introduction

It is a feature of Henry Neuburger's work in the fields of transport and economic evaluation that he tackled issues that are still at the forefront of analysis and policy, and did so with his characteristic blend of academic rigour and awareness of the practical policy environment. His papers of the early 1970s go way beyond the somewhat simplistic cost–benefit analysis (CBA) techniques common in transport at the time to address issues such as the aggregation of benefits when prices of alternative modes and routes change simultaneously (Foster and Neuburger, 1974), and the appraisal of transport proposals involving land use changes (Neuburger, 1971a). He recognised the need to allow for traffic induced by road schemes some 25 years before this became a part of official appraisal procedures. Having an appraisal method able to tackle such issues is of course an essential element of implementing an integrated transport policy. His paper on the economics of heavily congested roads (Neuburger, 1971b) prefigures a hot debate on the nature of supply/demand relationships for urban roadspace (Evans, 1992; Hills and Evans, 1993). This seemingly arcane subject is in fact critical for the correct evaluation of pricing measures currently under review by government. More recently, Neuburger and Fraser (1993) attempted a more radical revision of the methods of economic appraisal to overcome what Neuburger came to see as totally unacceptable assumptions behind existing techniques.

In this chapter, we will trace the development of project appraisal techniques in transport in Great Britain from the early studies of the Victoria Line and the M1 motorway through to the 'new' appraisal methodology now in use. We will see that, although the trend has been towards seeing the economic appraisal as part of a wider multicriterion analysis, the need to tackle this with rigour has not diminished; indeed, arguably the scope for simple errors such as incompleteness or double counting has increased with the new approach. Finally we shall offer some views on the way forward for transport appraisal.

The development of transport appraisal techniques

The first applications of social CBA to transport projects in Britain were the studies of the Victoria Line (Foster and Beesley, 1963) and the M1 motorway (Coburn, Beesley and Reynolds, 1960). These studies were developmental rather than being a formal part of the decision-taking process, but they prepared the ground for the introduction of the use of CBA on a regular basis, first to the road system (Searle,1972) and then to public transport both in the case of rail closures (Ministry of Transport, 1969) and investment receiving government grants, for instance under Section 56 of the 1968 Transport Act (Department of Transport, 1989).

The key elements in these early appraisals were the capital, operating and maintenance costs of the transport system, travel time and accidents. These were forecast over the life of the project with and without the scheme, in the case of road schemes usually on a fixed demand matrix basis – that is, making the assumption that putting in the scheme would not lead to trips diverting between different destinations, changing modes or to totally new trips being induced. Quantification and valuation of the costs were relatively straightforward, but travel time and accidents raised more issues. The approach taken to the valuation of journey time was to seek evidence on the value people place on travel time savings from their choices in either real or hypothetical circumstances in which they faced alternatives that varied in cost and time. Having obtained such a valuation, the journey time could be valued in money terms and added to the money cost of a journey to obtain the 'generalised cost'. With respect to accidents, the initial approach was to examine all the impacts on Gross Domestic Product (GDP) of accidents, including via the loss of labour inputs from injury or death – this was valued by assuming that the gross wage equalled the value of the marginal product of labour. However, it was recognised that part of the cost of death or injury – the so-called 'warm blooded cost' of pain and suffering – was omitted by this procedure, and a politically determined element was added to represent these costs. Later, these were replaced by a valuation based on stated preference techniques examining choices involving varying degrees of risk.

In the early 1970s there was growing opposition to new road building, mainly on environmental grounds. The above approach to appraisal completely ignored environmental effects, at least in the formal appraisal; these were considered separately on a judgemental basis. Following a number of extremely contentious public inquiries, the government decided to set up an independent committee to consider the methods used in the appraisal of trunk roads. This was the Advisory Committee on Trunk Road Assessment (ACTRA), chaired by Sir George Leitch. It concluded (ACTRA, 1977) that the appraisal method in use was essentially sound, but unbalanced in terms of the attention it paid to costs and time savings relative to environmental issues. The report proposed that appraisals should be undertaken by means of a 'framework' approach; essentially a matrix of costs and benefits to different sectors affected by the scheme which owed much to the Planning Balance Sheet approach (Lichfield, 1968). The costs and benefits would be measured in money terms where possible, but for environmental and development effects they would be purely described in terms of physical measures or written descriptions. This framework approach became the forerunner of the methods still in use today. Moreover, ACTRA became SACTRA, the Standing Advisory Committee on Trunk Road Assessment, a body which also continues to play an important role in the development of appraisal methodology, as will be seen below.

Three key issues which remained contentious were all the subject of reviews by SACTRA in the 1990s. These were the degree to which it was possible to value environmental effects in money terms (SACTRA, 1992), the degree to which new road building generated traffic which otherwise would not have existed (SACTRA, 1994) and the degree to which transport investments generated economic growth (SACTRA, 1999). We will return to these below. But first we consider the analytical basis of CBA as applied to transport projects.

The analytical basis of transport appraisal

The basic approach taken to transport appraisal in Britain is that of social CBA. This has its roots in welfare economics, and presumes that the aim of government decision taking is the pursuit of economic efficiency. Therefore, the essential information required to decide whether a road investment or other transport project is justified is whether it passes the compensation test – that is to say whether the beneficiaries from the project are willing to pay enough for those benefits to fully compensate the losers and still be better off themselves. In general, it is assumed that market prices reflect the value of costs or benefits. But where goods are untraded, such as time savings or accident savings, recourse has to be made to revealed or stated preference surveys to discover the willingness to pay or to accept compensation.

There are numerous criticisms of this approach, and many of these were drawn together in Neuburger and Fraser (1993) (see also Chapter Four of this book by Neil Fraser). First and foremost is the assumption that the sole objective of transport projects is economic efficiency. This is seldom true of governments, or of the electorate from whom governments obtain their mandate. Thus the attempt to impose this as a sole objective may be seen as profoundly undemocratic. Indeed the mismatch between the appraisal system and the objectives of government has been an enduring feature of the transport sector. For much of the time that CBA has been the fundamental method of transport appraisal, governments have put forward a set of objectives for the transport system that is not necessarily consistent with the sole pursuit of economic efficiency. For instance, it has consistently seen the economic development effects of transport investments as important, even where the appraisal methodology has regarded these solely as transfers between locations and therefore to be ignored. More fundamentally, it may be argued that people have rights – to healthcare, education, a clean environment and so on – that should be pursued regardless of their willingness to pay for them, and that the democratic way of trading off these rights is through the ballot box rather than through the market.

A second key objection is with the proposition that market prices really do reflect willingness to pay or to accept compensation. In the case of outputs, market prices will only reflect willingness to pay if the attributes of the alternatives are properly perceived. This is a particular issue in transport, where a long strand of research suggests that people persistently underperceive the costs of private motoring. This means that the value to them of additional private trips will be overstated if it is based on what they actually pay for them (Neuburger, 1971c). That paper also reminds us that where transport policy has effects on the part of consumers' budgets which might be classified as 'overheads', for example the propensity to own cars, these overheads or ownership effects should be fully considered when evaluating the policy. For inputs, market prices will only reflect the cost of their use in the project if they are traded in perfectly competitive markets, and if the markets for the goods they could otherwise have been used to produce are also perfectly competitive. In that case, their market price will represent the opportunity cost of the goods foregone, in terms of the compensation that would be needed for society to be as well off without them.

A third problem relates to the measure of benefit to use when several prices change simultaneously. For instance, where public transport generalised cost is reduced, and as a consequence road congestion is reduced, the end point is one where there is lower generalised cost on both modes. If they are substitutes, then the demand curves for both modes will also shift. The same situation arises where there are alternative road routes, and reassignment of traffic leads to a change in the level of congestion on all of them. There is an ambiguity about the Marshallian measure of consumers' surplus in these circumstances, as its value will depend on the order in which the modes are examined. By contrast, the compensating variation measure of consumers surplus, which represents an exact measure of willingness to pay or to accept compensation, is invariant with the order in which the different goods are examined, but cannot be readily observed from market data. However, Foster and Neuburger (1974) show that in practice, in most circumstances, the difference between the measures will be small.

Fourth is the concern as to whether the range of costs and benefits examined is really too narrow. For instance, it has been stated above that road investment appraisals until recently typically took the approach of assuming the same pattern of trips with and without the project. This assumption misses both the benefits of extra trips and their costs in terms of effects on congestion, accidents and the environment. A related problem is how to measure benefits when transport projects actually lead to land use changes. For instance, suppose that construction of a new road attracts new development and consequently generates trips to it. Or alternatively suppose that the road scheme leads to people from the area relocating further away to avoid the environmental consequences of the road, or simply because of the reduced housing and employment in the district. A standard transport appraisal would suggest that these extra, or longer, journeys are a result of reduced transport costs, and thus represent benefits from generated trips. However, a full measure of benefits would take account of the changed attractiveness of the origins and destinations of the trips in question before and after the new road is built. Neuburger (1971a) shows formally how to derive such measures, but in practice the necessary models to do so are rarely developed and cruder measures which ignore resulting land use changes are usually applied. Moreover the land use changes will have broader environmental costs and benefits not associated with trip-making patterns which also need to be taken into account.

But the most widespread and longstanding criticism of this form of CBA relates to the problem of distribution. It is commonly argued that most individuals, and most governments, do not care solely about economic efficiency but also care about distribution. The traditional textbook response to this is to assume that governments can achieve their distributive aims through non-distorting taxes (essentially lump sum transfers) so that transport decisions may be taken on pure efficiency grounds. This is clearly not the case. Transport decisions do affect distribution by the way in which gains and losses are spread across the community.

The main UK response to this problem has been to replace willingness to pay values for time and safety in the evaluation of public roads with standard or equity values. So the values of non-working time used are not those of the particular recipients of the benefits – stockbrokers in Surrey, or call centre operatives in Leeds – but a single average value. This device is a remarkably robust survivor from the days of Barbara Castle's tenure at the MoT (Ministry of Transport) and is far better than nothing. It is however crude, and may lead to the government spending money to achieve time savings when the individuals concerned would prefer lower fares or other financial benefits.

Formally the most commonly advocated improvement to this is to conclude that the actual incidence of costs and benefits must therefore be traced, so that costs and benefits can be weighted in accordance with a social welfare function. The starting point of this process would still be to measure willingness to pay and willingness to accept compensation, but this would have to be for the ultimate recipients of benefits and costs (so, for instance, in the case of cost reductions in road haulage, it might be reasonable to assume that – in a competitive market – the ultimate recipients will be the consumers of the goods in question; for time savings to commuters, the ultimate recipient might be property owners). But these values would then need to be weighted, both to reflect differences in the marginal utility of income, and to reflect judgement as to the social value of additional utility to the group in question (the latter weights might therefore simply give extra weight to people on lower incomes, or might give extra weight to people disadvantaged in other ways, for instance through disability). It may be noted that anyone who rejects the notion of utility as a cardinal concept that is measurable on a comparable basis for different individuals will reject this approach. Moreover, even if the general approach is accepted, it remains the case that no convincing method of measuring differences in marginal utility has yet been devised, so the adjustment for differences in the marginal utility of income is a matter of judgement rather than scientific evidence.

In practice, the difficulties in obtaining agreed values for the weights in question might lead to an approach in which distribution is investigated but no explicit weight is given to it in the appraisal, this being left to the judgement of the decision taker. Transport appraisal has moved a degree in this direction, inasmuch as the framework approach has always distinguished between categories such as road-users, householders, those concerned with heritage and so on . But no thorough distributive analysis is normally taken into account, and certainly the ultimate incidence of costs and benefits is not investigated. Somewhat surprisingly the one situation in which successive governments have wished to be able to divide benefits according to incidence has been to be able to disregard benefits to public transport users. The context in which this has been the case is that of Section 56 grants for public transport investments under the 1968 Transport Act. The rules for these grants were that they were given solely in respect of benefits to groups other than public transport users, who were expected to pay for benefits through the farebox. The origins of this rule seem to be a wish to ensure that such grants do not distort market competition within the public transport sector, and that they are not dissipated in projects which encourage low fares rather than improvements in service. The rule was introduced in 1989 and survived until the guidance on local transport plans was issued in 2000 (DETR, 2000).

The overall weight of these and other arguments led Neuburger and Fraser to advocate replacement of CBA by a new approach, which they call 'democratic decision analysis' (see Chapter Four by Neil Fraser). Essentially they describe this as a cost effectiveness analysis (CEA) of measures to achieve politically determined objectives. Interestingly, the 'new approach' to transport appraisal certainly moves in this direction, as it has at its heart an analysis of the contribution of a project to achievement of the government's strategic objectives for transport. The degree to which it succeeds in this aim will be considered below. But first we discuss some technical issues in the appraisal process.

Key developments in transport appraisal

Following the creation of the Framework approach by the Leitch Committee, the state of the art of transport appraisal was static during much of the 1980s. But right at the end of that decade came a watershed year in which events combined to open up the appraisal scene once more. This in itself is a useful reminder that, much as technicians may dislike it, the appraisal regime operates within a policy context. Changes in the policy or political climate are the main drivers of change in the appraisal process.

What happened to create the need for change at the end of the 1980s? Essentially there were two sets of events with a linkage between them. The first of these was an enhanced concern with the environmental impacts of roads and transport. Before this time, environmental impacts were seen as essentially scheme-related issues to do with the local environment. But around 1989, a range of strategic issues came to the fore – some related to global warming and other strategic pollution effects, others which viewed loss of assets such as Twyford Down and the threat to Oxleas Wood in South-East London as of far more than local or regional significance. These issues struck a chord both within the establishment (see for example RCEP, 1994; 1997) and with counterculture activists with whom the name Swampy is indelibly associated.

The second set of events was rather paradoxically associated with the publication of two papers by the DoT, the National Road Traffic Forecasts, 1989 (NRTF) and *Roads for Prosperity*, a policy document announcing the largest road-building programme in history. The 1989 NRTF forecast traffic growth through to 2025 running at about 2-3% per annum compound, that is 83-142% over the period. It was soon apparent that a conjunction of environmental, social and financial processes made this a very difficult scenario to deal with. Particularly once the Lawson boom burst, it was pretty clear that the road programme envisaged in *Roads for Prosperity* was simply undeliverable. 'Predict and provide', if it had ever existed, was dead[1]. But this left a big problem in appraisal terms. With the new road traffic forecasts, scheme appraisals were more often running up against problems of capacity, so that the fixed matrix assumption that traffic volumes would be the same with and without new capacity enhancing schemes was becoming less credible. A report for the Department from that time found that,

> ... of the schemes that have been reappraised in the light of NRTF 1989, almost one third are experiencing serious capacity problems in the 'Do-Minimum'. It is not merely the case that the forecast growth would lead to a certain amount of congestion which might need to be taken account of in the assessment process; rather it is often infeasible for the 'Do-Minimum' to accommodate the predicted growth of traffic, in some cases even in the off-peak. The presence of a significant number of schemes where the existing methodology is inappropriate, without modification, means that the option of ignoring congestion in interurban appraisal is unsustainable (MVA/ITS, 1990).

So the question of the treatment of induced traffic in scheme appraisal, considered by Neuburger (1971a), was back on the agenda.

Against that background, we comment briefly on developments in appraisal in relation to three specific areas before assessing overall progress.

Environment

It is probably fair to say that at the policy level, considerable progress has been made towards integrating consideration of environmental impacts fully within the appraisal process. Only ten years ago, Twyford Down was destroyed by the M3 project at Winchester. Today, much of the Channel Tunnel Rail Link is in tunnel, and the chosen option for the Stonehenge road scheme is also a relatively expensive tunnel. Though we have not moved all the way to a set of non-tradable rights to environmental assets, in practice, social valuation of these assets has risen substantially and their weight in the appraisal process is correspondingly greater.

At the technical level, there is much work still to do. Progress toward monetary valuation of environmental impacts has been relatively slow. The 1992 SACTRA report concluded that some environmental impacts including the loss of unique or sacrosanct assets could not sensibly be monetised. But that still leaves the noise, pollution and land-take impacts which are typical of most schemes. Here, SACTRA supported money valuation as an aid to consistency in decision taking. It does seem peculiar that we have been willing for many years to place money values on changes in safety risk, but not on changes in noise or pollution. Given how much the safety values and even their underlying rationale have changed over time, it does seem that different standards are applied to the two sets of impacts.

Induced traffic

In this field, there has been significant progress. The Department gave SACTRA the remit of advising on,

> the evidence of the circumstances, nature and magnitude of traffic redistribution, mode choice and generation [resulting from new road schemes] especially on inter-urban roads and trunk roads close to conurbations; and to recommend whether and how the Department's methods should be amended and what, if any research or studies could be undertaken.

SACTRA's 1994 report reached three main conclusions:

(1) that induced traffic can and does occur, probably quite extensively, though its size and significance is likely to vary widely in different circumstances;
(2) that induced traffic matters; there are circumstances where induced traffic can seriously affect the economic value of road schemes;
(3) that induced traffic is of greater significance where the network is operating close to capacity and/or the elasticity of demand with respect to travel costs is high and/or where the implementation of a scheme causes large changes in travel costs.

It is worth noting a couple of points, since SACTRA's report has sometimes been misinterpreted subsequently. SACTRA did not say that induced traffic automatically reduces the benefits of road schemes; it noted cases where induced traffic adds to the benefits, as had been the conventional wisdom. Still less did the SACTRA report say that road building makes congestion worse or is automatically self defeating. In general, induced traffic will only occur as a consequence of new capacity making conditions better. Although cases can be cited in which the final equilibrium is worse than the initial position (Mogridge et al, 1987), such cases relate to capacity improvements to radial routes in big cities where public transport has a large market share and significant mode switching may occur. This line of thought has proved useful in developing the case for road space reallocation within cities, but is probably not relevant to inter-urban roads. For the general run of trunk road schemes, the questions are 'how much induced traffic is likely to occur' and 'how much will it modify the fixed demand benefits upward or downward'? This is exactly the same question as the difference between Method 1 and Method 2 of Neuburger (1971a).

SACTRA drew two main recommendations from its findings. The first was that variable demand methods, that is, methods which allow the level and pattern of traffic to vary with the quality of the road network, should become the standard appraisal tool for trunk road schemes. In other words, we should at last move from Method 1 as the standard to Method 2. The Department accepted this recommendation and has provided guidance on how to incorporate induced traffic within the overall appraisal (DETR, 1994, 1996).

The other recommendation for strategic area-wide appraisal, was in a way even more far-reaching. The government's approach to road planning was essentially at two levels. At national level, forecasts of economic growth, population and car ownership were made and fed into the National Road Traffic Forecasts. These forecasts then fed scheme appraisal at local level. SACTRA felt that neither the national level nor the scheme level was really the appropriate unit for economic appraisal of road investment, for various reasons. Individual schemes are often elements in wider plans or strategies. Environmental and land development consequences of schemes need to be considered at area-wide level particularly if there are knock-on effects elsewhere in the corridor. Induced traffic is likely to be a function of network service quality; the scheme level with a tightly drawn study area is too small a unit at which to represent this adequately. Lastly the economic development consequences of road investment cannot sensibly be considered at scheme level.

Although the Department's response to SACTRA on this was initially cautious, in practice, policy has now gone very much in this direction. Following the White Paper and the Roads Review, a series of corridor and area-wide studies has been launched, many of them multimodal. Without in any way underrating the practical difficulties of doing strategic rather than scheme appraisal, this is in principle the right level at which to consider the complex interactions between transport policy, the economy and the environment. At the political level this has links too with the incipient regional government institutions.

Transport and the economy

A major problem area for the social appraisal of transport projects is the interrelationship between transport performance and final economic performance. On the one hand, technical appraisal has focused on the direct impacts of projects, on the basis that these are capable of measurement and provide reasonable proxy indicators of the final economic impacts. On the other hand, political assessment of infrastructure projects regards the likely effects on competitiveness and economic regeneration as extremely important for two reasons. First, there is the possibility that when the transport benefits are transmitted through market processes into final economic benefits, their magnitude changes – there is the possibility of wider economic impact additional to the direct transport and environmental impacts. Second, there is the point that distributive impacts may be important – do the final impacts occur to target areas, such as regeneration areas, or to relevant economic groups such as consumers, producers, travellers or landowners or to relevant social groups such as the unemployed? A standard transport CBA does not deal with any of these issues.

The difficulties of assessing wider and economic impact do not lie essentially at the conceptual level. Neuburger (1971a) and Williams (1977) have shown that the principles of transport-user benefit analysis could be extended to the comprehensive evaluation of transport, land use and economic changes. The main problems are with estimating the strength of the interactions between transport, land use and economic development.

In its report included in SACTRA (1999), David Simmonds Consultancy lists six requirements which need to be satisfied before benefits can be computed from land-use/transport interaction models:

(1) the model should contain an appropriate representation of behavioural response in the land-use and transport sectors;
(2) it should adopt an adequate level of segmentation;
(3) the strength/elasticity of each behavioural response should be calibrated;
(4) the model should respond to money and to non-money impacts such as time;
(5) the model should link together the full set of behavioural responses in a way that reflects their real world interrelatedness; and
(6) the responses should be represented in incremental form starting from the base situation.

This is a hugely demanding research agenda, but one where insights from new economic geography and spatial computable general equilibrium models (for example Venables and Gasiorek, 1999) have much to contribute at the strategic level. For the appraisal of all but the very largest schemes such as Crossrail or the Channel Tunnel, however, a full multisectoral CBA approach is not justified. Improved qualitative assessment of the wider economic impacts to complement the assessment of the direct transport and environmental impacts is the way forward at scheme level.

The new appraisal methodology

In the previous section, we reviewed progress in three individual elements of appraisal. In this section, we consider how the appraisal process as a whole has developed. Along with its comprehensive review of transport policy, culminating in the White Paper (DETR, 1998c) the new Labour government determined to revise the approach to transport appraisal first in respect of road schemes, but ultimately for multimodal appraisals and local transport plans too. It is part of the implementation of an integrated transport policy covering all modes of travel and also integrating transport policy with policy on land use, health, education and so on. Thus the policy towards urban regeneration, aimed at concentrating new housing on brownfield land, and raising densities, is an essential element of the policy to reduce transport demand and thus emissions (see also the chapter by Jenny Neuburger). The new approach to appraisal (DETR, 1998a, 1998b; Price, 1999; Glaister, 1999) is a progressive development rather than a revolutionary change. Several features are worth mentioning.

The new approach (NATA) links appraisal information more explicitly than previously to the government's stated criteria – contributions to environment, safety, the economy, accessibility and integration. The first three of these had always been there; elements of the last two would have been presented within the Leitch Framework, but are now given enhanced attention. Compared with COBA and the Framework, we have now moved to an objectives-related approach, but not to an objectives-led approach.

The new approach also brings in new subcriteria which were not previously always included in the assessment. For example, within the environment section, the effect of run-off on water pollution is now a serious concern and is included in the assessment. Under economy, the first steps are being taken towards modelling the effects of schemes on journey time reliability, recognising that impacts on the variance of travel times as well as impacts on the mean can be important. Also included is a very simple economic regeneration indicator – whether or not the road serves a regeneration area. This is unsatisfactory on several grounds, not least that it risks significant double counting with the journey time benefits but as discussed in the previous section, developing a usable set of indicators or measures with which to replace it will take some time.

The greatest advance made within the new approach is presentational. The weakness of the Framework approach was that the Framework document became unwieldy, including every individual impact in each dimension. It therefore became an exhaustive compendium which was very difficult for the Public Inquiry Inspector to use to weigh the scheme in the balance. The 1992 SACTRA report had called for the introduction of an Assessment Summary Report which would be a summary table plus an executive summary of the scheme impacts and performance. The NATA provides the summary table for each scheme on a single sheet of A4. Moreover it does so on a consistent basis; standard indicators are used which show the impacts of schemes in terms of their contribution towards the criteria and subcriteria. As with the Leitch Framework, these indicators are a mixture of money values, physical measures and verbal descriptions. However, whereas the old framework data were simply presented in their natural form, under the new approach the verbal descriptions are also converted into a set of numerical scores on a seven point scale showing the scale of the contribution of the project under each criterion and whether it is positive or negative.

There is currently no official procedure for aggregating the scores under the various criteria. So there is no explicit trade-off between performance under the various objectives of government policy. This is surprising given that the most difficult part of achieving such a trade-off has already been achieved in the scoring process.

Possibly the newest part of the new approach is the way in which the appraisal summary tables (AST) are to be used. For all trunk road schemes, major local transport plan schemes, and schemes developed within the multimodal studies, ASTs will be drawn up which enable the absolute performance of schemes to be examined and compared. The first exercise within which this was done was the 1998 Roads Review, under which the ASTs for sixty-eight trunk road schemes were made public, together with the Minister's decisions on whether to accept the schemes, refer them for further consideration, or reject them. This is a considerable step towards openness in what had always been regarded as a sensitive political area.

The publication of the 68 ASTs (DETR, 1998b) presents an opportunity to try to infer the values or weights placed by Ministers on scheme performance in the dimensions represented by the subcriteria. This is not the same as assigning values based on behavioural evidence for values of noise or pollution – they are political values, not economic values. But it might be argued that in some areas of the appraisal, particularly for impacts such as landscape, biodiversity and heritage, political values are the relevant index of social values anyway.

A recent paper finds a reasonable explanatory model for the decisions taken by Ministers in the 1998 Road Review, with significant coefficients on noise, landscape heritage, safety, journey time, cost, reliability and regeneration (Nellthorp and Mackie, 2000). The model correctly replicates 50 of the 68 decisions and also gets right the decision to accept the tunnel option rather than any of the other three options at Stonehenge. The implicit values per point on the seven point scales, with quite wide confidence intervals, are for landscape £18 million of present value, heritage £12 million, reliability £29 million and regeneration £41 million. Although this is a small-scale study on a limited data set, the results are sufficiently encouraging to imagine that advances from the position we have been stuck in since the 1960s, with monetary values for time, safety and cost, and no money or other explicit weight for the other impacts, may not be too far off.

Conclusions

Relative to the state of the art 30 years ago, there have been some significant advances in appraisal practice. They have come through developments such as the Framework, the improved treatment of induced traffic, and much more attention to environmental impacts. The synthesis within the NATA is itself a step forward. Indeed the last few years have probably been the most positive for serious transport appraisal for many years.

Beyond the details of appraisal practice a more fundamental shift has occurred. In the 1960s, the language and culture was engineering dominated. The discussion was all about questions of providing for growth, and economic appraisal was sometimes seen as a rather unfortunate necessity to convince the Treasury. Now, a form of appraisal which incorporates transport, environmental and economic impacts is at the heart not just of investment decisions, but also broader transport policy making. The new framework is to be applied systematically to all modes of transport through strategic multimodal studies as well as at the individual project level. It incorporates monetary and non-monetary measures of performance relative to politically determined objectives; these measures are systematically combined into scores which feed into a judgement on whether the scheme should go ahead. This has facilitated the start of the sort of dialogue between decision takers and analysts foreseen by Neuburger and Fraser, in which the weights implied by their initial decisions are being fed back to decision takers for future information. In total, this represents a significant shift away from traditional CBA towards the sort of democratic decision analysis advocated by Neuburger and Fraser.

However, there is still a big agenda ahead of us. There is still no clear rationale regarding what is and is not valued in money terms within the appraisal. There is still no adequate treatment of distributive impacts. Reducing social exclusion is an explicit goal of transport policy but it is far from clear how impacts of transport decisions on improving or worsening social exclusion are to be measured and valued. Treatment of risk and uncertainty remains very limited. Good quality appraisal in a multimodal, multi-agency, cross-sectoral world continues to present many challenges for modelling, forecasting, evaluation, presentation and decision making.

Note

[1] A similar change in housing provision took a little longer; see Jenny Neuburger's chapter.

References

ACTRA (Advisory Committee on Trunk Road Assessment) (1977) *Report*, London, HMSO.

Coburn, T.M., Beesley, M.E. and Reynolds, D. J. (1960) *The London–Birmingham motorway*, Road Research Technical Paper 46, London: HMSO.

DETR (Department of the Environment, Transport and the Regions) (1994, 1996) *Guidance on induced traffic. Design manual for roads and bridges*, vol 12, section 2, part 2, London: HMSO.

DETR (1998a) *Guidance on the new approach to appraisal*, London: HMSO.

DETR (1998b) *Understanding the new approach to appraisal*, London: HMSO.

DETR (1998c) *A new deal for transport: better for everyone. The government's White Paper on the future of transport*, Cm 3950, London HMSO.

DETR (2000) *Guidance on full local transport plans*, London, DETR.

DoT (Department of Transport) (1989) *Section 56 grant for public transport*, Circular 3/89, London: DoT.

Evans, A.W. (1992) 'Road congestion pricing: when is it a good policy?', *Journal of Transport Economics and Policy*, vol 26, no 3, pp 213-43.

Foster, C.D. and Beesley, M.E. (1963) 'Estimating the benefits of constructing an underground railway in London', *Journal of the Royal Statistical Society*, Series A, vol 126, no 1, pp 46-58.

Foster, C.D. and Neuburger, H. (1974) 'The ambiguity of the consumer surplus measure of welfare change', *Oxford Economic Papers*, vol 26, no 1, pp 66-77.

Glaister, S. (1999) 'Observations on the new approach to the appraisal of road projects', *Journal of Transport Economics and Policy*, vol 33, no 2, pp 227–34.

Hills, P.J. and Evans, A.W. (1993) 'Road congestion pricing: when is it a good policy? Comment and rejoinder', *Journal of Transport Economics and Policy*, vol 27, no 1, pp 91-105.

Lichfield, N. (1968) 'Economics in town planning: a basis for decision making', *Town Planning Review*, vol 39, no 1, pp 5-20.

Ministry of Transport (1969) *The Cambrian coast line*, London: HMSO.

Mogridge, M., Holden, D., Bird, J. and Terzis, G.C. (1987) 'The Downs/Thomson paradox and the transportation planning process', *International Journal of Transport Economics*, vol 14, no 3, pp 283-311.

MVA Consultancy and ITS Leeds (1990) 'Modelling the effects of congestion on interurban highway networks', Unpublished report to Transport and Roads Research Laboratory.

Nellthorp, J. and Mackie, P.J. (2000) 'The UK roads review – A hedonic model of decision making', *Transport Policy*, vol 7, no 2, pp 127-38.

Neuburger, H. (1971a) 'User benefit in the evaluation of transport and land use plans', *Journal of Transport Economics and Policy*, vol 5, no 1, pp 52-75.

Neuburger, H. (1971b) 'The economics of heavily congested roads', *Transportation Research*, vol 5, no 4, pp 283-94.

Neuburger, H. (1971c) 'Perceived costs', *Environment and Planning*, vol 3, no 4, pp 369-76.

Neuburger, H. and Fraser, N. (1993) *Economic policy analysis: A rights-based approach*, Aldershot: Avebury.

Price, A. (1999) 'A new approach to the appraisal of road projects in England', *Journal of Transport Economic and Policy*, vol 33, no 2, pp 221-26.

RCEP (Royal Commission on Environmental Pollution) (1994) *Transport and the environment*, Eighteenth Report, London: HMSO.

RCEP (1997) *Transport and the Environment – Development since 1994*, Twentieth Report, London: HMSO.

SACTRA (Standing Advisory Committee on Trunk Road Assessment) (1992) *Assessing the environmental impact of road schemes*, London: HMSO.

SACTRA (1994) *Trunk roads and the generation of traffic*, London: HMSO.

SACTRA (1999) *Transport and the economy*, London: HMSO.

Searle, G.A.C. (1972) 'COBA: a computer programme for the economic assessment of road schemes', *Traffic Engineering and Control*, vol 14, no 8, pp 376-81.

Venables, A.J. and Gasiorek, M. (1999) *The welfare implications of transport improvements in the presence of market failure*, Report to SACTRA, London: HMSO.

Williams, H.C.W.L. (1977) 'On the formation of travel demand models and economic evaluation measures of user benefit', *Environment and Planning*, vol 9, no 3, pp 285-344.

TWELVE

Housing and urban renaissance

Jenny Neuburger[1]

Introduction

When he joined the DETR in 1997, Henry Neuburger was drawn into the debate on the household projections, housing density and Urban Renaissance (although he was officially working on construction statistics). With characteristic enthusiasm, he immediately questioned the basic assumptions and parameters of the debate. What is meant by density? What is the goal of an urban renaissance? Who benefits? What is the relationship between households and houses? He rejected the limits of the greenfield versus brownfield approach, widening the debate to look at the distribution of the existing housing stock and to question the basis on which household projections are used to forecast future housing requirements. I have used his short writings, statistical analyses and lively discussions on this subject to present and expand the issues he raised.

How can we balance the demand for more housing against the desire to improve our cities and preserve our countryside? It is predicted by the DETR that 3.8 million additional households will form in England between 1996 and 2021, if past rates of population growth and household formation continue. Over the past 20 years, English cities have continued to depopulate, London being the exception, and low-density suburban development has continued to increase. The government's Urban Task Force, set up to investigate the solutions to urban decline, suggests that housing requirements can be met and more sustainable patterns of growth can be achieved through recycling urban land and building houses at higher densities. Economists counter that restricting greenfield development will push up house prices, thus preventing migration and reducing affordability in areas of economic growth. Missing from this debate has been a distinction between a demographically based measure of housing requirement or need and an economist's concept of housing demand.

The purpose of this chapter is to provide pointers to a framework modelling the trade-offs between: meeting housing needs (defined to a socially agreed standard); the market demand for housing; environmental and economic objectives. First, it provides a brief guide to the current debate over the location and density of housing development. Second, it gives an overview of the use and distribution of the existing stock. This gives an indication of the potential capacity of the existing stock to absorb new households. Next, it highlights the problems with the 'predict and provide' approach, which has characterised housing policy in the past. It questions the current use of the household projections in planning for housing. Finally, it suggests policies that would lead to a more efficient, equitable and environmentally sustainable use of our land and housing.

The current debate: are higher densities the answer?

The government's Urban Task Force (UTF) proposes the re-densification of our towns and cities as a way to accommodate future households in a more environmentally sustainable way. First, it emphasises recycling of urban land and suggests ways in which the government's target of 60% of new housing to be built on previously used land by 2008 can be met. Its key contribution is the construction of a National Land Use Database (NLUD) providing information on available vacant and derelict brownfield land in England. The evidence from the NLUD suggests that one third of derelict land, about 5,600 hectares, could be suitable for housing, producing about 164,000 new dwellings. Together with vacant land and the use and conversion of empty buildings, it suggests that, at a density of around 30 dwellings per hectare, around 1.8 million additional dwellings would be possible (UTF, 1999, pp 180-7). It proposes a mixture of planning regulation, tax breaks and other financial incentives to encourage brownfield development. Second, it suggests that densities for new housing should be increased from current average national levels of 25 dwellings per hectare to around 50-70 dwellings per hectare (UTF, 1999, pp 57-60). It emphasises the fact that 70% of projected new households consist of single people living alone. It suggests that the housing needs of these smaller households can be met through smaller homes and higher density forms of development. Further, it emphasises the costs of depopulation and benefits of higher densities in cities, generating demand for goods and services. It argues that this requires initial investment in public transport, infrastructure and other services in order to make urban living an attractive and viable choice.

Some economists and housing groups such as Shelter have questioned whether this vision of urban living is feasible in reality and what the effects of implementing some of the proposals would be (Holmans et al, 1998; Kleinman et al, 1999; Shelter National Inquiry, 1999). They point out that household behaviour is continuing to produce overall trends and patterns of settlement in the wrong direction. Further, they highlight the undesirable economic and social effects of restricting these trends. First, they argue that holding back greenfield land, through the planning system, in order to achieve a recycling rate of 60% would push up land and house prices, particularly in areas of high demand. For example, analysis has shown that planning constraints on land supply contributed to house price increases in Cambridgeshire and Herefordshire in the period 1981-91 (Monk et al, 1995). They argue that large amounts of brownfield land are unsuitable for housing or are in the wrong location in relation to jobs and services, for example, larger brownfield sites in Kent (Whitehead et al, 1999). They also suggest that the effect of planning restrictions would be to prevent migration into areas of jobs growth and to reduce affordability, causing labour shortages and hardship, particularly for lower income groups (Whitehead et al, 1999). Second, they point out that the trend toward lower density living is a natural effect of people's preference for privacy and space, made effective by growing household incomes. The 'young, professional' niche market is limited and single-person households on average take up more than five times more space per person than households containing six or more people, not less (Shelter National Inquiry, 1999; DETR, 1998, pp 29-30). They argue that pushing up densities, either through planning permissions or as a side effect of reducing land releases, would be difficult in practice and that "the only people who end up living in high density urban developments may be those who have little or no choice" (Shelter National Inquiry, 1999, p 39).

The use and distribution of the existing stock: what kind of density do we care about?

The issue of who is demanding (and getting) more housing has been somewhat sidelined within this debate. An analysis of the use and distribution of the existing dwelling stock provides some important insights into the allocation of housing in the past and the potential to meet housing needs in the future. It is important to be clear on which densities we care about in relation to re-densifying our cities and making more efficient use of our land and housing stock. The relationship between land and physical structure (planning density) is not the same thing as the density at which people occupy dwellings (household density), which is different again from the ratio of people to land (population density). These different types of density are related, but depend on a number of different factors. For example, although the UTF's model for urban living, Georgian terraces, have a relatively high number of dwellings and rooms to the hectare, in areas where only one or two wealthy people occupy each house, population density remains low.

Evidence from Census housing volumes and the English House Condition Survey suggests that the way in which households occupy structures is an important factor in relation to density. Nearly all households have more bedrooms than, according to the official bedroom standard, they need. In 1996, only 450,000 (2.3%) were below the bedroom standard, while 6.3 million (32%) had two surplus bedrooms (DETR, 1998, p 31)[2].

Overcrowding is a limited problem in England today. However, a minority of households in the social and private rented sector still live in overcrowded conditions. The greatest levels of overcrowding exist in the social sector, around 4%. Over 14% of households from ethnic minorities live in overcrowded conditions (DETR, 1998, p 31). In the private sector, overcrowding represents a mismatch between the housing that people need and the housing that they can afford. Despite an overall increase in floor space per person between 1991 and 1996, there has been a decline in space standards within the private rented sector. The numbers of private tenants below bedroom standard have increased significantly (from 2.1%) to levels nearer to the social sector (DETR, 1998, p 31).

Underoccupation is far more common, reflecting wealth and history. First, housing demand is income-elastic with respect to space, that is, as people get richer they occupy bigger houses. It is closely related to tenure: around 40% of owner-occupiers have two or more surplus bedrooms, compared to less than 17% of local authority tenants. In 1996, some 760,000 households reported that they had a second home. Second, elderly households tend to underoccupy as partners die and children leave home. In 1996, there were 2.8 million older households (where the nominal head is aged 60 years or more) comprising lone persons or couples living in homes with three or more bedrooms (DETR, 1998, pp 31-3).

Population and household densities are significant in a regional and urban/rural context. The overall population density of England is one of the highest in Europe, with 3.6 residents per hectare, but there is significant regional variation and urban densities are generally low. Population density in inner London is 78.1 residents per hectare, compared to 34.9 in Manchester and 23.2 in Newcastle (Power and Mumford, 1999, p 9). In 1996, 798,000 dwellings were vacant, an increase of 159,000 since 1991. Half of these were classified as 'problematic vacants', as opposed to 'transactional vacants', representing a housing resource that was not being utilised (DETR, 1998, ages 30-4)[3]. Over 230,000 homes in England have been empty for more than a year (Shelter National Inquiry, 1999, p 12). These are mainly concentrated in areas of some northern cities. In Leeds, where demand is high overall, the level of voids in council housing increased by 75% between 1996 and 1999. Manchester reported that 12 out of 23 housing areas had "significant demand problems' (Keenan, 1999, p 709). In contrast, there is a desperate shortage of council properties in most London boroughs. Significantly, a study of four neighbourhoods in Manchester and Newcastle found that the quality of most housing in the areas is 'good' or 'excellent' (Power and Mumford, 1999). Despite this, no one wants to live in these areas and large numbers of homes are being demolished.

Clearly, the problem lies beyond immediate housing quality and affordability issues. The major cause of low demand has been chronic job losses in manufacturing. A study of 90 authorities with a housing surplus showed that in 60 of these areas, the rate of jobs growth was below the national average, while 51 had experienced a net loss of jobs between 1981 and 1995 (Bramley, 1996). In some areas, the loss of jobs has created a spiral of decline, with cumulative problems of depopulation, falling property values, services closing down, deprivation and rising crime (Power and Mumford, 1999, p 100).

In rural areas, the housing problems related to density are different again, with underoccupation of commuter, second and holiday homes combined with a shortage of affordable housing to meet local needs. Underoccupation, particularly by richer households, also means a lack of demand for local services and public transport, making rural poverty and homelessness a more isolating and less visible problem.

The above analysis suggests that as well as the proposed emphasis on brownfield sites and building new housing at higher densities, there should also be measures to encourage more effective use of the existing and future housing stock. In an unpublished note on this, Henry wrote,

Figure 12.1: Average number of rooms per person by household size 1981-91

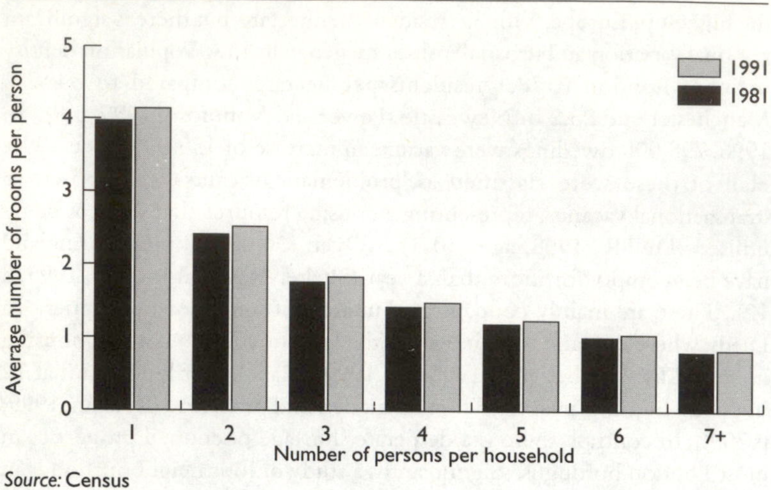

Source: Census

"Reviving towns means more than building on old gasworks; it means having more people living civilised lives in what are at present abandoned, under-occupied or neglected residential areas".

Plan, monitor and manage: An end to predict and provide?

The problems of the 'predict and provide' approach to housing provision are illustrated by the experience of the last 20 years. Between the census years of 1981 and 1991 there was an increase of just over 2 million households. There were about 2 million houses built; so it looked as if the sums added up. But if we look at what happened to people, a different story emerges. Census housing volumes contain a table showing the number of people in a household and the number of rooms they occupy. In an unpublished note, Henry analysed the statistical data to show trends in the distribution of housing (see Figure 12.1).

In both 1981 and 1991, the population divided roughly into half; with the half in smaller households having two thirds of the rooms and the other half having one third. As the figure shows, between 1981 and 1991 the number of rooms per household increased for all household sizes, but the gains were largest for the small households. For instance, one and two person households – 49% of the 1991 population – together benefited from 56% of the gain in rooms per person[4]. Those in households of five or more persons – 17% of the 1991 population – together benefited from only 9% of the gain in rooms per person. During the 1970s when there was a larger social element to housing there was also an imbalance of this kind but it had been less pronounced with for instance the quarter of the population in the largest, most crowded households benefiting from 20% of the gains in numbers of rooms for different household sizes (calculated from Census Housing Volumes, 1981 and 1991).

The 1996 English House Condition Survey shows that the trend continued into the 1990s, with small falls in the number of households below the official bedroom standard, while there was a sharp increase in the number of households with two or more bedrooms above standard (DETR, 1998, p 31).

The government has announced a change from a 'predict and provide' approach to a system of 'plan, monitor and manage' (DETR, 2000a)[5]. The Deputy Prime Minister, John Prescott, announced that 43,000 additional dwellings per year should be built in the South East and 23,000 per year in London, rather than announcing a figure for the next 20 years. However, sceptics have pointed out that the South East figure (if it is not monitored and managed) adds up to an additional 860,000 dwellings over 20 years, lower than the Crow report recommendation[6], but higher than the SERPLAN (the local authorities of the South East) figure. The figure for London would mean a 22% increase on the current rate of building. In this sense, the role of the household projections in determining housing and land requirements has not been fundamentally questioned.

Household projections are trend-based predictions of the future increase in the number of households produced by the Department of the Environment (DoE) (now DETR). They are based on two key sets of variables: population growth, dependent on the estimated rate of births, deaths and internal and international migration, and headship rates which chart trends in household size, formation and break-up. The starting point is the population projection. This figure is disaggregated by age, gender and marital/cohabitation status. Within each category, household membership rates are projected from historical data derived from Censuses and Labour Force Survey data[7]. The subnational projections are adjusted to be consistent using a process referred to as 'regional controlling'. Present projections show an increase in the number of smaller and single-person households; household growth reflecting people rearranging the way they live in houses, rather than more people, *per se*. In 1996, the DoE recognised that the projections "cannot be regarded as precise predictions for future years and the sources of uncertainty have to be borne in mind … including international migration, economic and policy changes…" (DoE, 1996). However, this qualifying statement does not recognise the fundamental problems in the way in which the projections are used. They are treated as if they were an exogenous variable, rather than an extrapolation of past trends.

Planning is the way in which government influences the amount, location, density and type of housing that is built, in contrast with a free market situation. Ideally, it provides a "democratic interface for reconciling different interests in land use" (UTF, 1999, p 191) and a way of promoting the collective interests of society, such as environmental protection. The government's Planning Policy Guidance for Housing states that local planning authorities should "plan to meet the housing requirements of the whole community … provide sufficient housing land … create more sustainable patterns of development and make more efficient use of land" (DETR, 2000a). The planning system regulates development through the release of land for housing and through permitted building densities. However, at present, the household projections are used as a basis for land designations for housing. This means that, rather than steering the housing market, the planning system is enabling past patterns of household formation and demand to continue. There would be no problem with this approach if there were not a limit on the supply of land, with environmental costs, other externalities attached to its use and also costs attached to unbalanced regional economic growth. However, there are negative impacts upon the environment, in terms of increased congestion, destruction of the countryside, on the quality of life of existing residents (as they keep on telling us) and on areas that are allowed to depopulate as a consequence. Since these externalities exist, there is a strong case for planning. There are three main problems with the current method.

First, the projections do not distinguish between the housing needs of a growing, changing and ageing population with reference to some socially agreed standard and the market-expressed demand for housing, linked to income growth. Housing need refers to people's basic housing requirements, regardless of their ability to pay market rents or prices. In practice, the calculation of need depends upon fitness standards and upon political decisions about who is entitled to housing (Holmans, 1995). It does not mean forcing households to share. It includes the needs of families that have split up or adult children living at home. However, through agreeing a basic standard, the social goal of an adequately housed population can be prioritised over meeting the demand for extra housing.

Housing demand refers to the quantity of housing that people are able and willing to buy at market prices, including their demand for luxury attributes such as spare bedrooms, large gardens and second homes. Also, for people working from home, it includes the demand for a study or working area, although if patterns of living and work change dramatically in the future, it could be classified as a housing need at some point. More significantly in the UK, where 68% of households own their homes, it includes the demand for housing as a financial investment. This is a particularly tricky area since, on one side, this demand reflects financial speculation on the property market, while on the other, it is for a degree of security against future increases in house prices and rents.

In practice, particularly in areas of high demand, the indiscriminate release of land for housing based on the household projections has resulted in the development of high cost housing for commuters and wealthy retired households, rather than low cost housing for local residents (Goodchild, 1997, p 265). In Hertfordshire, it was reported that

> district councils in the county have all overshot their initial targets for house building by an average of 33 per cent … yet we are still a long way from meeting the local needs requirement. Because the land has been used up for private house building, this gives the anomaly of too much housing, but not enough to meet needs. (Shelter National Inquiry, 1999, p 6)

A second, related issue is that there is a circular relationship between planned provision for housing and the number of households that actually form or locate in particular areas. Bramley has produced a model that shows that the supply of land for housing significantly impacts on the rate of household formation at a local and regional level through patterns of internal migration (Bramley and Watkins, 1996, p 53). Where extra land is released for housing, this will tend to pull in extra households. This suggests that new building on greenfield sites may "cut against inner-city regeneration where there are problems of over-supply" (Keenan, 1999, p 704). For example, Newcastle City Council has recently released more greenfield land for housing while inner city areas, particularly in the West End of town remain depressed with large amounts of empty housing (Shelter National Inquiry, 1999, p 11).

Third, using household projections to determine total dwelling requirements leaves no room to plan for the use and distribution of the stock. The outcomes of 'predict and provide' indicate a circular relationship between the release of land for housing and the demand for more space. A useful analogy can be drawn with the roads debate of the 1960s and 1970s. People then argued that growth in car ownership implied a massive building programme. However, others argued that the construction of more roads would merely result in more people using cars and taking more and longer car trips, rather than reducing congestion (see Christopher Nash and Peter Mackie's chapter). Holmans contends that this is a false analogy with respect to housing, since the households will simply be forced to share if supply is limited. However, given that people tend to occupy bigger homes as they get richer, this analogy is useful with respect to the demand for the luxury attributes of housing, particularly space and to housing as an investment. This would suggest that under the present system "large land releases are ... an ineffective and environmentally damaging way of meeting housing need" (JRF, 1994, p 7).

So, rejecting 'predict and provide' means adopting a housing and planning policy that identifies the needs of people in dwellings, rather than focusing on total dwellings built. It is not about preventing people from being allowed more space or more bedrooms than the bedroom standard, but it does mean prioritising basic housing need. Further, it means balancing the market-expressed demand for more housing against the needs of the environment, the economy and the desire of people to preserve the countryside. The evidence of the last 20 years suggests that the link between the household projections and land designation for housing is less clear than people think. It is not simply a case of projections being proved right or of requirements being fulfilled, but of the planning system following the market and producing housing outcomes that are inequitable, inefficient and environmentally unsustainable.

Policy implications

Fiscal and policy measures could usefully be used to promote a more equal distribution and effective use of the existing stock. Annual new building comprises less than 1% of the total housing stock. This suggests that affordable housing need for the overcrowded and housing poor should be addressed directly by making more of the existing stock fit and available through a range of administrative and financial instruments. This includes tackling the £19 billion repair and modernisation backlog in social housing announced in the government's Housing Green Paper (DETR,

2000b). Acquisition of vacant private properties by local authorities, as well as investment in Low Cost Home Ownership and new affordable rented housing is vital.

Addressing underoccupation is difficult to do, since the aim is to limit the use of extra space and the wealth aspects of housing, not to reduce security for households or to punish lower income or elderly households for living in areas where house prices are going up. Positive measures and incentives directed at 'unhappy underoccupiers', particularly elderly households where single living is not a matter of direct choice, could include moving grants, national 'care and repair' schemes currently run by some local authorities, monitored schemes and financial incentives to encourage secure and comfortable ways of sharing accommodation or taking in lodgers, and initiatives to identify alternative homes.

More radically, it would imply reform of Britain's system of property taxation. John Hills and Holly Sutherland analysed the structure and distributional effects of the Council Tax, which replaced the Community Charge (poll tax) in 1991. They argued that it was not mainly a property tax, but a hybrid: "part household tax, part poll tax, part property tax and part income tax" (Hills and Sutherland, 1991, p 4). They demonstrated that the 'property tax' or banding element was a more progressive part of what was an overall regressively distributional tax. Further, they showed that making the size of the bill rise more steeply with band of capital value (or imposing a straightforward tax on capital values) would result in gains at the bottom end on the income distribution and more losses at the top[8]. A more recent analysis also shows that the council tax is highly regressive within each local authority and across regions (Muellbauer and Cameron, 2000a). Strengthening the 'property taxation' element of council tax would be one way of making richer households pay a fairer amount toward the environmental costs and wealth aspects of their larger, more expensive homes. Muellbauer and Cameron (2000b) propose that the tax should be more proportionate to property values, and that there should be regular revaluation, for instance, every 2-3 years. They also suggest that elderly people (as in the US) could be offered an option to defer payment to be settled on eventual sale of the house.

Another important measure would be to remove council tax exemptions on second homes, which currently pay half the council tax (on the basis that households use less council services) and the removal of tax exemptions on vacant properties. These measures would not only encourage a more efficient use of the stock, removing incentives to underoccupy and own rural second homes, but would also be a way of addressing inequalities in housing wealth.

Planning policy should use the household projections for what they are: indications of what will happen if past trends continue. Planning should prioritise meeting housing need: projecting the number of households likely to need affordable housing and the likely availability of such housing. More direct ways of meeting housing need, without inflating housing demand should be devised. A dynamic modelling of the relationship between land releases and household formation at a regional and local level is one aspect of this. A second aspect is the relationship between house prices, housing demand and housing need (Bramley and Watkins, 1996). Modelling would be a more effective way of monitoring and managing the housing outcomes of planning and other policy decisions. The trade-offs between meeting housing need, housing demand and protecting the environment would then be a matter for democratic decision analysis (see Chapter Four of this volume by Neil Fraser). Within this framework, the establishment of a hierarchy of rights and 'functionings' would mean that the right to basic shelter would be prioritised over the demand for additional space (Neuburger and Fraser, 1993, pp 52-3).

Conclusion

In conclusion, the primary objective of an urban renaissance and housing policy is improving people's quality of life and their satisfaction with their homes and environment. The degradation of the urban environment, increasing car dependency, congested roads and declining urban and rural services clearly impact upon people's wellbeing, now and in the future. On the other hand, individual and household preferences for more personal space are increasingly made possible as incomes rise. This chapter suggests that the issue of the use and distribution of housing is an important factor, both in terms of meeting housing needs and preserving the environment. If we monitor the quantity and physical quality of the housing stock but not its use, there is a danger that regeneration will turn into gentrification, with poorer households excluded by high rents and prices, as is happening in parts of London, Leeds and other cities. Ensuring the adequate provision of affordable housing is central to meeting need. In relation to future housing requirements, abandoning 'predict and provide' should not mean the end of modelling and forecasting, but the development of more flexible, policy-led models that focus on distributional issues (see also Simon Wren-Lewis's chapter). The policy measures suggested to tackle these problems are controversial in the current political climate. However, unless we address underoccupation and limit the wealth and luxury aspects of housing as a financial asset, it is unlikely that we will achieve the social and environmental goals of an urban renaissance.

Notes

[1] The author is very grateful to Anna Brueton, Tania Burchardt, John Hills and Christine Whitehead for help and advice.

[2] The bedroom standard compares the number of bedrooms available to a household with a calculation of its bedroom requirements. For the General Household Survey a separate bedroom is allocated to each cohabiting couple, anyone else aged 21 or over, each pair of young people of the same sex aged 10-20, and each pair of younger children (regardless of gender).

[3] This figure falls to 35% if dwellings undergoing modernisation or awaiting demolition are ignored.

[4] Comparing the actual numbers of rooms for households of different sizes in 1991 with the number of rooms each group would have had if densities for each had remained the same as in 1981.

[5] For a critique of predict and provide and an alternative modelling approach see Bramley (1996) and Bramley and Watkins (1996).

[6] This recommended building over one million new homes ('Regional Planning Guidance for the South East Public Examination Panel', September 1999).

[7] The official definition of a household is one person living alone with own housekeeping or two or more people who share a common housekeeping or share a living room (DETR, 1998).

[8] Interestingly, they showed that the addition of higher tax bands for larger, more expensive properties had relatively minor distributional effects (Hills and Sutherland, 1991, p 15). See Figure 6.4 in John Hills's chapter, for the overall distributional impact of the British tax system.

References

Bramley, G. (1996) *Housing with hindsight: Household growth, housing need and housing development in the 1980s*, London: HMSO.

Bramley, G. and Watkins, C. (1996) *Steering the housing market. New building and the changing planning system*, Bristol: The Policy Press.

DETR (Department of the Environment, Transport and the Regions) (1998) *English house condition survey 1996*, London: The Stationery Office.

DETR (2000a) *Planning policy guidance note no. 3: Housing*, London: DETR.

DETR (2000b) *Quality and choice: A decent home for all*, the Housing Green Paper, London: DETR.

DoE (Department of the Environment) (1996) *Projections of households in England to 2016*, London: HMSO.

Goodchild, B. (1997) 'The management of urban growth', in B. Goodchild, *Housing and the urban environment*, Oxford: Blackwell.

Hills, J. and Sutherland, H. (1991) 'The proposed council tax', *Fiscal Studies*, vol 12, no 4, pp 1-21.

Holmans, A. (1995) *Housing demand and need in England 1991-2011*, York: Joseph Rowntree Foundation.

Holmans, A., Morrison, N. and Whitehead, C. (1998) *How many homes will we need? The need for affordable housing in England*, London: Shelter.

JRF (Joseph Rowntree Foundation) (1994) *Inquiry into planning for housing*, York: JRF.

Keenan, P. (1999) 'Housing abandonment in inner cities – the politics of low demand for housing', *Housing Studies*, vol 14, no 5, pp 703-16.

Kleinman, M., Aulakh, S., Holmans, A., Morrison, N. and Whitehead, C. (1999) *No excuse not to build. Meeting housing need through the existing stock and the planning framework*, London: Shelter.

Monk, S., Royce, C. and Whitehead, C. (1995) *Planning for housing. Lessons from recent research*, Cambridge: Department of Land Economy, University of Cambridge.

Muellbauer, J. and Cameron, G. (2000a) 'The tax reform Gordon forgot', *Roof*, July/August, pp 32-3.

Muellbauer, J. and Cameron, G. (2000b) '5 key council tax reforms and 12 reasons to enact them, *New Economy*, vol 7, no 2, pp 88-91.

Neuburger, H. and Fraser, N. (1993) *Economic policy analysis: A rights-based approach*, Aldershot: Avebury.

Power, A. and Mumford, K. (1999) *The slow death of great cities? Urban abandonment or urban renaissance*, York: JRF.

Shelter National Inquiry (1999) *An urban and rural renaissance: Planning for the communities of the future*, London: Shelter.

UTF (Urban Task Force) (1999) *Towards an urban renaissance: Final report*, London: DETR/E & FN Spon.

Whitehead, C., Holmans, A., Marshall, D., Royce, C. and Gordon, I. (1999) *Housing needs in the South East*, Cambridge: Property Research Unit, University of Cambridge.

THIRTEEN

The main priority in priority setting in healthcare

Gavin Mooney

I best remember Henry Neuburger professionally for his work on discounting and cost effectiveness league tables. He worked on health at a time when these priority-setting devices were particularly fashionable and when health economists and Henry in particular brought a combination of skill, optimism and enthusiasm to the tasks of priority setting in healthcare. He also provoked a major discussion of the question of discounting future health gains.

In cost effectiveness analysis (CEA) and Quality Adjusted Life Years (QALYs) or cost utility analysis (CUA) league tables (see Chapter Four by Neil Fraser), health economists had something to offer health planners and policy makers in sorting out priorities. To provide a formula for such priority setting through cost-effectiveness and QALY league tables was a process of beauty. Rational economics could stand against the unthinking ethics of the romantic clinicians.

Earlier in my career I had been made aware of the risks associated with attempting to apply economics in healthcare. This was when I was considering a move from the Ministry of Transport, where I had first worked with Henry, to the Department of Health. Humphrey Cole, a senior economist in the Ministry of Transport and son of G.D.H. Cole, counselled caution and suggested that economics could never have its rightful place in healthcare as it was so dominated by the medical profession's power. He may well have been right and perhaps both Henry and I would have saved ourselves much anguish had we heeded Humphrey's words!

Henry and I shared much in common not only professionally but also ideologically. We were, however, only in part fellow travellers on the CEA and CUA league table road. Together with Karen Gerard, we worked on a review of CUA studies (Gerard, 1992). Today I think we can safely say that CUA league tables have their rightful place in health economics and in health policy (Gerard and Mooney, 1993) even if that place is less grand than Henry, Karen and I had envisaged in those earlier days.

Priority setting in healthcare

This chapter looks at where priority setting has now reached in healthcare and where it might be heading. It examines the reasons for the partial demise in popularity of CEA and CUA league tables, arguing that it is not just a question of the techniques *per se* being flawed or at least inadequate, but also the environment in which they are applied being infertile soil. The opportunity is then taken to look at some recent developments in priority setting which may provide a way forward to develop more acceptable and more relevant techniques and approaches in the future.

The techniques

It is relevant to note that the time when Henry and I first worked together in the late 1960s in the Ministry of Transport in London was the heyday in many ways of cost–benefit analysis (CBA), and that transport provided one of the most fruitful fields for its application (see Chris Nash and Peter Mackie's chapter). The value of time had been well researched and that meant that the key variable in the return on road investment was both measurable and could be valued in money terms.

Cost-benefit analysis was also applied in healthcare at that time – although much less so, and with less acceptance of the technique and less agreement about the valuation process. The human capital approach to valuing life was still prevalent and the valuation of pain and suffering at best rudimentary. Indeed, it was not until 1976 that Mike Jones-Lee published his book on valuing life (Jones-Lee, 1976) and my own work appeared a year later (Mooney, 1977). Strangely too the early work of George Torrance, Alan Williams and others on health state valuation was completely separate in the literature (Williams, 1985; Torrance, 1986) from that on valuation of life. This did not involve monetary valuation for the purposes of CBA but a health-related quality of life numeraire where the relatively simple trade-off was between length of life and quality of life in what, some years later, came to be placed under the heading of 'extra-welfarism'. Even today this paradigm has problems with any efforts to value life, perhaps because it is 'death' that it tries to deal with rather than dying. The notion of placing the state 'death' on a health-related quality-of-life-scale which measures states of the world rather than changes in the states of the world seems at times bizarre, in my view, even if it is frequently attempted.

At least as important, however, is that the techniques of CEA and CUA are severely limited in that, at best, they can handle technical efficiency and not allocative efficiency. Democratic Decision Analysis (DDA) is an attempt to extend CEA so that allocative efficiency is handled (see Chapter Four by Neil Fraser). It is allocative efficiency that is required when faced with issues of priority setting between different healthcare programmes or between different potential recipients such as poor versus rich people or young versus old people.

CEA ranks options on the basis of cost per unit of output where that output is defined in terms of some single dimension, such as lives saved or years of life saved. It is to be noted too that units of such output must be valued equally in terms of, for example, the age at which the life is saved so that no distinction is drawn in CEA between saving a 10-year-old or a 90-year-old. Of course that potential problem can be partly overcome by using years of life saved, but that in turn means that a year of life saved is valued the same whether the recipient is aged 10 or 90.

It is also to be noted that no consideration is given in CEA to any concept of diminishing marginal value or utility of the output. Thus 20 units of gain to one person are valued the same as one unit of gain to 20 people.

Cost utility analysis

Accepting that the single-dimensioned nature of the output in CEA was problematical, CUA was developed in healthcare. It needs to be stressed that while this is called cost *utility* analysis, it is a weak form of utility that is embraced in this context. It is weak in at least two ways. First the utility involved is only the utility of health where all else is held constant. Thus there is a 'utility trade-off' between length of life and quality of life but that is all the change from CEA. It is an important change but it is limited to that and that has to be stressed. Thus to call it 'cost utility analysis' is at best stretching a point.

Second, it remains the case, as with CEA, that nothing but health is included in the output. There is also no ability to take diminishing marginal utility or value into account in the way in which CUA is normally applied. It follows that the premise that underlies the use of

CUA is that health services are about the maximisation of health from the health service budget.

This is most apparent when the results of CUA studies are used in 'QALY league tables'. Most commonly the unit of measurement in CUA studies is the QALY. When the results of CUA studies are brought together to consider the marginal gain per dollar from investment in new services or interventions and ranked by marginal cost per QALY gained, this produces a 'QALY league table'. Implicitly it is being assumed that investment in health services is aimed at maximising the health gain as measured by QALYs.

That can readily be questioned, especially as information, various process variables and distributional considerations may well be relevant. There are also concerns here with respect to the sources of entries in any QALY league table – as suggested elsewhere (Gerard and Mooney, 1993). Ideally what is sought is to have available the results of studies that are local to the budget that is being appraised and perhaps to changes to that local budget. This means that the marginal costs and benefits (or QALY gains) need to be determined locally and indeed ideally that the QALY values be derived locally. (It is quite possible that the trade-off between length and quality of life will vary from one country to another and indeed from one region to another, even within the same country.)

Cost-benefit analysis

It can of course be argued that all will be resolved through the use of CBA. Certainly in principle CBA allows all relevant social costs and benefits to be taken into account and it can also allow for diminishing marginal utility of the good in question, in this case healthcare (or perhaps even health). It has the very real potential advantage that it allows people to include in their valuation of any intervention whichever attributes of the good they want. In most cases this might be seen as a bonus, but the advocates of CUA would probably want to question that. They suggest that there is some external judgement that health services are about health only, and then health maximisation only, resulting in other attributes not being valued (see for example Culyer, 1989). This is a very strong position to adopt and suggests that health is indeed, in this sense at least, a merit good. This is the basis of 'extra-welfarism' (Culyer, 1989).

The most serious criticism of CBA vis-à-vis CUA is normally seen as being related to the distributional consequences. With CUA everyone's health gain counts equally. Clearly with CBA, where willingness to pay is assumed and will vary between different income groups, *ceteris paribus*, the health of the rich will be valued in money terms more highly than the health of the poor. This is, for many health services, unacceptable, which is a part of the reason why CUA is often seen as more appropriate.

It is also the case, however, that some people have some ethical objections to the whole question of placing money values on pain, suffering and death. This is based on a mistaken view of what is involved as, within any programme where there is a limited budget, there will be some – at least implicit – values attached to the outputs. The fact that the outputs here are more emotionally based than elsewhere does not alter the basic principle involved.

A more fundamental problem still may be the fact that the value base of CBA is that of individuals' preferences, and the aggregation of such preferences to produce the benefits side of the comparison of costs and benefits in an implied social welfare function. It is the same, if simplified, base upon which CUA also rests.

A fundamental tenet of CBA is that individual preferences count and that these are to be summed in some manner to allow the social benefit to be constructed. Further, it is assumed that individuals in stating or revealing their preferences are doing so with the intent of maximising their own welfare or utility. Certainly externalities can be incorporated whereby, for example, my health may enter your utility function. There is, however, no place for 'commitment', as Sen (1977) has called it, which is a counterpreferential value and which, when present, means that individuals choose to do something or act in some way or consume in such a manner that, as individuals, they do not maximise their own welfare. This behaviour is intentional. CBA does not allow for that; nor does CUA.

For some who believe in such individual, essentially liberal, values, this is not a problem. For others who see a need for a more community based focus, even a communitarian focus, the situation is different. What would emerge if we were to adopt a more 'social value' stance and, going still further, a more communitarian stance? It is to these issues that the rest of this chapter is devoted. The top priority for health economics in the future is to determine whether we are to continue to face the communitarian values of healthcare with health economics techniques founded on utilitarian, individually-based preferences which embrace only consequences and ignore the value of processes. This is especially important for issues of allocative efficiency, given how we currently deal with priority setting in healthcare.

A communitarian constitutionalist future?

Investigating a more communitarian rather than an overtly individualistic, liberal, basis on which to build a paradigm for health economics seems to me potentially central to the future of health economics. Communitarian philosophy places the community at the centre of its analyses and its value system, arguing against the atomism of modern liberalism (Avineri and de Shalit, 1992). There is a value to the community *per se* and a value in being a part of – being embodied in – the community. While some have expressed the view that communitarianism is inevitably conservative this is by no means universal. It is a more radical communitarianism that I believe will be relevant in future health economics, one that can more readily embrace concerns, for example, for equity.

This 'economic communitarianism' is expressed along the following lines by Boswell (1990):

> ... the most effective cultural and attitudinal nurture for public cooperation comes from a deeper source. It springs from a conviction that public cooperation forms part of a wider search for community which has value in itself ...; from an assignation of top priority, in its own right, to the quality of interpersonal and intergroup relationships.

John Broome (1989) has proposed that "a 'claim' to a good involves a duty that a candidate for that good should in fact have it". I have previously extended this idea (Mooney, 1998) to "communitarian claims" which "recognise first that the duty is owed by the community of which the candidate is a member and secondly that the carrying out of this duty is not just instrumental but is good in itself"[1].

To pursue this approach in future, questions of rights, claims and needs in general and specifically in healthcare will need to be investigated as potential contributors to alternative bases for a health economics paradigm in priority setting. As Hausman and McPherson (1993) state: "On consequentialist views, the problem of rights articulation can be formulated as one of selecting rules that maximise good consequences." The work of James Buchanan (1986) on 'constitutional' choices is relevant with consideration of choices about setting the general 'rules of the game'. This notion of a 'constitution' – which dates back to Adam Smith – is likely to prove central in future work in health economics in priority setting. As Vanberg (1994) describes it, "the constitutional paradigm ...[concentrates not] on the 'goals' that organizational action is supposedly *directed at* ... [but on] the procedural foundations that organizational action is *based upon*".

A 'beyond consequentialist' value theory needs to be developed. This will have to embrace three issues. First, values will be based in the embeddedness of communitarianism or the 'atmosphere' of the institutionalists (Williamson, 1973). Second, the theory will be non-consequentialist. Third, it will endorse the view that a greater element of participation will be demanded in future healthcare organisations than currently obtains (as Jan, 1998, has indicated). Part of the problem to date has been that the assumption of market failure in healthcare is built mainly on information asymmetry and does not take account of the problems of 'fuzzy' or unformulated values of health. At present, while many analysts are prepared to accept that greater emphasis on community participation in economic evaluation would be 'a good thing', this idea is most often dismissed as being too costly.

It has to be that people are the source of values. However, the emphasis on individuals' values should be replaced by a concern for the values of people as citizens, as members of a community. There is not space here to discuss at length what is meant by 'community'. All that the term implies is a grouping of individuals with some common bond, which in history has been most often that they live in the same geographical location, but today might be a university department or some running club or reading society. A community is a grouping where mutuality and reciprocity are present; the sum of individuals' utilities may be less than the social welfare in total; and externalities are present – but also not just Sen's 'sympathy' (which looks very much like standard positive externalities – Sen, 1977) but also 'commitment' which Sen describes as 'counterpreferential'. Neither utilitarians nor neoclassicists can allow for the counterpreferential as, in their terms, that is irrational. Indeed, from their perspective the question has to be asked why anyone would do or consume anything which would be counterpreferential. When, however, we allow for reciprocity and a sense of community, an important change occurs. No longer is it the case that individuals seek to maximise their own utility. Rather they seek to maximise the community's welfare. Individual consumption decisions may be 'counterpreferential' at the individual level but the commitment to the common good means that they are not counterpreferential as judged by the community (or more accurately perhaps as judged by the individual as he or she perceives the welfare of the community).

Thus it remains the case, or can remain the case, that utility is maximised at a community level, but not through the maximisation of individuals' utility. The emphasis is on giving individuals the opportunity to set their preferences in a wider context than is typically the case in either neoclassical economics or in the standard approach to economic evaluation and hence to priority setting in healthcare.

As indicated above, extra-welfarism as used currently tends to assume that all that healthcare services produce is health. Much effort has gone into the measuring of health, particularly QALYs. When QALYs are used in practice, there is an 'external judgment' that variations in preferences for own health are not permitted to count: a QALY is a QALY (although recent work has begun to question this).

A prior question arises: does society want individual preferences to count? As Rice (1998) has put at least part of the question here: "do people know what is good for them?" Yet more to the point is the question: for which issues do people want their preferences to count? This in turn raises the question of whether the community might not want to be involved in determining at least the social decision rules which could then be used to guide resource allocation.

Within that branch of institutionalist economics called 'constitutionalist economics', Vanberg (1994) emphasises the 'constitutional perspective'. This embraces both "the question of to whom the organisation's constitution assigns rights to take part in organisational decisions [or 'procedural rules'] and, second, the question of whose interests are *de facto* taken into account by those who are authorised to make organisational decisions".

Investigation is thus needed on whether communitarian claims can be used to allow a democratic setting of the principles (social rules, constitution or procedural rules) of healthcare which can then be adopted as a guide for policy makers. This view of social choice theory follows Bergson (1954), one of the fathers of welfare economics, who states, "[The public official's] one aim in life is to implement the values of other citizens as given by some *rules of collective decision making*" (emphasis added). Citizens do not need to be asked their values for every public service good but rather to be involved in setting the rules of collective decision making.

The main impetus for this development lies in questioning the value base on which much of current health economics rests and then tracing the implications of this for the subdiscipline in terms of both a new conceptual paradigm and at a policy level. Important revisions of the methodological base will lead to making health economics more relevant to priority setting in healthcare. It will also allow economic evaluation and priority setting techniques to extend beyond the rather narrow confines of consequentialism. Further it will provide a set of principles for examining, for instance, what the objectives are of healthcare systems, how best to finance these and to set incentives to motivate the key actors – especially medical doctors. It will focus attention on the failure to appraise citizens' wants for their health services.

This work may have significance within economics more generally in the growing recognition within the discipline that we cannot continue to ignore moral and ethical values. Such recognition is not wholly new – Adam Smith was Professor of Moral Philosophy when he wrote *The wealth of nations* but for much of this century concerns by economists about moral sentiments and ethics have been at best muted.

As economists, we normally take preferences as given. The fact that preferences over beliefs are typically not investigated perhaps more than anything explains our relative lack of interest in moral and ethical matters. As Hausman and McPherson (1993) point out, utility theory cannot be viewed as a positive theory "without further assumptions concerning the extent to which people are rational ... because rationality is itself a normative notion".

Questions of values, the choosing of values and the eliciting of values underlie much of what needs to be questioned in current health economics related to priority setting. These echo the sentiments of Victor Fuchs (1996) in a recent Presidential Address to the American Economic Association. He suggested that health economists, 'must pay more attention to values than we have in the past'. This is endorsed by Uwe Reinhardt (1992) who suggests that "to begin an exploration of alternative proposals for the reform of our [US] health system without first setting forth explicitly, and very clearly, the social values to which the reformed system is likely to adhere is ... a waste of time".

What this might mean in practice is currently less clear. There have been some efforts to try to consult communities about healthcare services as in Oregon (Dixon and Walsh, 1991) and New Zealand (Core Services, 1994). These have fallen short of eliciting their preferences for healthcare and at best have been an aggregation of individuals' values or middle-class values regarding priorities as opposed to objectives or principles. Trying to build the notion of a community and community values other than as a sum of individuals' values is no easy task. It may be that economists in this context can learn from health promotion where the concept of community 'capacity building' is approaching the basic idea here. With colleagues I am also endeavouring to work with Aboriginal communities (Wiseman and Jan, 2000; Mooney, 2000) to see what they want from their health services – as opposed to the former model of white Australians proposing what is good for them. The key here is to put flesh on the bones of the idea of Habermas (1997) of citizens 'laying siege' to the democratic institutions of modern economies – including in this context healthcare services as social institutions.

Conclusion

Much of the work in health economics in the last two decades has been building up to a new paradigm. The ideas raised above represent this health economist's views as to where health economics ought to travel in the next few years. The hope must be that the main impact on health economics will be to build a cohesive whole out of what has been a rather disjointed series of developments. At the level of healthcare policy there remain many policy makers who for various reasons do not see the worth of health economics. The future direction outlined here would assist in overcoming some of these reservations. It emphasises the role of the community and the prospects for the community to inform healthcare decision making with their values, that is the healthcare system as a social institution.

In so far as this work will make health economics more relevant to policy and embraces a greater element of community participation in this social institution, it would have been dear to Henry Neuburger's heart.

Note

[1] Communitarian claims may well have relevance elsewhere in economics; this paper deals only with their relevance to healthcare.

References

Avineri, S. and de Shalit, A. (1992) 'Introduction', in S. Avineri and A. deShalit (eds) *Communitarianism and individualism*, Oxford: Oxford University Press.

Bergson, A. (1954) 'On the concept of social welfare', *Quarterly Journal of Economics*, vol 68, pp 233-52.

Boswell, J. (1990) *Community and the economy: The theory of public co-operation*, London: Routledge.

Broome, J. (1989) 'What's the good of equality?', in J.D. Hey (ed) *Current issues in microeconomics*, London: Macmillan.

Buchanan, J.M. (1986) *Liberty, market and state: Political economy in the 1980s*, New York, NY: New York University Press.

Core Services (1994) *Core Services for 1995/6*, Wellington: Ministry of Health.

Culyer, A.J. (1989) 'The normative economics of health care financing and provision', *Oxford Review of Economic Policy*, vol 5, pp 34-58.

Dixon, J. and Walsh, H.G. (1991) 'Priority setting: lessons from Oregon', *The Lancet*, vol 337, pp 891-4.

Fuchs, V. (1996) 'Economics, values, and health care reform', *American Economic Review*, vol 86, pp 1-24.

Gerard, K. (1992) 'Cost utility in practice: a policy maker's guide to the state of the art', *Health Policy*, vol 21, pp 249-79.

Gerard, K. and Mooney, G. (1993) 'QALY league tables: handle with care', *Health Economics*, vol 2, pp 59-64.

Habermas, J. (1997) 'Interview on questions of political theory', in J. Habermas, S. Rendell and P. Hohendahl (eds) *A Berlin republic*, Nebraska: University of Nebraska Press.

Hausman, D.M. and McPherson, M.S. (1993) 'Taking ethics seriously: economics and contemporary moral philosophy', *Journal of Economic Literature*, vol XXXI, pp 671-731.

Jan, S. (1998) 'A holistic approach to the economic evaluation of health programs using institutionalist methodology', *Social Science and Medicine*, vol 47, no 10, pp 1565-72.

Jones-Lee, M.W. (1976) *The value of life: An economic analysis*: London: Martin Robertson.

Mooney, G. (1977) *The valuation of human life*, Basingstoke: Macmillan.

Mooney, G. (1998) 'Communitarianism and health (care) economics', in M.L. Barer, T.E. Getzen and G.L. Stoddart (eds) *Quality and inequality: What care, whose costs, whither quality?*, London: Wiley.

Mooney, G. (2000) 'Vertical equity in health care resource allocation', *Health Care Analysis* (forthcoming).

Reinhardt, U. (1992) 'Reflections on the meaning of efficiency: can efficiency be separated from equity?', *Yale Law and Policy Review*, vol 10, pp 302-15.

Rice, T. (1998) *The economics of health reconsidered*, Chicago, Il: Administration Press.

Sen, A. (1977) 'Rational fools, a critique of the behavioural foundations of economic theory', *Philosophy and Public Affairs*, vol 6, no 4, pp 317-44.

Torrance, G. (1986) 'Measurement of health state utilities for economic appraisal', *Journal of Health Economics*, vol 5, pp 1-30.

Vanberg, V.J. (1994) *Rules and choice in economics*, London: Routledge.

Williams, A. (1985) 'Economics of coronary artery bypass grafting', *British Medical Journal*, vol 291, pp 326-9.

Williamson, O.E. (1973) 'Markets and hierarchies: some elementary considerations', *American Economic Review*, vol 73, Papers and Proceedings, pp 316-25.

Wiseman, V. and Jan, S. (2000) 'Resource allocation within Australian indigenous communities: a program for implementing vertical equity', *Health Care Analysis* (forthcoming).

Part Four: Henry Neuburger's contribution

FOURTEEN

Making economic policy in the Labour Party, 1980-1990: Bringing economists back in

Mark Wickham-Jones[1]

Introduction

Between 1979 and 1997, years in which it was out of office, the economic policy to which Labour was committed underwent a dramatic transformation, as did many other aspects of the party's activities and organisational structure. In this chapter I examine the development of Labour's economic programme between 1980 and 1990. I identify some of the significant changes to the party's proposals that took place during this period. For reasons of space, my account focuses inevitably on some issues and not others. I do not discuss in detail the contribution of John Smith as shadow chancellor in emphasising the significance of macroeconomic stability and designing the party's policies in the run-up to the 1992 general election (Wickham-Jones, 1995). Nor do I consider either the measures articulated by Roy Hattersley as the party's Treasury spokesperson in the mid 1980s or the policies that Tony Blair and Gordon Brown identified as being at the heart of the New Labour project in the 1990s. Instead, I aim to give a general account of how the social democratic project was modified between 1980 and 1990.

There are two wider dimensions to the chapter. The first concerns the role of party officials and academic economists in policy formation: I argue that much of the relevant academic literature plays insufficient attention to these actors in analysing the determinants of policy programmes adopted by political parties. I discuss this matter in more detail in the next section. In this chapter, focusing on Henry Neuburger's contribution, I outline the role played in policy formation by advisors.

Henry Neuburger is unusual in working for Labour across the 1980s: he was the economic advisor to successive leaders, going to work for Michael Foot in 1981 and joining the Kinnock team in 1983. (Derek Scott, his predecessor as economic advisor to the leader of the opposition, also worked for two leaders, but his appointments with James Callaghan and Tony Blair were separated by nearly fourteen years in which he left the party, became a member of the Social Democratic Party (SDP), and then rejoined Labour.) Neuburger also worked for Bryan Gould between 1987 and 1990. His contribution to a variety of economic groups, such as the Labour Economic Strategies Group, may also be atypical but serves to illustrate the potential broader role played by expert advisors to the party. Neuburger's status is not, however, unusual: he was one of a number of economists employed by Labour to advise on policy matters during the 1980s and 1990s.

The second wider dimension relates to where Labour's economic policies from this era stand in relation to the measures articulated by the party now led by Tony Blair. A key point frequently made by Tony Blair is that only with his accession to the leadership did the dramatic changes necessary to render the party electable occur. This claim is made with some consideration: the Labour leader is careful not to ignore the contributions to the party's recovery of his two predecessors, Neil Kinnock and John Smith. Nevertheless, Blair's assertion is that only after 1994 did the modernisation project take a firm grip over Labour (see, for example, Blair, 1995, p 11). Similar judgments are to be found in much of the academic literature surrounding New Labour (Butler and Kavanagh, 1997, p 64; Hay, 1998; Panitch and Leys, 1997, p 14).

Academic conceptions of Labour Party policy making

The book that has defined much of the terrain for an exploration of Labour politics is Robert McKenzie's classic account of British political parties. McKenzie's argument was straightforward: whatever the formalities of the Labour Party constitution, he claimed that effective power lay with the leadership of its parliamentary arm (PLP). The leadership was autonomous from the other, essentially subordinate, elements of the party. Policy was made by the leaders, who were held to account only at periodic general elections. Writing of members of the research department and other officials, McKenzie argued:

> There can be no doubt, however, that ultimately the members of the professional staff are the servants of the NEC and its sub-committees. If they are sufficiently persuasive and able they may succeed in exerting personal influence on the formulation of policy; but it would be inaccurate to suggest that the professional staff in any sense dominates or controls policy-making within the party. (1964, pp 569-70)

In turn, McKenzie asserted that "The views of [policy-making] committees are unlikely to be at variance with those of the majority of the PLP itself" (1964, p 527).

In the 1970s, the generalised nature of McKenzie's account was criticised, in a qualified way, by Lewis Minkin. Minkin argued that power was much more dispersed between Labour's constituent elements. Trade union leaders were not as subordinate and unquestioning in their loyalty as McKenzie concluded. Authority was divided: the parliamentary leadership had power but so too did the NEC, the unions, and even the party's activists. Developing an organic model of intra-party democracy, Minkin suggested that the annual conference was able to exert pressure on Labour's trajectory. Trade union power was often discrete, concealed, and negative in terms of shaping agendas (1980, p 53). Minkin acknowledged, "The research department has developed an important place in party policy-making" (1980, p 49). Its members drafted party statements: "Consequently its officers often had a significant role in the policy process, if only in establishing the orientation and framework of a document" (1980, p 50). He did not, however, emphasise the role of officials, unlike senior figures in the PLP, union leaderships, and delegates to conference, as one of the "divergent authoritative sources of policy" (1980, p 319). Other scholars voiced similar criticisms of McKenzie. Samuel Beer described Labour as "boisterously pluralistic" (1965, p 188). Samuel Finer argued, "The important thing to note here is the incompleteness of the leader's control of the party" (1980, p 79). Beer argued, "The only possible agency that could properly be charged with this task [the formation of policy] is the mass membership of the party.... Discretion as to details, timing and so forth, must, no doubt, be left to the organs charged with leadership. But the decisive will and the main thrust of ideas must come from the rank and file" (1965, p 88). These authors did not place any weight on the role of officials in policy making.

In a second book, published in 1991, Minkin qualified his account of Labour's internal politics. Assessing developments during the 1980s, he moved closer to the stance originally adopted by McKenzie. Rather than policy making being driven by a model of intra-party democracy, he accepted that the parliamentary leadership had become predominant. Though noting their role, he did not explore in any depth the role of party officials in this process. Indeed Minkin suggested that, for much of the 1980s at any rate, the influence of TUC officials was "usually far greater than their party counterparts" (1991, p 403). The increase in so-called 'Short money' (state aid given to opposition parties) promoted independent policy making within the PLP. The result was that, by the mid 1980s, the leader was in an extremely powerful position. Rather than assessing their independent input into policy making, Minkin presented advisors as strengthening the leader's own position (1991, p 409). Similar perspectives, downplaying the role of party officials, are to be found in the general literature about political parties (see Maor, 1997, pp 99-113; an exception is Panebianco, 1988, pp 220-35). (There is a literature addressing the role of advisors in terms of bureaucratic policy making but it does not address political parties. See Barker and Peters, 1993; Burchardt, 1997.)

The neglect of party officials and advisors from any theorisation of policy making is problematic. Party policy making reflects numerous inputs: these are likely to include material preferences and ideological values. But the construction of a programme by a party does not take place in a vacuum and proposals cannot be based on perceptions of either electability or ideology alone. It is intuitively the case that any party programme will require some sort of 'evidential' or 'knowledge' driven base (for a discussion of this point and the role of experts see King, 1999, pp 28-44). Knowledge provides the basis for what constitutes a plausible policy that a party can seek to implement with a reasonable chance of success. Party officials and other advisors are central as key sources of the expertise on which more electoral or ideological policies are based. Advisors and officials have access to the knowledge and expertise that will legitimate any claim made by politicians that the proposals they offer are viable. They can also shape the wider discourse within which ideas are shaped (King, 1999, pp 28-9). For reasons of space and subject matter, I do not develop a formal model based around the role of officials in any party's policy-making procedure: rather I suggest, through a discussion of Labour's experience in the 1980s, that officials are a significant and potentially autonomous input into that process.

Labour's alternative economic strategy

Between 1980 and 1983, under Michael Foot's leadership, Labour's economic strategy was dominated by what became known as the Alternative Economic Strategy (AES). The party's adherence to such policies dated back to the early 1970s and to the adoption by it of *Labour's programme 1973* (Wickham-Jones, 1996). The AES consisted of six interlocking elements. The first, a commitment to reflation, was straightforward. The others were more radical and unusual. They were: a commitment to public ownership; the introduction of planning agreements; the utilisation of price controls; the development of industrial democracy; and (added later than the other elements), a reliance on import controls. The strategy involved considerable intervention in markets on the part of the state, it offered far-reaching transformative goals, and it was characterised by considerable hostility to private firms.

In the early 1980s the AES was advocated in enthusiastic and robust terms by Leftwingers within Labour and a variety of groups (some outside the party). Rightwingers within Labour, including members of the shadow cabinet, were much less certain in their attitude towards it. Michael Foot took little part in arguments over economic policy. His energies as leader were focused on a variety of other matters, often ones internal to the party: to the extent he was interested in policy matters, he took a fairly traditional Leftwing stance and endorsed the objectives and policies of the AES. His views were close to those of Henry Neuburger, who was already active as a proponent of the AES within the London group of the Conference of Socialist Economists (CSE) before going to work for the Labour leader.

In November 1982, Peter Shore launched a document drafted by the shadow Treasury team entitled *Programme for recovery* (named authors, alongside Shore, were Robert Sheldon, Robin Cook and Jack Straw). Based around reflation and devaluation, the 70-page statement was focused on the demand side of the economy. Though it accepted the need for the introduction of a new institutional apparatus for planning, it offered little detail as to what such measures would amount. Neuburger was closely involved with *Programme for recovery*, having worked with Jack Straw in drafting the package and having tested it on the Treasury model (*Financial Times*, 27 November 1982). (In effect, Neuburger divided his time between Foot and Shore.) Much of the document laid out the results obtained: the key prediction was that Labour's target of cutting unemployment to under one million could be met by the end of 1986 (Shore et al, 1982, p

57). (Arguably, the Lawson boom of the late 1980s combined a similar combination of measures to those laid out by Shore.)

Neuburger's alignment as a supporter of both the AES and *Programme for recovery* is interesting because the Shore package proved controversial. It had not been through Labour's formal policy process (*Financial Times*, 27 November 1982). Austin Mitchell, a Labour MP, claimed subsequently that it was an attempt by the Treasury team to distance themselves from party policy (1983, pp 62-3). Shore's programme was subject to an astonishing assault from Roy Green, an official in Labour's research department; writing in a personal capacity, he criticised it as a retreat from planning: "it is in reality a systematic attempt to roll back the advances made by the trade union movement in developing a positive role for collective bargaining as a central element in economic policy" (1982). Robin Cook and Jack Straw (1983) replied: "Our document frankly recognises that macro-economic management alone cannot return us to full employment, but must be accompanied by a parallel programme of industrial planning". Green described it later as an attempt to hijack the party (personal communication, May 2000). Earlier, Cook and Straw (1982) had offered a striking and defensive definition of their job, perhaps one which reflected the internal turmoil in the party: "The job of party spokesmen is not to make policy but, in government, to implement it, and, in opposition, to show how it can be implemented". Their defence did not satisfy critics: Andrew Wilson, a co-author of Roy Green and a member of one of the party's policy-making committees, responded (1983): "Their *Programme* is inconsistent with the Labour Party's because it states that macroeconomic policy will provide the main general instrument for achieving the targets on unemployment".

Many critics saw *Programme for recovery* as an attempt by Shore to get reluctant union leaders to accept incomes restraint as an integral part of policy. The modelling was based on the presumption of some form of wage restraint: where the assumption was relaxed, the predicted result was higher inflation and balance of payments difficulties (Shore et al, 1982: appendix, p 7). Andrew Wilson (1983) asserted polemically, "In their determination to squeeze a commitment from the unions to incomes policy, the authors of the *Programme* have inflicted incalculable damage on Labour's electoral prospects". Some supporters of Shore may not have been so concerned about the implication that there should be an incomes policy of some sort. Henry Neuburger, along with other party officials, felt that an arrangement on incomes was a necessary element in economic strategy. The party had proposed that there would be a national economic assessment but the form that any agreement on pay and profits would take remained uncertain. There was a line of thinking in the party, closely associated with Michael Foot, that the social contract of the mid 1970s had not been a disaster and that Labour could return to something not dissimilar (Henry Neuburger, interview, October 1993). From a Leftwing standpoint, Roy Green and Andrew Wilson (1983) articulated a series of criticisms about the document that they accused Cook and Straw of sidelining.

Whether the kind of measures involved in *Programme for recovery* could have been reconciled with the AES is an open question. For Neuburger, both were straightforward attempts to reduce unemployment and tackle the grip that monetarist theory had on economic policy making. His view was that many within the party were agreed about both the range of policy possibilities and the central goal of full employment. Later, he accepted that some members of the shadow Treasury team might have seen Shore's plan as a means by which to bypass the Bennite Left. The London Conference of Socialist Economists (CSE) group (1979, p 91), before Neuburger joined it, had ruled out devaluation as being "generally regarded as incompatible with the AES". The book-length CSE version to which he did contribute did not discuss the exchange rate.

As well as working for Shore and Foot, Henry Neuburger contributed to the CSE and to the foundation of the *Socialist Economic Review* (*SER*) in the early 1980s. Both forums were designed to further the case for the AES in intellectual terms; the debates within both, especially the CSE, were indicative of the support for as well as the opposition to the AES in what were tumultuous and unusual times. Adherents of the AES perceived such debates to be important in demonstrating the feasibility and legitimacy of their approach. Within the CSE, it is noteworthy that much attention was given to discussions about reformist possibilities. Some economists were dismissive of the kind of goals that were embedded within the AES and the organisation was split between ultra-leftists and supporters of the AES who took on the mantle of cautious reformists, in contrast to perception of their stance within Labour (see the appendix in London CSE Group, 1979, pp 89-91; and CSE London Working Group, 1980, pp 44-5 and 133-40).

Several points can be noted about this discussion of Labour Party politics and the AES during the early 1980s. First, party officials played an important role in the shaping of Labour's policy. For the most part, such officials were based at its Walworth Road headquarters and worked with the policy-making subcommittees of the NEC. These committees and the advisors who serviced them determined the detail of Labour's policy: "the economic and industrial programme ... was drafted by a handful of youngish researchers" (*New Statesman*, 22 July 1983, p 14). Second, party officials were also important in shaping the discourse surrounding Labour's radical economic strategy. On occasion interventions took the form of public disputes as in the case of Roy Green's criticism of Shore's economic policy and much about the discourse remained unresolved. Third, this period was an unusual one, not in terms of the policies put forward by the party, but in that way that Labour's politics were characterised by disunity and internal conflict. The public gave little attention to the substance of the party's commitments. With hindsight many appeared overambitious: at the time they reflected a widespread view that an alternative to the quasi-monetarism of the 1974-79 Labour government and to the dogmatic monetarism of the Thatcher administration was possible.

Labour's long road to recovery between 1983 and 1987

In June 1983 Labour went down to a crushing defeat at the general election. Within days of the election it was clear that there would be major changes to Labour's structure and policy commitments. Geoff Bish, the party's Leftwing research secretary and much associated with Labour's AES, produced a series of papers. His analysis of the party's existing procedures was scathing: "the party has failed to get over to the electors those few key policies – the priority issues – upon which the success of our whole programme rests.... We have also over-burdened ourselves with a complex policy-making apparatus" (Bish, 1983a, p 2). He argued Labour needed new priorities, including a new focus on campaigns (Bish, 1983b, p 3).

Neil Kinnock, who became party leader in October 1983 following Foot's resignation, took up many of Bish's themes. He outlined the case for reforms to the party's structure and campaigning in his speeches during the summer of 1983. Some radical ideas remained in these, but given that he was a Leftwing candidate for the leadership, Kinnock was remarkably candid about what he perceived should be done. He told one audience, "The party must become more communication conscious and the quality of its communication with the public must be raised" (1983a). He went on, "Our campaigning role must be a permanent activity and organised as such between elections". In another speech, he argued that Labour had "failed to convince the relatively advantaged about the merits of its case and its commitment to efficiency" (1983b, p 7). Kinnock outlined a detailed series of Labour's organisational deficiencies, calling for clearer lines of authority, a reformed policy research process and better communication both within the party and with outside contacts (1983a). Kinnock did not feel reforms should be confined to structural matters: some policies would be reasserted by the party, but others, including the commitment to leave the European Economic Community would be reappraised (*Tribune*, 15 July 1983).

On becoming leader, Kinnock took on Henry Neuburger to work on economics, along with Dick Clements, another of Foot's policy advisors and a couple of others already in the leader's office. Neuburger blamed Labour's defeat on the lack of a clear strategy, a failure to use the media and polling properly, and the inadequate manifesto and poor organisation (1983a, p 10). Like others, he argued that the party had to reconfigure the balance between campaigning and policy making. In 1984 he argued "Policy formulation must go on but quietly and not interfere with campaigning" (1984, p 6). Kinnock's new press secretary, Patricia Hewitt concluded (1983, p 2), "The party must become a campaigning and propaganda organisation". Neuburger (1984, p 6) was blunt about the party's problems: "Research and policy have a traditional relationship in the party which owes more to organisation than to common sense". Hewitt concurred (1983, p 9): she had suggested earlier, "The NEC will need to reduce work on research and policy-making to the minimum priorities". Neuburger (1983b, p 2) was also realistic about the difficulties that Labour's policies had encountered before 1983: "Where our policies are not obviously relevant we must work hard at making sure people understand the connections". Many figures within the party concluded that sweeping reforms were needed if Labour was to recover: it is manifest that there was much support within the leader's office for a programme of reorganisation.

Kinnock soon instigated the first in a long series of reforms to the party. In October 1983, he set up a Campaign Strategy Committee to oversee the party's campaigning activities and ensure that they were accorded a higher priority than hitherto. The new committee allowed him to sidestep the NEC on certain issues at a time when he was not certain of support within it. At the same time, important changes were made to the party's policy-making process to simplify it and to integrate members of the PLP formally into it. The subcommittees of the NEC that had carried out much work in developing the AES were abolished. Bish (1983c, p 5) argued that they were too removed from the PLP and that their membership fluctuated too much creating policy instability. Neuburger (1983a, p 11) was equally critical: "the present system of policy formulation in the party is neither democratic nor effective. A vast number of committees with overlapping responsibilities exist. They seem to be largely self-appointed and only a small fraction of their membership attend any given meeting". In a paper in the autumn of 1983, Jack Straw (1983, p 2), newly elected to the shadow cabinet, took a different view to policy formation to that he had given in *Tribune* earlier that year:

> Moreover the prime responsibility of the researcher has been to service the NEC sub-committees and working parties. The system has encouraged an unhealthy and unnatural gulf between Walworth road and the party in parliament; and in so doing has wasted resources and effort, and tended to institutionalise and exacerbate conflict between the PLP and the NEC, when the machinery should ensure that conflicts are properly resolved.

Straw proposed relocating staff from Walworth Road to Westminster. Kinnock (1988) was equally contemptuous about the process.

The old process was replaced with new bodies, called Joint Policy Committees, made up equally of members of the NEC and senior figures from the PLP. The result of the new structure was a shift in influence over policy formation away from party headquarters towards the PLP. This development was evident in Labour's first initiative in terms of economic policy after the 1983 election campaign, the jobs and industry campaign, launched in April 1985. For the first time in over fifteen years, moderate members of the shadow cabinet, including Roy Hattersley and John Smith, played a central role in the formation of the Labour Party's economic policy (Wickham-Jones, 1996). One important feature of the new process was that it was directly aligned to campaigning. Geoff Bish (1984) told Patricia Hewitt, "They [the committees] will be asked to look at specific areas of policy – linked to forthcoming campaign work – with a view to preparing 'campaign statements' rather than detailed blueprints". It was an approach with which Neuburger (1983a, p 11) was in agreement, "Given that we probably have enough policy to be going on with, the focus should now be on expounding the policy". Another official remembered, "The feeling was that we've got to campaign, that there had been far too much policy in the past" (interview, May 2000).

The party's new policy-making process generated an informal and new role for advisors to senior figures within the PLP, and especially for members of the leader's office. In January 1986, Kinnock took on John Eatwell, a Cambridge economist, to work alongside Henry Neuburger. Eatwell dealt with speech writing and focused on macroeconomic policy, Neuburger tackled policy issues and party links, concentrating also on industry and social security. Eatwell became especially important in contributing to the formation of party policy: he drafted many of Kinnock's speeches and liaised with some members of the shadow cabinet in shaping the emergence of policy commitments. The role played by Eatwell and Neuburger was indicative of a shift in policy influence away from party officials at Walworth Road to those based at Westminster. "Party officials were not greatly important in this period. There was enormous suspicion of Bennites in Labour's headquarters … a feeling that the party as a machine was not interested in change" (interview, policy advisor, May 2000). Another former party official remembered, "Relations between Walworth Road and Westminster were patchy. In some subject areas people barely spoke" (interview, May 2000). Neuburger (1983a, p 10) had advocated a shift: "If we are to aim for a more streamlined research organisation at Walworth road, there is a strong case for making some more formal arrangements for researchers in the House [of Commons]". Under Kinnock, the leader's office grew larger and became much more involved in the formation of party policy: Foot had had three policy advisors (one of whom, Neuburger, was effectively shared with Shore), Kinnock had at least seven policy advisors, though a direct comparison of roles within the two offices is difficult. Likewise Roy Hattersley, the new shadow chancellor, established a team of academic advisors which proved to be important in reshaping the party's macroeconomic stance.

In place of the AES, Labour articulated a new set of policies as part of its jobs and industry campaign in 1985. These themes were reiterated in the run-up to the 1987 general election during which documents and speeches sought to establish, with limited success, Labour as 'the party of production'. Kinnock placed considerable emphasis in interviews and speeches, often little noticed, on the importance of creating wealth, as opposed to distributing it (see, for example, 1986a, p 13). Between 1985 and 1987 Labour argued that Britain's poor economic performance could be explained in terms of a failure by private firms to invest. The party highlighted three problems. First, firms did not invest because they were concerned with short-term profits and inadequate demand. The threat of takeover heightened this bias against long-term investment and Labour promised to alter "the priority given to short-term profitability" (Labour Party, 1985, p 6). Second, employers did not allocate sufficient resources for research and development, partly because of the poor availability of finance and the short-termism of decision making (TUC-Labour Party Liaison Committee, 1985, pp 14 and 23). Third, companies failed to train their workforces (TUC-Labour Party Liaison Committee, 1985, p 13). Together, these three market failures provided the explanation for Britain's disappointing economic record. John Smith, shadow trade and industry spokesperson argued, "There are three engines of recovery for the British economy. The first is investment, the second is education and training and the third is research and development" (*Labour Party Annual Conference Report*, 1985, p 216). The conception of three engines of growth was used in later documents outlining Labour's policies.

To be sure, between 1983 and 1987, there remained ambiguities about Labour's economic strategy and at times a rhetoric was deployed which was more radical than the substance of the party's proposals. The party still referred on occasion to planning agreements and industrial democracy. Social ownership, as a replacement for the term public ownership, was discussed in a 1986 document. Such policies reflected the exigencies with which the leadership was confronted. One party official described the period as a rather 'confused' one (interview, April 2000). Kinnock was an inexperienced leader who lacked a firm base of support within the party's NEC. Time was diverted both by the year-long miners' strike of 1984/85 and by the lengthy dispute between the Thatcher government and several Labour local authorities. At one point in Kinnock's early years of leadership, Neuburger was concerned about discussions over a possible *World in Action* documentary that would, he felt, exaggerate the kind of industrial strategy articulated by Labour, with too great a focus on enterprise boards (Leader's office, no date).

By the time of the 1987 general election, Labour repeated its commitment to reflation from its manifesto of four years earlier. Little else was retained in terms of the core features of the party's then economic strategy. The proposal for a national economic assessment remained though much was uncertain as to what it would amount. Planning agreements, price controls, the plans for industrial democracy, and import restrictions had all gone. Social ownership was mentioned but little detail was given as to what would be involved and the idea did not represent the kind of sweeping public ownership Labour had proposed in 1983. Unsurprisingly, in the aftermath of June 1983, support for the AES had diminished: Neuburger (1987, p 2) noted later that "the debate [in the early 1980s] within the party had itself become rigid and sterile". He went on to criticise those who held on to the kind of policies involved in the AES: "few of its original adherents would now advance [such measures] without embarrassment" (Neuburger, 1989a, p 8). It can also be noted that changes to Labour's policy did not only involve its economic programme but also included, amongst other areas, the party's proposals for industrial relations and social security.

A number of contrasts can be drawn between the AES and the policies articulated by Labour between 1983 and 1987. First, the sweeping direction of the economy by the state envisaged by the AES had been replaced with a much more limited set of interventions. In speeches before the 1987 general election, Kinnock emphasised his conception of the 'enabling state', one far removed from the kind of state envisaged in the AES.

Second, the policies outlined in the jobs and industry campaign and subsequently were modest in their goals. Kinnock did offer a commitment to reduce unemployment by a million in two years. Many around the Labour leader recognised it to be a mistake and only with some difficulty was a detailed package put together, with little input from the shadow chancellor, as to how the reduction would be secured. The package owed much, in the event, to Bryan Gould, a Treasury spokesperson, and members of the leader's office. Neuburger was involved in testing the proposals. For the most part, though, Labour was cautious about what could be achieved.

Third, the party abandoned its sharp hostility to the private sector. Under the AES, firms had been blamed for Britain's economic decline. The only way to reverse that decline it had been argued was to intervene directly in the way companies made decisions. After 1983 Labour accepted, somewhat implicitly at first, that it could work with firms. By 1985 documents emphasised the importance of a Labour government working in partnership with private companies.

Fourth, the documents contained a different attitude to the market from that embedded in the AES. Labour had suggested that markets were inherently problematic because of their inevitable tendency to monopoly and their uncompetitive nature. Hence the extensive state intervention required. By the mid 1980s, Labour accepted that markets fulfilled an essential role in the running of the economy and went on to argue that state intervention was only needed in specific (though nonetheless significant) cases of market failure. (The acceptance of the market's role did not extend to all areas of the party.) Kinnock (1986b, p 94) described the market as a "remarkable co-ordinating mechanism". One colleague remembered Henry Neuburger as believing that "markets allocate some goods well and some goods badly. [He felt] you needed to tackle market failure but that markets had a role" (interview, April 2000). Neuburger wrote later (1989b): "the market can work very effectively, but it requires constant vigilance to ensure that it does not lead to concentrations which have damaging political and economic consequences".

Party officials and academic advisors played an important role in shaping this strategy. The speeches drafted for Kinnock during 1985 and 1986 indicated a very different attitude to the private sector from that articulated in documents and speeches before 1983. Kinnock accepted that most of the investment for recovery would come from the private sector. A draft speech from Roy Green (1985, p 8), previously a supporter of the Left's industrial strategy, stated: "we recognise that the state cannot direct the behaviour of companies. It cannot compel employers to invest. But it can help to change the atmosphere in which decisions are taken". A draft speech for Kinnock in 1986 stated, "The main task of modernising British industry will fall to the private sector operating under the competitive pressures of the market" (Leader's office, 1986a). At a meeting with business in the same year this line was repeated: "Some of this investment will be undertaken by the public sector. But in our mixed economy much of it will depend upon the private sector" (Leader's office, 1986b, p 3). This attitude to the private sector reflected that set out in a memorandum by Eatwell (1985, p 5) to Kinnock in 1985: "But the main task of modernising British industry will fall to the private sector. This is inevitable. Whether we like it or not Britain is a market economy embedded within the market economy of the West". Neuburger's strength within the leader's office at this time lay, in many ways, in his ability to outline a plethora of ideas and appraise analytically their strengths and weaknesses. He may have been uncomfortable with the increasing pace of change within Kinnock's office and in 1987 he moved over to work with Bryan Gould.

The role of party officials was not confined to their direct input into Labour's formal policy commitments. Advisors played a role in shaping the wider discourse within which the party's policies were discussed and, hopefully, legitimated. For example, on one occasion, Roy Hattersley (1987a) noted the use of bringing the economist, David Currie, in to help the party in policy discussion, as he had been "consistently involved in giving our policies public academic respectability". Henry Neuburger was involved in several initiatives including the formation of Labour Economic Strategies Group in 1985. Another project concerned the so-called Kaldor group, named after Nicholas Kaldor, in which a series of economists met in semi-secrecy during 1985-86 to discuss Labour's policy proposals. Neuburger and Eatwell acted as links to the leader's office. The objective of the Kaldor group was ambiguous. Many economists sought to shape the party's proposals; the leader's office hoped for a rather different impact whereby members of the group would shape public discourse through the publication of articles in the popular media. The Kaldor group produced a detailed set of economic policy proposals that does not seem to have much impact on Labour's policy commitments. Moreover, the document indicated some of the weaknesses of policy making by economists with insufficient political input. A couple of proposals had to be removed because they were likely to prove electorally problematic. Andrew Graham (1986), the group's convenor, wrote to Kinnock, "The sensitive areas concern contingency plans for controls on trade and payments which we believe ought to be prepared". A similar group, organised around Tony Blair, met a few times in Cambridge in 1985, though little came of it. Last, in 1985 some economists formed the Industrial Strategy Group to advise John Smith.

Labour's policy review

Following Labour's June 1987 general election defeat a review of the party's policy commitments was set in motion. The Policy Review intensified the changes to the party's policy-making structures and proposals that the Kinnock leadership had already initiated. One of seven policy groups, The Productive and Competitive Economy (PCE) group tackled macroeconomic measures and industrial strategy and for a time it dominated the party's overall economic policy. It was co-chaired by Bryan Gould, the party's trade and industry spokesperson. In this period, those working at Westminster, including the members of Labour's newly formed Economics Secretariat, dominated policy formation. Officials at Walworth Road liaised with staff at Westminster. They did not have the kind of autonomy that they had before 1983. Some members of the shadow cabinet had little confidence in Bish (interview, party official, April 2000). The shift of policy-making power to Westminster was furthered by the creation of the shadow cabinet economics subcommittee in 1987. At first a rather discursive forum in which theoretical material was discussed informally, it became more important in shaping the party's economic outlook by 1990.

The final report of the PCE group, 'Competing for prosperity', was published as part of *Meet the challenge, make the change* in May 1989. The review focused on market failures as collective action problems and the necessity of state intervention to resolve them: "Without government co-ordination and organisation in areas like research and development and training, individual firms will find that the rational course is not to invest but to try – as free riders – to benefit from the investment of others. When everybody is a free rider, however, nobody rides" (Labour Party, 1989, p 10). The review proposed a Medium Term Industrial Strategy for the United Kingdom under which the focus for intervention would be a reinvigorated Department of Trade and Industry. Policy proposals included new incentives for research and development, investment in infrastructure (especially communications), and the establishment of a national training fund financed through a levy on company payrolls. There would be tighter rules on takeovers. A battery of new institutions was designed to coordinate Labour's interventions.

The macroeconomic strategy outlined alongside these industrial policies was limited. Labour was at pains to jettison its image as a high-spending and fiscally irresponsible party. Neuburger argued (1989c, p 1), "The rejection of Tory criteria [on spending] does not mean that we are free to spend immediately as much as we think the needs of society justify". He went on (1989c, p 2) to recognise the constraints that confronted Labour: "Broadly if public spending is funded by borrowing then it will increase pressure on productive capacity with consequences for inflation and the balance of payments". The economics subcommittee (1989) concluded that Neuburger's approach was "too rigid". The Policy Review was vague about the control of inflation, hinting at the use of some form of credit controls. Neuburger, like Gould, favoured their use.

By 1989 further developments had taken place in the party's policy proposals. Labour's commitment to public ownership, stated in a rather nebulous fashion in the 1986 document, *Social ownership*, was further watered down. At the time of the 1987 election, the party proposed to extend social ownership and to renationalise British Telecom and British Gas by converting private shares into new securities. The Policy Review repeated the pledge to renationalise BT, though it now proposed simply to raise the public stake from 49% to 51%. The review recognised that there were financial constraints to further renationalisations and electoral considerations to be made in this context. Neuburger (1988a, p 1) argued, "The main aim of policy making in this area was to solve a political dilemma – how to avoid contradicting our policy of no compensation beyond the nominal value of shares and avoid the electoral embarrassment of not compensating people". In any case, he noted (1988a, p 3), the record of public monopolies was often uninspiring: "There is little ground for saying that they were well managed socially". Accordingly, emphasis was placed on the need to design a regulatory framework within which the performance of any natural monopolies could be shaped (1988a, p 3): "There is a case to be made that a good regulatory agency and well drawn company articles can achieve a lot in terms of social responsibility". The PCE group (1988) concluded, "in many privatisations there was no case for renationalisation and much could be achieved by other methods". Major utilities would be designated 'public interest companies': and each subject to regulation from a new commission. The commitments marked the evolution of Labour's strategy towards limited state ownership, diverse forms of control and the strong regulation of utilities. The shift away from public ownership was unproblematic for Neuburger. In advocating the AES, he had conceived of planning agreements as a means of bypassing the issue of nationalisation (1988b): "by the early seventies, this [public ownership] was replaced by the concept of planning agreements which implicitly downgraded the role of ownership".

There was some tension in the review between the policies articulated by Gould and those endorsed by Kinnock. Gould's conception of the new role for the Department of Trade and Industry (DTI) drew heavily on David Marquand's (1988) 'developmental state' thesis (see Gould, 1989, p 7). Such an approach was too interventionist for the Labour leader; he favoured a conception of an 'enabling state' with a more limited role, though Patricia Hewitt (1988, p 6) appeared supportive of Marquand's argument. John Eatwell, having once favoured the developmental state approach, was critical of Gould's attitude to the market and the extent of state intervention proposed (*The Guardian*, 7 April 1989). Gould and Eatwell also differed over the exchange rate: Gould, having been close to Peter Shore in the early 1980s, continued to favour devaluation. Eatwell, concerned by the potential impact of devaluation on inflation, came to favour UK membership of the ERM. Early in 1989, Eatwell (1989) wrote to Gould, "I was astonished to hear Keith Cowling [one of Gould's advisors] claim that changes in the exchange rate do not have a major impact on domestic prices". Eatwell continued, "There is a severe danger of inflation and devaluation being mutually reinforcing". Neuburger (1988a, p 6) accepted that inflation "remains a chronic weakness" and continued to favour the adoption of some form of incomes policy, an idea that was politically unacceptable to most within the Labour Party.

Eatwell (no date) was also critical of Neuburger's proposal for an Industrial Investment Fund, financed by a business levy:

> However much as we try to argue differently this will be portrayed as a tax on business and will lose us any credibility in the business community that we might have. There is no call for this measure in the business community. They will see it as an imposition. Nobody else will care. We lose.

The proposal was dropped.

There were significant disagreements between John Smith, the shadow chancellor, and Gould. Smith felt (as did his deputy, Gordon Brown) that Gould tended to give too wide a remit to industrial strategy. When Gould suggested that there might be limitations on dividend payments, Kinnock swiftly corrected him. Soon afterwards, in October 1989, Gould was demoted in a reshuffle and switched to the less important portfolio of the environment (though he kept his place on the shadow cabinet economics committee). Between 1989 and 1992, advised by David Ward and Andrew Graham, John Smith played an important role in shaping Labour's economic strategy, emphasising the party's commitment to economic stability and the modesty of its economic objectives.

During the Policy Review, Bryan Gould made considerable use of the Industrial Strategy Group, having taken it over from John Smith. It met regularly, tracking the PCE group, on which its convenor, Keith Cowling, sat as a member. One party official remembered, "Bryan was always one for taking on new ideas. He had strong opinions but he was very open. Some members of the shadow cabinet thought he was too open and not safe enough in terms of focusing on the election as a priority" (interview, April 2000). Many of the ideas raised by members of the Industrial Strategy Group filtered into the review's proposals (though some of these were already party policy). Equally, many wanted some of the party's proposals to be pushed further, as the title of the group's collected volume, *Beyond the review*, suggested. Keith Cowling (1989) suggested that sweeping powers would be needed by the DTI and, together with Malcolm Sawyer (1989), he proposed a complete ban on mergers between large companies.

Beyond the review proved to be controversial. Henry Neuburger, writing with Sawyer (1989, p 49), suggested that moderate inflation was not intolerable: "But when inflation is relatively low (say below 10% per annum), these dangers do not exist and the control of inflation should receive relatively low priority (as compared with unemployment, improving industrial efficiency etc)". Though economically defensible, the claim was problematic for those in the Labour leadership seeking to establish the party's anti-inflation credentials. As front page news, *The Sunday Times* picked up on it and the possibility, that Neuburger and Sawyer noted, of a run on the pound (1 October 1989). The BBC pressed John Smith in an interview about the extent of the party's commitment to price stability, much to his discomfort: "I explicitly disavow it [Neuburger's claim about the priority of inflation] here and now" (transcript, *On the record*, BBC, 1 October 1989). He emphasised that Labour's target was to bring inflation down to the G7 average (at 4.8%, well below 10%). Peter Mandelson, then the party's director of communications, was incensed by the comment on inflation. Neuburger and Sawyer (1989, p 51) also concluded, "In the longer term, the maintenance of full employment will be undermined by inflationary pressure unless some (implicit or explicit) incomes policy is in place". This proposal also attracted media attention (*The Guardian*, 4 October 1989). When the Industrial Strategy Group's essays were reprinted a year later as a book, both observations were dropped. The word 'agreement' replaced 'policy' with regard to incomes (Neuburger and Sawyer, 1990, pp 122 and 127). Just before publication of the volume, one of the editors was rung up and harangued by a senior frontbench spokesperson, who warned that if publication went ahead its contributors would not be involved in Labour's policy making in the future. The episode indicated one of the weaknesses of economists in making policy is that they may be politically innocent about the electoral realities constraining politicians.

The 1989 shadow cabinet reshuffle had far-reaching consequences for Labour's policy commitments. Although the Policy Review was formally completed in the summer of 1989, important shifts were made afterwards in the orienting of economic strategy. In the autumn of that year, after discussions with European social democrats, Smith and Brown became convinced that Labour should commit the United Kingdom to joining the European Exchange Rate Mechanism (ERM). The final decision to commit Labour to the ERM was taken by Smith and Brown, together with Kinnock and Eatwell. It was confirmed by a meeting of the shadow cabinet economics committee in March 1990. Henry Neuburger was probably not as hostile as Gould to the ERM: as early as 1986 he had noted that there was a tension between the pro-European rhetoric deployed by Kinnock and the substance of the party's conditions for joining the ERM, noting with Jane Ashley (1986, p 2), that "Some members of the committee [of the Confederation of European Socialist Parties] were puzzled at our cautious position on joining EMS, having read Roy Hattersley's and Neil Kinnock's pronouncements as a clear shift in our position". He also felt that Labour's hostility to the European monetary system, within which the ERM was located, was driven by its anti-Europeanism (1988c, p 2). He was, however, sceptical about the kind of benefits associated by some with the European single market (see Iain Begg, Chapter Nine in this volume).

Conclusions

In this chapter, I have outlined some of the ways that Labour's economic policy changed between 1980 and 1990, a period in which the party went from a position of advocating the strongly interventionist AES to one of endorsing the ERM as a means of attaining price stability. Assessing the role of party officials and advisors in the formation of Labour's policy under Kinnock's leadership is difficult. After 1983 a resurgent shadow cabinet, especially Neil Kinnock and John Smith, played a much more direct role in the construction of the party's economic programme. Much of the archival evidence about policy formation is rather fragmentary. It is also manifest that, on becoming leader, Neil Kinnock had a clear view of the kind of changes that were needed in terms of policy and organisation if the party was to be rendered electable.

I suggest, however, that the input into policy formation from economists and other experts should not be neglected. Many party officials, as well as members of the PLP, shared Kinnock's outlook in the aftermath of the 1983 defeat. Assessing their role is problematic: many advisors worked well with politicians taking policy in the same direction. Nevertheless the parameters of policy reformulation after 1983 left much about the party's programme unspecified and unresolved, issues that were addressed by advisors over the next decade or more with resultant changes to Labour's commitments. Economic advisors such as John Eatwell and Henry Neuburger played a significant role in translating the Labour leader's general ideas into specific theories and proposals for the economy. The detail of the party's policy owes much to the advisors and party officials working for it. For example, the emphasis placed on the private sector in promoting economic recovery was a strong theme of Eatwell, which he frequently injected into speeches for Kinnock (before the theme emerged in party documents). Likewise, the need to design an effective framework for the regulation of utilities was emphasised by Neuburger after 1987. It is also the case that the environment in the leader's office under Kinnock was one in which economic ideas and their relevance for policy were discussed openly. (Of course, Gould's attitude to ideas was even more manifest.) For example, in July 1986 Kinnock was given a paper by Meghnad Desai on Labour's economic policy. Desai argued:"the emphasis in the current debate is far too much on fiscal and monetary policy for short run reflation to tackle the unemployment". Clearly sensitive to Desai's charge, Kinnock wrote in the margin:"Not really true. See all the party of production material". Desai claimed that Labour was 'dodging' issues of money and technology. Kinnock noted acerbically, "No dodging. No one has yet unveiled a system for spending money that you don't know you are going to have or can reasonably expect" (details in Kinnock papers, box 254).

The Labour leader placed considerable weight on the opinions of his economic advisors, especially those of Eatwell (interview, party official, April 2000). A 1986 briefing for him before a meeting of Labour's home policy committee stated, "An assessment needs to be made here as to whether or not the paper is worth putting forward" (Leader's office, 1986c). The paper in question was an economic policy document entitled, 'The party of production'. The briefing noted that, whilst Smith and Hattersley were in favour, Bish, Eatwell and Neuburger were against, and David Blunkett favoured postponement. The equal weighting given to Labour's officials is noteworthy: in the event the document was replaced with a much briefer statement to the annual conference. One party worker recalled of the various contributions to Labour's policy process:

> It is true that party officials contributed to policy-making. What other sources were there? Labour listens [an exercise to find out members' views in 1988] was a failure. Backbench MPs didn't come up with other things … I did a lot of drafting but it was supervised and the text went back and forth. (Interview, April 2000)

It is understandable why advisors were important: the Labour leader's office, even in its expanded state under Kinnock, was under-resourced in comparison to what was available to the government. Labour politicians relied upon advisors for ideas and proposals about what was feasible as well as briefings and information. Such advisors often brought in economists on the basis of personal contacts to challenge the economic arguments mobilised by the Treasury. From the mid 1980s onwards, on budget day, a range of economists came in to critique the government's strategy. They shaped the opposition's immediate response. The practical implication of this account is that anyone seeking a point of entry to the policy making process should pay regard to the accessibility of advisors and officials as much as that of politicians.

Alongside their direct input into policy making, the contribution of party officials and economists in shaping the wider discourse surrounding policy should not be neglected. Neuburger chaired the Labour Economic Strategies Group in the mid 1980s as well as contributing to the SER, the Kaldor group and the Industrial Strategy Group. Modellers for Socialism, a group designed to make better use of econometrics, met at various times under his direction. For several years in the late 1980s he wrote a biweekly economic column for *Tribune*. Assessing the impact of these activities is by no means straightforward. The 1980s were a difficult period in which many ideas about socialist economic strategy were marginalised from public discourse. A tentative conclusion might be that without such activities as those of Neuburger such marginalisation would have been heightened and intensified.

Where do the economics of the 1980s stand in relation to those of New Labour today? New Labour's economic programme is characterised by the modesty of its goals and the extremely limited nature of its interventions. Great emphasis is placed upon securing macroeconomic stability through the tight control of inflation attained via an independent Bank of England. Many commentators conclude that New Labour has made a decisive break with the party's past in terms of its economic policy.

Some significant links can be made, however, between the arguments articulated by Labour in the aftermath of the 1983 general election defeat and those made by senior figures within New Labour today. One official remembered, "1983-85 was a formative period, an exercise in turning the ship around" (interview, May 2000). Key features of the party's policy between 1983-87 included the following: the abandonment of sweeping intervention, the rejection of far-reaching transformative goals, the advocacy of a partnership with the private sector, and the endorsement of the market. All these are to be found at the centre of the economics of New Labour. To this list might be added, the emphasis on the management of public utilities through regulation given in the 1989 Policy Review, again an approach to found within New Labour. Although many of the policies of Tony Blair's party may be different, many of the ideas and theories with which they are underpinned are to be found in the arguments deployed by Labour from the mid 1980s onwards. The centralisation of Labour's policy making process began after 1983 and from then on those involved in the formation of strategy were aware of the need to take electoral considerations on board. As early as 1986, Blair himself was arguing in an internal memorandum, "We must distinguish carefully between borrowing to invest and borrowing to consume" (1986, pp 5-6). At the same time, Roy Hattersley noted the importance of the debt-GDP ratio for the economy (1985, p 18). He promised a target for the ratio, one that required at most a small increase in it, in line with that in other countries (1987b, p 77). Subsequently the idea that borrowing should only fund investment and that the ratio of debt to GDP should be stabilised became part of New Labour's code for fiscal responsibility: both had been a feature of the party's outlook well before the mid 1990s.

In February 1999, Stephen Byers, one of Blair's ministers claimed, "the reality is that wealth creation is more important than wealth redistribution". Yet it is striking that from 1983 onwards, Neil Kinnock (1983b, p 7) emphasised the importance of wealth creation (though no doubt he had different views from Byers about the necessary policies to secure higher output). In his first extended television interview as leader Kinnock (1984, p 11) lamented that production "has been obscured to a certain extent by the welfarist identity that has been taken on by Labour". From this perspective, it is important to emphasise the evolutionary nature of the changes undergone by Labour and to recognise the impact of the 1983 general election as a watershed, rather than any subsequent date, including Blair's own election to the party leadership.

Note

[1] My thanks to Chris Allsopp, Jane Ashley, Iain Begg, Dan Corry, Roy Green, John Hills, Desmond King, David Jordan, Emma Maclennan, David Metcalf, Stuart Quayle, Tom Quinn, Fiona Ross, Malcolm Sawyer, Roger Sugden, Simon Wren-Lewis, and several former party officials and advisors who remain anonymous for their help in writing this chapter. At several points in the text I draw on these anonymous interviews. I also draw on an interview with Henry Neuburger in October 1993. Responsibility, of course, is mine. I am also grateful to the Nuffield Foundation, the Harold Wincott Foundation and the Arts and Humanities Research Board for financial assistance with some of the research upon which this chapter is based.

References

Note: The prefix RD refers to the relevant number of internal memorandum produced by the Labour Party research department.

Ashley, J. and Neuburger, H. (1986) 'Report of the meeting of the Economics Committee', RD (I): 381, Kinnock papers, box 437.

Barker, A. and Peters, G. (eds) (1993) *The politics of expert advice*, Pittsburgh, PA: Pittsburgh University Press.

Beer, S. (1965) *Modern British politics*, London: Faber and Faber.

Bish, G. (1983a) 'Future policy development', RD:2806/July 1983.

Bish, G. (1983b) 'The failures and some lessons', RD2808/July 1983.

Bish, G. (1983c) 'Programme of future work 1983/84', RD:2889/October 1983.

Bish, G. (1984) letter, 13 February 1984, Kinnock papers, box 482.

Blair, T. (1986) 'Public expenditure', internal memorandum, Labour Party archive, Manchester: National Museum of Labour History.

Blair, T. (1995) 'Power for a purpose', *Renewal*, vol 3, no 4, pp 11-16.

Burchardt, A. (1997) *The Broyd papers*, Nottingham: Spokesman.

Butler, D. and Kavanagh, D. (1997) *The British General Election of 1997*, Basingstoke: Macmillan.

Byers, S. (1999) Speech, Mansion House, 2 February.

Cook, R. and Straw, J. (1982) 'Our plan to end mass unemployment', *Tribune*, 3 December.

Cook, R. and Straw, J. (1983) 'Of course, we believe in planning', *Tribune*, 14 January.

Cowling, K. (1989) 'The strategic approach', in Industrial Strategy Group, *Beyond the review*, Edinburgh: ISG.

Cowling, K. and Sawyer, M. (1989) 'Merger and monopoly policy', in Industrial Strategy Group, *Beyond the review*, Edinburgh: ISG.

CSE London Working Group (1980) *The alternative economic strategy*, London: CSE Books.

Eatwell, J. (1985) Memorandum, 28 November, Kinnock papers, box 176.

Eatwell, J. (1989) Letter to Bryan Gould, 27 February, Kinnock papers, box 167.

Eatwell, J. (no date) 'Industrial investment fund', Labour Party archive, Manchester, National Museum of Labour History.

Economics Sub-Committee, (1989) Minutes, 28 February, Kinnock papers, box 59.

Finer, S. (1980) *The Changing British Party System 1945-79*, Washington, DC: American Enterprise Institute.

Gould, B. (1989) 'Introduction', Industrial Strategy Group, *Beyond the review*, Edinburgh: ISG.

Graham, A. (1986) Letter, Neil Kinnock, 10 July, Kinnock papers, box 58.

Green, R. (1982) 'The economy: Has Labour bought the Treasury line?', *Tribune*, 31 December.

Green, R. (1985) 'Unemployment and economic strategy', draft speech, February 1985, Kinnock papers, box 179.

Green, R. and Wilson, A. (1983) 'The future course of planning', in T. Topham (ed) *Planning the planners*, Nottingham: Spokesman.

Hattersley, R. (1985) *Government borrowing: What Labour would do*, ECSTRA working paper.

Hattersley, R. (1987a) Letter to Neil Kinnock, 22 January, Kinnock papers, box 127.

Hattersley, R. (1987b) *Economic priorities for a Labour government*, Basingstoke: Macmillan.

Hay, C. (1998) 'That was then, this is now: the revision of policy in the modernisation of the British Labour Party, 1992-97', *New Political Science*, vol 20, no 1, pp 7-33.

Hewitt, P. (1983) 'Rebuilding the party', July, Kinnock papers, box 89.

Hewitt, P. (1988), 'The strategy for phase 2', December, Kinnock papers, box 562.

King, D. (1999) *In the name of Liberalism*, Oxford: Oxford University Press.

Kinnock, N. (1983a) Speech, Stoke, 12 September, Kinnock papers, box 245.

Kinnock, N. (1983b) Speech, Wandsworth, 8 September, Kinnock papers, box 247.

Kinnock, N. (1984) *Weekend World*, 12 January, Kinnock papers, box 250.

Kinnock, N. (1986a) Fabian lecture on the New Right, Manchester, 11 September, Kinnock papers, box 245.

Kinnock, N. (1986b) *Making our way*, Oxford: Basil Blackwell.

Kinnock, N. (1988) 'PRG', notes, Kinnock papers, box 46.

Labour Party (1985) *Investing in Britain*, London: Labour Party.

Labour Party (1989) *Meet the challenge, make the change*, London: Labour Party.

Leader's office (1986a) 'Party of production', draft speech, Kinnock papers, box 176.

Leader's office (1986b) Draft introduction to Business International meeting, May, Kinnock papers, box 179.

Leader's office (1986c) Briefing, 14 July, Kinnock papers, box 586.

Leader's office (no date) Note for Neil Kinnock, Kinnock papers, box 261.

London CSE Group (1979) 'Crisis, the Labour Movement and the Alternative Economic Strategy', *Capital and Class*, no 8, pp 68-93.

McKenzie, R. (1964) *British political parties*, London: Heinemann.

Maor, M. (1997) *Political parties and party systems*, London: Routledge.

Marquand, D. (1988) *The unprincipled society*, London: Jonathan Cape.

Minkin, L. (1980) *The Labour Party Conference*, Manchester: Manchester University Press.

Minkin, L. (1991) *The contentious alliance: Trade unions and the Labour Party*, Edinburgh: Edinburgh University Press.

Mitchell, A. (1983) *Four years in the death of the Labour Party*, London: Methuen.

Neuburger, H. (1983a) 'What went wrong', 24 June, Kinnock papers, box 89.

Neuburger, H. (1983b) 'Polling and strategy', 31 October.

Neuburger, H. (1984) 'Campaigning, policy and research', 16 February, Kinnock papers, box 239.

Neuburger, H. (1987) 'ECSTRA into the nineties', *ECSTRA News*, p 7.

Neuburger, H. (1988a) 'Compensation for nationalisation', PD: 1469/March.

Neuburger, H. (1988b) 'Social ownership', PD: 1792/November.

Neuburger, H. (1988c) 'A useful exchange rate mechanism', Kinnock papers, box 563.

Neuburger, H. (1989a) 'The information revolution gives no succour to Thatcherism', *Tribune*, 31 March, pp 8-9.

Neuburger, H. (1989b) Economic commentary, *Tribune*, 23 June.

Neuburger, H. (1989c) 'Public spending implications of the Policy Review proposals', ESC 89/4.

Neuburger, H. and Sawyer, M. (1989) 'Macro-economic policies and inflation', in Industrial Strategy Group, *Beyond the review*, Edinburgh: ISG.

Neuburger, H. and Sawyer, M (1990) 'Macro-economic policies and inflation', in Keith Cowling and Roger Sugden (eds) *A new economic policy for Britain*, Manchester: Manchester University Press.

Panebianco, A. (1988) *Political parties: Organisation and power*, Cambridge: Cambridge University Press.

Panitch, L. and Leys, C. (1997) *The end of parliamentary socialism*, London: Verso.

PCE (Productive and competitive economy group) (1988) minutes, 29 March.

Shore, P., Sheldon, R., Cook, R. and Straw, J. (1982) 'Programme for recovery', unpublished paper (mimeo released to press), 23 November.

Straw, J. (1983) 'Shadow cabinet support', 12 October, Kinnock papers, box 587.

TUC-Labour Party Liaison Committee (1985) *A new partnership, a new Britain*, London: TUC and Labour Party.

Wickham-Jones, M. (1995) 'Anticipating social democracy, pre-empting anticipations', *Politics and Society*, vol 23, no 4, pp 465-94.

Wickham-Jones, M. (1996) *Economic strategy and the Labour Party*, Basingstoke: Macmillan.

Wilson, A. (1983) 'We won't win with an incomes policy', *Tribune*, 11 February.

FIFTEEN

Henry Neuburger: A personal appreciation

Andrew Burchardt[1]

I have adopted a chronological structure in describing Henry's career to facilitate keying the chapters of this book into the phases of Henry's developing interests. Although the posts Henry held were necessarily consecutive, it is more helpful to see his interests as cumulative. A case in point is economic modelling and forecasting, his enthusiasm for which developed while he was at the Treasury (early 1970s), but which remained an absorbing interest after he left in 1981 despite the fact that his next post was in the office of the Leader of the Labour Party. Even when Henry re-entered the civil service it was several years before this interest found expression again (in his work for Customs and Excise and again while he was at the Office for National Statistics, in the 1990s). As it was rare for Henry to lose interest in aspects of economics that had once engaged him, and as he moved from one post to another fairly rapidly, his range of expertise became singularly extensive. The curriculum vitae below will therefore be more effective in indicating when Henry's interest in a particular topic might have originated, than when work based on that topic was completed. Henry's concern with quality of life indicators (see Gavin Mooney's chapter), for instance, was not particularly strong before his period at the Department of Health in 1990, but long survived his move from that Department, and can be detected in some of his work on satellite accounts undertaken at the Office for National Statistics in 1997.

Henry's university education began in 1961 at St. Catherine's College, Oxford, where he read Politics, Philosophy and Economics. He followed this with a B.Phil. in Economics, also at Oxford, on industrial location in London. He then started what was to become a long and varied career in economic policy making with a post in the Ministry of Transport. In 1966 he joined the Department, which was at that time led by Barbara

Castle, to work under Christopher Foster in the economic planning division (see Christopher Nash and Peter Mackie's chapter).

By 1971 Henry had moved to the Treasury where in due course he became Head of Economic Assessment. This was a formative period for Henry and laid the foundation for his long-standing interest in modelling and forecasting (see Simon Wren-Lewis's chapter). No other Department was able to hold him for as long as the Treasury. After seven years he left (temporarily) for an unusual reason, which was however typical for Henry: the arrival of his first daughter. When she was 6 months old he took 12 months off formal work (1978).

Henry returned to the Treasury in 1979 but the political climate had changed and Henry left to spend several years trying to ensure the return to power of the Labour Party. In 1981 he became Economic Adviser to the Leader of the Opposition, working mainly to Michael Foot, a period he greatly enjoyed partly because he was close to policy making but partly also because of his respect for Michael Foot.

Before this Henry had become an active member of the Conference of Socialist Economists (CSE), although he never wrote for their journal *Capital and Class*, which he felt failed to relate the theoretical issues discussed to practical policies. Henry did, however, contribute to a number of other publications, of which the most widely known was *The Alternative Economic Strategy* (CSE London Working Group, 1980). The ideas collected in that book represented an important focus for Labour Party thinking, particularly in the years running up to the 1983 general election (see Mark Wickham-Jones's chapter).

In 1981, Henry supported the launch of a new journal, the *Socialist Economic Review*, for which he wrote a number of articles, including one in 1982 entitled 'Does manufacturing deserve special status?'. Here, Henry challenged the conventional wisdom, as he loved to do, and, long before it was generally fashionable among economists, argued that non-manufacturing industries were a perfectly viable basis for an advanced economy. In the 1983 edition of the *Review* he returned to the subject of forecasting models.

He became Economic Adviser to Neil Kinnock in 1983, and was much involved in preparing the latter's speeches on economic issues (a period covered in detail by Mark Wickham-Jones in his chapter). As well as writing for *Tribune*, Henry produced a number of pamphlets during this period. In 1984 two came out under the imprint of the Low Pay Unit. In one (on the minimum wage) Henry based a brief econometric analysis on an analogy with a physical law on the compressibility of solids (see

David Metcalf's chapter). This long pre-dated Paul Ormerod's headline-grabbing recommendation that economists should borrow techniques from the physical sciences. He left the Labour Leader's Office in 1987 to work for Bryan Gould, who was then Shadow Minister for Trade and Industry. They were very much on the same wavelength and worked together effectively. During this period Henry was instrumental in setting up LABECSTRA, the Labour (Party) Economic Strategies Group, a policy discussion forum which was also designed to present the Labour Party's economic policies persuasively in the media. This was to be achieved by a combination of local groups and individual economists. The former would become knowledgeable about the application of Labour's policies to the peculiarities of their region or town and take up issues in local forums and media. The latter would be specialists in particular aspects of Labour's economic policy and would be able to comment immediately and expertly at the moment when an issue broke in the news. This was an ingenious formula which will surely be applied repeatedly. Henry chaired LABECSTRA from its launch in 1985 till the Group was on its feet in 1988. In 1986 Henry co-authored, with four others, a book which took the Alternative Economic Strategy further, emphasizing in particular the need for democracy in planning (Gilhespy et al, 1986).

In 1990 Henry returned to the civil service, working initially in the Department of Health. While there the book he had been working on for many years with Neil Fraser was published (Neuburger and Fraser, 1993; see Neil Fraser's chapter). This to some extent articulated Henry's doubts about Cost-Benefit Analysis, the seeds of which had been planted during his time in the Ministry of Transport. Instead Henry and his co-author proposed an unorthodox non-neo-classical method of evaluating proposed policies. Attacks on utilitarian and neo-classical economic theories were not new. What was path-breaking in the book was that it advocated a positive counter-proposal, namely democratic decision making (DDA). Couched in the terminology of Kant, Rawls and Sen, the authors proposed that political decision making be based on a hierarchy of functionings – life, physical health, etc – that can only be assigned weights through the political (here called democratic) process.

After some two years in the Department of Health Henry transferred to H.M. Customs and Excise where he was once again involved in pre-budget planning and forecasting, though his work on smuggling and VAT avoidance was more eye-catching.

In July 1995 Henry left Customs and Excise to become head of the newly-formed Economic Assessment and Strategy Division at the Central

Statistical Office (later renamed the Office for National Statistics) and returned to some of his earlier interests. An ex-colleague's impression was that it was typical that unlike many economists Henry regarded the processes of compiling economic statistics as an intellectually exciting as well as worthy activity. The post gave him scope to pursue many of his interests: for instance, insuring that economic thinking fully informed the technical process of constructing economic statistics, and particularly the national accounts (see Anne Harrison's chapter); economic modelling; and developing ideas for measuring areas of economic activity previously thought intangible and unmeasurable, such as the information economy. In *Economic Trends*, October 1997, he promulgated the concept of satellite accounts for the UK, and published (with Prashant Vaze) the first UK environmental accounts, as well as laying the foundations of current UK work on household accounts. Henry's contributions to these areas, and his enthusiasm for his endeavours, has had a lasting influence both on his ONS colleagues and on national accountants overseas.

In January 1998 Henry returned to a policy-formulating department, joining the new Department of the Environment, Transport and the Regions to head the Construction Market Intelligence Division. He made significant progress in updating the electronic base of the London and Bristol branches for which he was responsible, and in modernising the understanding of the economics of construction. He also participated fully, after the 1997 election, in the discussions within the Department on housing, urban and rural regeneration (see Jenny Neuburger's chapter), and, using his Customs and Excise experience, VAT.

In the twenty years that Henry worked as a civil servant, and excluding his time at the Treasury, he spent on average only two and a half years at each of the five Departments in which he held positions. Despite these relatively short stays, there was no Department where he did not make a significant contribution: a remarkable achievement in an environment with a built-in respect for procedures and precedents for someone who, in his enthusiasm for the matter in hand, frequently overlooked the grade of the person he was addressing (Burchardt, 1997). To this contributor it appeared, further, that although such things are by their nature hard to quantify (a challenge Henry would have enjoyed) his contributions were steadily becoming more significant. His untimely death in December 1998 deprived the country of what could have been yet more exciting insights.

Note

[1] This chapter will assist the reader who wishes to place the individual chapters of this book in the context of Henry's burgeoning interests and rapid career moves. I have restricted myself to Henry's career and have omitted his extensive knowledge of a wide range of subjects from architecture to bassoon playing and cookery. Even within economics Henry's interests were polymathic, stretching from building workers' holiday schemes to political and economic simulations.

References

Burchardt, A. (1997) *The Broyd Papers: Industrial policy of the Civil Service and the case for open government*, Nottingham: Spokesman.

Conference of Socialist Economists London Working Group (1980) *The alternative economic strategy*, London: CSE Books & Labour Co-ordinating Committee.

Gilhespy, D., Jones, K., Manwaring, T., Neuburger, H. and Sharples, A. (1986) *Socialist enterprise: Reclaiming the economy*, Nottingham: Spokesman.

Neuburger, H. and Fraser, N. (1993) *Economic policy analysis: A rights-based approach*, Aldershot: Avebury.

Bibliography: Henry Neuburger's publications

This bibliography includes only the more academic pieces, written under Henry's own name. He also used a range of pseudonyms, while subject to civil service rules on publishing. There were numerous other pieces of a more political nature and reviews in newspapers and journals, such as *The Times, The Guardian, Today, New Statesman, New Socialist, Economic Affairs* and *Labour Party News.* Henry also published regularly over several years in *Labour Weekly* and *Tribune.*

Macroeconomics

(1983) 'The use and limitations of economic forecasting models', *Socialist Economic Review*, vol 3, pp 259-71.

(1983) 'Turning the clock back?', in J. Kay (ed) *The economy and the 1983 budget*, London: Institute for Fiscal Studies.

(1985) 'Why is unemployment so high?', *National Westminster Bank Quarterly Review*, May, pp 12-20.

(1986) *Socialist enterprise: Reclaiming the economy*, coauthored with D. Gilhespy, K. Jones, T. Manwaring and A. Sharples, Nottingham: New Socialist and Spokesman.

(1989) 'Productive and competitive economy', coauthored with D. Henderson MP and M. Mowlam MP, in Tribune Group of MPs (ed) *Discussion papers for Labour Party policy review.*

(1989) *Direct and indirect taxation: A socialist approach*, Fabian Society Taxation Review Background Paper No 5, London: Fabian Society.

(1990) 'Macroeconomic policies and inflation', coauthored with M. Sawyer, in K. Cowling and R. Sugden (eds) *A new economic policy for Britain*, Manchester: Manchester University Press.

(1993) *Economic policy analysis: A rights-based approach*, coauthored with N. Fraser, Avebury: Aldershot.

(1996) 'Life after economics? Economics wants surgery not a wake', *New Economy*, vol 3, no 1, pp 39-42.

Transport and planning

(1971) 'The economics of heavily congested roads', *Transportation Research*, vol 5, no 4, pp 283-94.

(1971) 'User benefit in the evaluation of transport and land use plans', *Journal of Transport Economics and Policy*, vol 5, no 1, pp 52-75.

(1971) 'Perceived costs', *Environment and Planning*, vol 3, no 4, pp 369-76.

(1974) 'The ambiguity of the consumer's surplus measure of welfare change', coauthored with C. Foster, *Oxford Economic Papers*, vol 26, no 1, pp 66-77.

(1976) 'The economic appraisal of land-use plans', coauthored with J. Wilcox, *Journal of Transport Economics and Policy*, vol 10, no 3, pp 227-36.

(1978) 'The ugly truth about consumers surplus', with C. Foster, *Zeitschrift für Nationalökonomie*, vol 38, no 3/4, pp 379-88.

(1985) 'Economics of planning', *Economics of Planning*, vol 19, no 3, pp170-3.

Industry

(1982) 'Does manufacturing deserve special status?', *Socialist Economic Review*, vol 2, pp 197-216.

(1989) *The economics of 1992*, London: British Labour Group of MEPs.

(1992) 'Energy demand in an era of rapidly changing oil prices. How OPEC did not save the world from the greenhouse effect', *Environment and Planning A*, vol 24, pp 1039-50.

Employment and pay

(1984) *Unemployment: Are wages to blame?*, London: Low Pay Unit.

(1984) *From the dole queue to the sweatshop: Minimum wages and government policy*, London: Low Pay Unit.

National accounts

(1996) 'How far should economic theory and economic policy affect the design of national accounts?', *Economic Trends*, vol 518, December, pp 48-64. (Also presented to the 24th General IARIW Conference, Lillehammer, Norway, August 1996.)

(1997) 'Competitiveness in manufactures', coauthored with M. Byme and Z. Chaudhri, *Economic Trends*, vol 523, June, pp 43-7.

(1997) 'A household satellite account for the UK', coauthored with L. Mugatroyd, *Economic Trends*, vol 527, October, pp 63-71.

(1997) 'How should economic statistics respond to information technology?', coauthored with D. Holt, *Economic Trends*, vol 529, December, pp 23-9. (Also presented to UN Statistical Commission meeting, February 1997.)

Health

(1992) 'Discounting and health benefits', coauthored with M. Parsonage, *Health Economics*, vol 1, pp 71-9.

Index

A

B

C

D

E

F

G

H

K

L

M

N

O

P

U

V

W